MW00917098

Plausible Gumption:

The Road Between a Christmas Toolbox and the Barker Bass

by

G. B. Lee Barker

Independently Published

Without you, these last thirty something years would have amounted to very little. But with you, they have been imbued with your art, peppered with your humor, melted by your voice on the phone, cooed by your smile, and enlarged by my knowing and loving you.

Without you, I would never have known and loved Andi, Patrick, Maya, Bjorn; and Joe, Sarah, Lily and Juni.

It has been grand, simply grand.

INTRODUCTION

Welcome. Thanks for showing up.

It's audacious to write a book about yourself. Only big-name stars and vainglorious politicians have that entitlement, and I'm just an average guy. *Gumption* made me do it.

Merriam-Webster fires this shot across the bow of *plausible*: 'Superficially fair, reasonable, or valuable, but often deceptively so.' We'll see how this plays out.

There are two threads through these tales. Music has been a part of my life from the beginning. I was an active musician for forty-seven years, give or take a few choruses. So that's one thread.

The other thread is work, from first job to last. After college, radio announcer. Tree planter. Carpenter. Writer. Househusband. Carpenter and Cabinetmaker. Finally, developer and maker of a unique musical instrument.

This book started because Maya, Lily, Bjorn, Juni, Emily, and Liam, our grandchildren, might someday want to know about Grampa's life before color photographs and pizza, espresso and earbuds. Your version is way shorter than theirs, and for that I accept your gratitude.

The Dry Canyon Filharmonhick Tour, Gearheads, Rainey, Dempsey, and Blake stories come from contemporaneous notes. The rest, my memory, which can be a little squishy these days. And I will cop to this: I am definitely better now/then than I was then/then.

At the end is the Appendix of afterthoughts. If this book is a ship, these are the barnacles.

Onward.

First, how about a cleverly appropriate quotation?

"...and in his brain, which is as dry as the remainder biscuit after a voyage, he hath strange places cramm'd with observation, the which he vents in mangled forms."

Shakespeare: <u>As You Like It</u>, act 2 scene 7

TIMELINE

Bernos and Me | 1946

	First recorded appearance,
1944	Fort Atkinson, Wisconsin
1946	Moved to Beloit, Wisconsin
1951	Moved to Big Timber, Montana; second grade
1958	Moved to Mountain Home, Idaho; Graduated High School 1962

1962-66 — Westminster College, Salt Lake City, Utah; Graduated B.A. English

Radio Announcer, KDBM Dillon, Montana, pop 3500

1966-68 — Radio Personality, KSLM Salem, Oregon, pop. 66,000; Married Diana (1969)

1968-70 — Freelance writer and photographer; Teaching Aide, Oregon School for the Blind; Tree Planter, U.S. Plywood Co

1970-71

1971-75 — Radio Personality at KALL, Salt Lake City, pop. 176,000

1976 — Moved to Bend, Oregon, pop. 17,263 Employed by McCaul Construction; Partnered with Rob Trout; Whistlepunk Construction. Licensed General Contractor #17771, Great Ned! Construction

1977 — Remodeling Contractor, Salt Lake City

1981

Moved to Redmond, pop. 7000. Opened Great Ned! Woodworks.

Grandpa Leo (Lee) Armstrong | 1945

	1983	Bought the Old Redmond Ice House
Divorced from Diana; physical custody of Guy and Joel	1986	
Married Linda; Blended family. Guy and Joel, meet Li Andra and Joe; Redmond pop. 7204	1991	
Sold Ice House and leased shop in the Airport Industrial Park	1993	

Jack Reidelberger,
(Uncle Broccoli) | 1945

Redmond pop. 15,288	2000	
Built Barker Bass prototype	2003	

	2010		Redmond pop. 26,215
Backburnered Barker Bass business; infilled with woodworking and furniture repair	2012	2013	Joe Post purchased tools and opened Nedson Woodworks. Last basses sold
	2015		

Home for good. Made whirligigs and wind chimes. Redmond pop. 28,654. Welded stuff together to resemble art. Built a cycle kart. Read a few good books and wrote an average one. Loved my wife and life and family and lived a positive attitude while avoiding fried foods.

Cathy and me | 1954
How at 10 year old holds his brand new baby sister

ONE

Learning to Work

I

I like work. Young kid, I watched the telephone man drill holes in the wall of our house to install the phone. By hand, a brace and bit. I hung around a welding shop where they let me use a helmet so I could watch the blinding sparks. I was nine when workmen added a bedroom to our house because my younger sister's birth was imminent. They had a noisy electric saw which cut through wood but when they set it down after cutting, the blade spun freely. I was baffled by the spring-loaded blade guard. It was a Skilsaw by brand, now an eponym for the tool genre.

Earlier, an important Christmas gift: a Montgomery Ward toolbox with hammer, saw, pliers, screwdriver, wrench set, zig-zag rule, and pencil. I still have the box, hammer and square.

First job: eighth grade, hired by the Mountain Home News to "catch papers" off the press, Wednesday afternoons. The raw paper, "newsprint," came to us precut, large sheets, which were fed singly into the monster cast-iron press which inked the lead type and pressed the paper onto it, lifted it off, and sent it to me. I would grasp each sheet and square it up with the rest of the stack to be transported later to the cutter and folder. Fifty cents an hour. The press, driven by a large, industrial electric motor, clanked and swooshed and hummed like a steampunk war machine. The paper dust stuck to my glasses.

I did a brief stint working evenings in a grocery store. I was a freight-buster. Hi-C was a brand new sugary fruit drink and it came in cardboard boxes which addressed me personally in large print: "Stack 'em Hi, C 'em Sell!" Hmm. Advertising can be not only clever but also in unusual places.

Then to Sav-Mor Drug, hired by Arden Drake, the owner and head pharmacist. Through high school I worked two hours after classes, until six, and eight hours Saturday. I opened freight, stocked shelves, swept floors, and washed windows. I cleaned the bathroom and made distilled water. Filled the pop machine. Grabbed a handful of nuts every time I walked past the backside of the Johnson's machine with its warming bulb and rotating center tray.

Fall, 1962, Westminster College, Salt Lake City: The easy way to earn money on campus was to work in the kitchen for Saga Foods, a franchise provider of food services. An hour a day every day paid a third of your board bill. I worked three, full board, no tax involved. I washed pots and pans, peeled potatoes, and stacked hot plates off the Hobart dishwasher. Summers, no classes, lived in a vacant campus building and worked maintenance and landscaping.

My 1951 Ford four door sedan, weak pea-soup green, with a flathead V8 and overdrive, delivered 30 mpg on the highway. Gas was about a buck a gallon. The toolbox was in the trunk.

Thus begins this memoir of my time as an employed college graduate person. However, we'll back up to catch the early years of my involvement with music and segue back to the rank amateur radio announcing that fell on Beaverhead County's seat in sixty-six.

An important Christmas gift

Tuning Up

My family of origin is somewhat musical. My father could hold his own tenor part in a barbershop quartet. He played brass instruments in high school. My older sister Bernie (short for Bernos, a French family name), was a clarinetist from fifth grade through college and can sing effortlessly. Cathy, the dilling, is also a natural singer who took up the guitar "as a prop" when she led church-affiliated group song or otherwise needed it. These years she and her husband Dick sing serious, difficult, and long classical choral music with orchestras and visiting baton slingers in Helena, Montana.

Mom and I differ from them. First, we are brown-eyed and left-handed. Those "others" are blue-eyed and adroit. Second, we are not singers. Once Bernie said I was "the only person I know who can change key during a note." This insightful observation was amplified in Pilgrim Choir rehearsal at church when the conductor, Mrs. Paulson, asked elementary-schooler me to sing a part by myself. "You certainly are a monotone," she said, not kindly. At supper that night I asked what "monotone" meant. Thank you, Mrs. Paulson, for your aid in my self awareness!

Bernie played in band before I did and she got to wear this colorful uniform and march in a parade. How cool! The clarinet did not interest me at all; I wanted to be the kid with the trumpet. Those guys stand up and play solos and get applause. But, on the day at school when the who-plays-what decisions were officially made, the daunting band director Mrs. Malcolm said, "You want to play tuba, don't you Lee," and it was not a question. So I nodded, totally intimidated, wobbly on my skinny legs and unsure what a tuba was.

I just held the image of those band jackets with the horizontal gold braided trim across the chest in lines that ended in three loops held in place by brass buttons, framed by the deeply-colored fabric.

Contrasting piping at the jacket seams. Some day, if I survived Mrs. Malcolm and made it to high school, I would have a uniform.

First day of grade school band: this thing is heavy! The silver, upright Eb tuba weighed thirty-five pounds. Typically they sit on the player's lap but that would have made it impossible for a person of my shortness to reach the mouthpiece. I had a special wooden chair with a six-inch length of small wood molding nailed on the front edge of the seat to prevent the horn from sliding off and taking me with it. This prescient task was accomplished by the school janitor, who simultaneously demonstrated (a) the value of carpentry skills, and (2) a modification to enhance musical instrument functionality. Foreshadows.

Despite the guard rail on the chair, I often contemplated the carnage of a rogue tuba incident, three journeymen plumbers with cutting torches and tin snips laboring for hours to extricate my bent and bloody body from the crushed metal coils. I hoped I would be brave and not cry.

At last! | 1957

I overcame those fears, but nothing alleviated the embarrassment I suffered every Friday when I had to ask my sister to carry my cased instrument home for weekend practice. I couldn't lift it, much less navigate the five block walk home.

High school! Band members got adventurous bus rides to away games, football and basketball, and the concert music was more engaging. Overall the experience was one of fraternity, team play, and an occasional mental sunrise when a majority of things went right and what we did bore some resemblance to what the composer had intended. And there were opportunities to hang around with Cheryl, the cute fluter.

I played some good quality brass King sousaphones, which are the more easily carried form of tuba, at Mountain Home High School. My senior year, the school purchased the Reynolds company's innovative response to all that brass avoirdupois: A fiberglass sousaphone which tipped the scale at a mere fifteen pounds. This was like entering the shot put at a track meet but using a tennis ball. The tone was not as rich as that from the brass horns—a seminal moment in my evaluating bass sounds.

I played bass solos like "Scherzo Pomposo" at high school music festivals and got ribbons, mostly blue, thanks in large part to the sainted classmate and pianist JoAnn Parsons whom I never thanked enough.

The sousaphone fetched me some scholarship money. At Westminster I played sousaphone whenever and wherever I was told to and got an unremembered number of dollars a year for laying down "ooms" and letting the french horns echo with the "pah-pahs." I was the only bass horn player those four years. History repeats: After I put a sign on the old brass horn, tagging it as "Westminster's Relic," and sported it in the basketball pep band, the college bought a new white, light, fiberglass sousaphone.

Westminster boasted an eponymous community symphony orchestra, directed by Dr. Kenneth Kuchler, who was not only the head of the music department but also the concertmaster of the Utah Symphony. I was expected to play in the former group, which proved to be an ear-opening experience which keeps me listening to classical music to this day.

The Scholars 1965-66

Gordon K. McBride, a percussionist and fellow member of the Westminster Community Symphony Orchestra, lived next door In the men's dorm. A barrel chested guy with a snazzy goatee,\ a captivating smile, and a warm voice.

Gordon played in a trio with bass player Doug Evans and guitarist Ed Casias (kuh-SEE-us) that gigged in bars. Two years later, Gordon and Ed approached me. Doug was headed off to graduate school that summer of 1965 and they needed a bass player. They would teach, I would learn, and get to wear snazzy outfits and Beatle boots to boot. "Sure," I said.

Doug sold me his Fender Precision Bass and Fender Bassman 100 Amplifier with the tweed cloth covering. I let my hair grow; joined the musicians union. I was one of The Scholars.

Ed's olive complexion gave him a European air. He was a dedicated husband with two daughters, Hollie and Heidi, and that motivation us booked and working.

Ed was a musician's musician. He had been drafted several years prior, and the army recognized his talent and assigned him to the NORAD (North American Air Defense Command) Band in Colorado. This elite group was top musicians from all branches of the US military as well as Canada's. At this writing I found Ed in several pictures of the NORAD band on the web. In his time off he studied with Johnny Smith, one of the all time great jazz guitarists. (Gibson made a Johnny Smith model guitar-now how about that!)

Despite Ed's tutelage, bass playing didn't come easy. We didn't work from sheet music as I knew it, we used lead sheets: lyrics with chord symbols above. I learned the bass fretboard but little background theory. I should have asked more questions.

I became an adequate bassist but being a non-singer was a negative, especially in the sparse vocal landscape of the trio. Musically, we were standing with a foot in the American Songbook/

standards bucket and the other foot in the Beatles/Dave Clark/
Chuck Berry bucket which sloshed of Love Potion #9. I developed
dazzling technique which supported elementary note selection. I had
no onboard cognitive tools, inborn or acquired, to pick up anything
new unless Ed wrote me a chart which I would then memorize.

The Scholars were well booked for the summer before, all of
my last school year, and the summer after graduation. I was paid
in cash and could afford an off-campus basement apartment.

Midyear, Gordon headed off to Eugene, Oregon to graduate
school and, after a brief teaching career as a PhD in history stamping
out ignorance in those who think there were only eight who were
crowned King Henry, went to seminary and became a prominent
Episcopal priest in Tucson, Arizona. In his spare time he wrote and
published three novels. He died in 2010.

In his place we hired fledgling drummer Steve Burton who
was as cute as Herman of the Hermits, which forced him to sing
"I'm Henry VIII, I Am."

The stomping, back-beaten repetitive rock'n'roll stuff was
undeniably fun but the lasting gift from this period of employment
was my introduction to jazz. We played standards that Ed improvised
over, tunes like "Satin Doll" and "Dancing on the Ceiling" and
"Sentimental Journey" and "Polka Dots and Moonbeams." Ed sang
the ballads—"Moonlight in Vermont" and "Softly as I Leave You"
come to mind. We cooked on "Love For Sale"and "Route 66" and
dipped into the blues vault for "Kansas City." Our theme song opener
and signoff was "Watermelon Man" and our break song was a short
and hellishly rhythmic version of Henry Mancini's "Batman." It was
after a ballad, occasionally, that someone would say to Ed, "You
sound like Johnny Smith." We loved that.

Our rock and roll and popular book included Beatles, of course,
and "Ferry Cross the Mersey," "King of the Road," and even Buck
Owens' "Tiger by the Tail." We tried nobly to assemble the folk rock
anthem "You Were on my Mind" but didn't have the personnel to
pull it off. Some you can, some you can't. I loved the ostinato bass
line in "We Gotta Get Outa This Place" but the lyric line "...see my
daddy in bed he's dyin'," was difficult to hear because that is exactly

what I'd witness on the rare occasions when I could travel to see my parents in Butte, Montana. His battle with cancer lasted over four years and involved too many "exploratory" surgeries.

.MEMORABLE MOMENTS FROM THE SCHOLAR YEAR:

- When Doug left and I started full time (I had been sitting-in a set or two per night) we were booked at the Porthole Lounge at the Holiday Inn in Ogden, Utah. We had played there a week, and finished up on Saturday night, leaving the drums and our PA setup on the stage. When we came back Thursday night for our 9 p.m. start. I was rattled to see our stuff had been moved off the stage and there was another band set up, getting ready to play. The manager of the bar tried to explain but it was wasted wind. We mumbled and grumbled and packed up and went home. I was disturbed; nothing in my life experience had prepared me for anything like this. But Gordon and Ed went out and found us another gig. We never went back to the Porthole. From that experience on I was wary of bar owners and managers.

- We had three band uniforms, all worn with white shirts with snap tab collars, black narrow tie and black shoes. Most impressive were the shiny silver suits with stingy lapels. Bands of the time attired themselves like this, clearly a vestige of the Vaudeville dress-better-than-the-audience-to-honor-them imperative.

- We played for several months at the Crow's Nest in downtown Salt Lake City. It was owned by two Greek brothers who liked our stuff and gave us free beer (not all owners would). Ed didn't drink so Steve and I took it upon ourselves to fully accept the brothers' generosity on Ed's behalf.

- One Crow's Nest night two men in black suits came in carrying bulky electronic devices in their hands. They walked determinedly about the floor, stopping at random places and staring at the gizmos and writing something down on a notebook. This puzzled me. I knew the whole Utah bar scene to be bizarre in other ways. For instance: you could buy beer (3.2% alcohol) or else "setups" which were small glasses with a bit of 7up or Coke or Sour. You brought in your bottle of liquor (usually in a brown bag) and added it to your setup. Leaving was a problem because there was a law against open containers in cars. My oh my, what to do? Leave the bottle there? Or drink it all before you leave so you can get your money's worth?

- But that still didn't explain the Black Suits. I asked one of the boss brothers at the break. "They're from the Liquor Control Commission. They're testing to see if it's too dark in here to be selling beer."

- A guy came in and jabbered with Ed while Ed was playing. Rude. Ed smiled and nodded his head and looked at me, his smile wide open. I noticed the visitor had a piece of inch-wide gray steel strap sticking up from his chest like it was glued to his necktie. It leaned out the front away from his chin and had a hole in it. When he came back there was a microphone screwed into the hole and three or four harmonicas in his sport coat pockets. He played along with us for the rest of the night and Ed was just crazy with laughter. It sounded OK. Meanwhile, beer flowed and no one cared.

- I learned how to set up Steve's drums. We played the song "Caravan" as a jazz instrumental and included a drum solo which went on as long as the drummer was moved to play. When he was done, he'd walk us back into some cadence patterns and Ed and I would get back on stage and strap on our instruments. On a slow Thursday Ed called the tune. Gave Steve the nod for his solo, always spontaneous and interesting. Steve was focused on his timbales, two smaller drums set just beyond and a little above his snare drum. Without thinking much I took away his floor tom. Then a cymbal on a stand. Steve was aware. I kept sliding stuff out of his reach until he had was the bass drum and his sticks, playing on its rim and on the wall behind. I fed the stuff back to him one item at a time and the solo built to a fantastic ending. It became a regular part of our arrangements. "Caravan" would have been a great act at a chili cookoff.

- I performed "I Was Cool," written and recorded by Oscar Brown Jr. You can't go wrong with a talkin' blues song in which the declaimer must cry, weep, and bawl with feeling and intensity that ascend through the three verses. It all ends with a punch line: "...the shot (BAM (drum rimshot)) whistled right on past that woman's head and killed my houn' dog dead!"

- We got booked in Provo, home of Brigham Young University, fifty miles south of Salt Lake. The joint was The Nugget and we quipped that "the parking lot is somewhat cleaner than the inside of the bar." But we thrived on our Tuesday through Saturday schedule there and we were loved. Indeed there were BYU students who were regulars. Tut tut.

- The owners, a couple, looked like a button down accountant and a professional women's motivational speaker. They always dressed well, in sharp contrast to the grittiness of the bar and its shabby décor. We were there for months.

When I started my radio career I sold my musical equipment and threw out my band suits and pointy-toed boots. There was no more making electric bass music of any kind until 1983, eighteen years later, when I had the temerity to ask if I could sit in and the bass player said, "No."

TWO

KDBM 1966 - 1968

I

I n the early summer of 1963, between my freshman and sophomore college years, I was approached by the Protestant campus minister at the University of Utah who wondered if I wanted to go to Washington DC. for a big national protest. I said "Sure!" and ended up one of fourteen Utahans who traveled across the country by train and stood in the muggy heat to hear Dr. Martin Luther King Jr.'s moving "I Have a Dream" speech on August twenty-third. That I was one of a quarter million people speaking in one voice which influenced history remains a singular, durable fiber in my being. Something tilted in the United States of America that day, and whenever I see the pictures I am stirred by the profundity of what Bayard Ruskin, Martin Luther King Jr., and others led us to do.

Westminster College was founded as a secondary school and has existed as an educational institution since 1875. Salt Lake (and Utah) are a center of western and Mormon conservatism, but Westminster has secured its identity as a liberal arts island of intellectual and educational openness. All this was not part of my decision to matriculate there. It was more about on-campus work opportunities, the right distance from home (300 miles; not a weekend option but doable twice a year), half tuition for being a preacher's kid, and a scholarship for playing the tuba (sousaphone).

Sears and Texaco had added a few hundred scholarship dollars to my Higher Education Boodle Bin.

My senior year of school I got to know Jack Bogut, the engaging and talented midday personality on KALL radio, which played middle-of-the-road music that was right down my teacup even though ubiquitous rock and roll had its back-beating attraction and I was earning money hammering it out six nights a week with the Scholars. Listening to KALL was a pleasant part of my memories of that downstairs studio apartment just off campus. Through Jack I got the notion that radio would be a cool career—something I ought to be thinking about, with graduation looming large.

II

I had entered college as a pre-theological student expecting to enter the ministry, not a deeply explored decision. The summer before my senior year I was hired to help the pastor at a UCC church in Ogden, thirty miles north of Salt Lake. He had had a stroke and could not speak well. So he stayed home and I spent three days a week there keeping the ship barely afloat and leading worship Sunday morning. I made sure the folks hiring me knew of my music job, detailed elsewhere in this work. They shrugged.

This casually-framed ecclesiastical intern experience canceled my career path. I was not wired for the church gig. Playing bass for Ed Casias was more fun, but I lacked the talent to be a full time professional musician. So that's two careers off the list.

I liked academia but couldn't imagine myself as a college teacher. In addition, I had read one too many lugubrious early English novels to consider graduate school, despite a flattering bit of scholarship money dangled by the University of Utah. I was emotionally ready for the world of work. I just didn't know where.

I found myself in front of a campus bulletin board with military recruiting posters. But wait, what's that? The Columbia School of Broadcasting? I took a brochure.

I nabbed the bait and communicated with salesman Jack Levitan at CSB over several weeks. Their deal: give us $1500 and record your homework onto a cassette tape, send it to us, and we'll send back helpful critiques from seasoned professionals. And there was a lot more blah blah blah. My introverted nature was attracted to the privacy of the education and the suggestion that, with this kind of credential, radio stations in major markets will be climbing all over each other trying to ink me to a lucrative, multi-year contract. This was looking good. But where the $1500 would come from was a nagging mystery.

Levitan was persistent and polished but failed to get me to sign on the dotted line. I shared all this with Bogut, whose comment was, "Yes, you could do that, spend the $1500 and after three months you'd still not have a job. Or," he added emphatically, "you could get hired at a one-lung station in some small town. Your mouth will be an open wound, but in three months you'd still have a job and no debt!" Compelling logic. I ended my conversations with Levitan, but I didn't know what to do next. Secretly I assured myself that my mouth would not be an open wound. How could it? I had studied Shakespeare! I could speak the speech trippingly on the tongue!

After graduation, late summer of 1966, I was driving to Butte with my sister Bernie to see our parents. I saw a radio station out in a field. I pulled right off the highway onto the gravel lane and, in an hour, as Bernie patiently sat, I had met the owner, Burt Oliphant, and accepted a job at Dillon's only radio station. Start in September. Forty-eight hours a week. Salary: $200 per month.

Amazing. KDBM: The same station where Jack Bogut had uttered his first words on the air.

I studied for and passed the test to become a Third Class Radiotelephone Operator. FCC regulations of the time required smaller stations such as KDBM to have one First Class Radiotelephone Operator on staff and anyone on the air to have a "Third Phone." There wasn't a lot of learning here—essentially I had to show I knew how to read dials and gauges—but I was proud of my blue certificate.

September, I packed up my stuff and my License to Use My Open Wound and left the familiarity of Salt Lake City and pointed myself at an isolated Montana town where I knew nobody.

I found lodgings, as was said often in those weighty English novels which I had read so diligently in preparation for an unrealized working life of academic fustiness, in the Hokum House. Once a rooming house, it had been reimagined as apartments. Thirty-five bucks a month for undeniably dreary digs. A spartan life is easy when all you own is clothes, books, a frying pan and one small Montgomery Ward toolbox.

I went to work in a squat rectangular building, about twenty feet by thirty feet. The front office had a desk, typewriter, a catalog of stock advertising texts and lots of album storage. And a bathroom. The transmitter room, separated from the control room with a windowed wall, was dominated by the fan-cooled, heat producing Marconi marvel that allowed us to work our magic on Southwestern Montana. Big tubes, and they glowed.

The production "room" was a windowed booth, about the size of a bedroom closet in a modest home. There we recorded commercials and did other sound production and from which someone, usually Burt, would read the local news live.

In the control room the on-duty person ("on the board") sat on a castered secretary chair and faced the control board, which was switches and volume controls for all the inputs that went into what you chose to send to those glowing transmitter tubes. To your left and right, three turntables, readily accessible current 45rpm records, players for the cartridges on which we recorded commercials and intros and outros for daily programs (and eventually Lee's goofy sound effects and musical bridges and bumps, used to transition from or punctuate the end of something creative, and sometimes even funny, that I did). "Carts" looked like 8 track tapes and were based on the same 'endless loop' concept.

Below to the left was the phone with a hook on the handset so you could hold it on your shoulder and talk and have two hands free to do whatever the instant required. On the right, at the end of that leg of the U, a playback and record tape deck above and an identical one below.

On the wall above the window into the production booth and just below the ceiling was the Grand Despot: The clock. You could not negotiate with it, you could not fudge it at the beginning and give it back at the end. Its absolute metronomic authority meant that, when the second hand clicked straight up, to twelve, the network news started. You'd better be done with whatever you were doing, have identified the station (call letters, city) per FCC regulations, and have the network channel clicked on and the volume at the right level. If you blipped it, Burt always found out and would mention it next time he saw you.

Burt lived in a modest home with his family of young children. He and his wife Peggy worked in tandem, from home. Burt wore a suit and tie all the time and had come to radio because of his voice.

Burt and Peggy had built the station from the ground up. Once it was on the air, Burt was working nine hours a day on the board and then, after 3pm, selling time and servicing accounts. He quietly wore the grit and determination characteristic of his generation as he created his version of the American Dream.

III

External forces can act in one's life even though one attempts to singularly focus on one thing; in this case, learning how to be a radio announcer. Some interruptions:

- Received notice from the IRS that I could not deduct the total cost of my Fender bass and amplifier from the income I had made playing rock and roll music in bars my last year of school. Had to be depreciated at 10% a year they said. I paid the adjusted tax.

- Bought a green corduroy sport coat at J.C. Penney's for $8.88. Still have it. Still kinda fits.

- Traded in my '57 Chevy for a brand new Datsun 1300 sedan (the only brand new car ever for me). I had to move the driver's seat back two inches so I could fit. It was a sweet little machine, the color of an olive which had misplaced its pimiento. I made payments, my first.

- Learned to fly fish. The Beaverhead River flows past Dillon; the Madison and the Big Hole rivers are nearby. All three are legendary trout fisheries. Evening fishing with royal coachman, brown bear brown, brown bear black and wooly buggers. Rainbows and browns. I could catch my dinner once I got the hang of casting. When I fished I smoked Tiparillos. When a brown trout hit the fly and took a plunge (Rainbows tend to come out of the water) one could chomp right through a regular cigar. I fancied myself the Izaak Walton of the Beaverhead.

- Trained a bunch of young men to be radio announcers, mostly students from the college. They could get part time work at the station and everybody benefited. Some were more dependable than others.

- Slid off the iced-up highway driving to work one winter morning. Unharmed, my Datsun sedan in the barrow pit on the opposite side of the road, facing back toward town. I walked to the station, made it in time to sign on at six. Burt kindly paid to get the car back on the pavement where it belonged.

- Became lifetime friends with two coworkers at KDBM: Don Richard, by far the best voice among us, who moved up to manage a station in Miles City, Montana until retirement, and Glenn Larum, who followed me to my second radio job at KSLM and went on to a career in Texas as a teacher, editor, highway department spokesman and, in retirement, published novelist.

- Brought my Christmas toolbox on my day off and built some cabinets in the little production booth to create more storage, less clutter. Les, the boss's father-in-law, made the doors as well as some disparaging comments about the squareness of my work. "Barker, better stick with radio, you're no good at woodworking."

- Got permission from Stan Lynde, who lived in Billings, Montana, to read his comic strip every morning on the air. "Rick O'Shay" was good western stories peppered with humor and colorful characters like Sheriff Rick's friend Hipshot Percussion, whose father was Rep. The action was in the town of Conniption. Reading a comic strip on the air was stolen from Will Lucas at KALL in Salt Lake City, who read Peanuts every weekday. If I had the chance again, I'd read Mary Worth. The opportunities to add sound effects (raspberries, trombone slurs, harp arpeggios, champagne cork pops) are deliciously dizzying. Oh, and doing the voices.

KDBM was affiliated with the ABC radio network and IMN, the Intermountain Network. It had separate Idaho, Montana, Wyoming and Utah bureaus and at its peak boasted sixty-seven station affiliates into North Dakota, Colorado and New Mexico. We aired several newscasts a day from the Montana bureau and one in the noon hour out of Salt Lake City. IMN's headquarters in Utah were in the same building as KALL radio.

A weekday at KDBM went like this:

6 A.M. SIGN ON, news and sports from ABC Radio Network along with album selections of (both kinds of) country and western music. The sportscast was Howard Cosell and often included his landmark interviews with Muhammed Ali. Theirs was a remarkable friendship and it made for great radio.

8-9 A.M. Don McNeil's Breakfast Club from the network.

9 A.M. - NOON, middle of the road (MOR) music and some radio personality stuff. This was when I'd make a case that you needed an actual membership card to be part of the KDBM Train Watching Society. I'd announce the impending passage of any southbound train, freight or passenger, and report a car count on northbounds which had cleared Dillon and were headed for the Continental Divide. You'd hear some semi-appropriate sound effects.

AT 10 A.M., for about twelve minutes, it was Mary Blaine Time. I'd bring her in with, "Ma---ry!........Ma---ry!.....Yoo Hoo, MA----RY! and start the tape, which always started with her calm "Hello." It was a sweet cooking show which we got free because she was financed by the Beef Growers of America or some such organization. Mary sounded like your aunt, the one with gray and tightly bunned hair. She never talked of poultry of any kind. When Thanksgiving was approaching she'd ease you into thinking the best possible thing you could do for your family would be to serve them a delicious pot roast. Before you knew you'd picked up a pencil you'd be writing down her recipe which was delineated with gaps   between the ingredients   and then more gaps   after three or four words   of the instructions   and if you were the person in charge at the   radio station   and doing something else and noticed the silence   youmightrunbackintothecontrol roomthinkingwewereofftheairorthetapehadbroken.

I started playing a little classical music between **11:45 AND NOON.** Nothing Wagnerian, just little puffy things short enough they'd be over before you could find my number and call me to complain.

NOON TO 1 P.M., an hour of information. It started with fifteen minutes of Paul Harvey's "news and comment" which should have gone on to say, "and you can't tell one from the other because he is so clever." Harvey's was a voice of conservatism, sneaky putdowns and heartwarming midwest-toned stories. He was pro Vietnam war until his son became draft-eligible. A fascinating, iconic broadcaster.

12:15 brought local news, sports news, IMN news and the Dillon Creamery Bulletin Board, chockablock with announcements of bake sales and pancake dinners and cheerleader car washes. Farm news next ("leans, lights, canners and cutters...heifers"...that stuff. I had no idea what I was reading). At 12:55, ABC Network news. It was a busy and complex hour for the person on the board but it was an important part of the community's life. Local news included obituaries and detailed reports from both Kiwanis and Rotary meetings as well as items from local schools and Western Montana College.

1-2 P.M., western music from albums, played without much patter because I was pattered out. Long hours six days a week was a demanding schedule but I was trying, failing, occasionally hitting the ball well enough to get on base, and learning all the time.

IV

Don Richard, Dillon native and college student, rolled in before two and opened the audio floodgates of "DR's Jam Session." At four he'd take "requests and dedications" from kids who usually wanted bubblegum rock.

5–7 P.M., "Sunset in Hi Fi." A great name. All instrumental, minimal announcer intervention, few commercials. Mantovani, 101 Strings, The Exotic Sounds of Martin Denny (Quiet Village). Put the Philco Bakelite radio by the chrome-legged kitchen table, sip a little sauterne and please pass the lime Jell-O marshmallow cottage cheese surprise.

7–10 P.M., The collegiate part-time announcers with popular stuff for their world.

The final program of the day was thirty minutes of Dr. Carl McIntire and "The Twentieth Century Reformation Hour." His program usually started sermon-like but moved quickly to topical political broadsides and harangues, all punctuated by affirmations from his on-mike cohort, "Amen Charlie." When he was done, you heard The Star Spangled Banner.

V

Burt did all the selling for the station and he was good at it. He wanted me to get involved too but I had no interest. I preferred to stay in my introverted comfort zone behind my disembodied, but friendly, voice.

Three thousand nine hundred and sixty souls were counted in Dillon in 1960. It is the home of thrice-renamed University of Montana-Western, which was founded as Montana Normal School in 1893. The campus is within the city limits yet seemed culturally isolated from the rest of the town when I lived there. (Dillon has increased in size only thirteen percent in the past fifty years. As Dwight Eisenhower said, "Things are more like they are now than they ever were before.")

I needed a haircut. I'd been in Dillon a month, so I went to Don and Marty's Barber Shop. It was the only one. I was in Don's chair and we carried on a desultory conversation while he hummed the clippers about my hirsute dome and little puffs of stuff tumbled down onto my bib like slow-mo fluffy dandelion heads. Abruptly he stopped and shut off the clippers, turning to his partner. "Marty, come look at this." Marty stopped combing mid-part and stepped over to my chair. "What does this look like to you?" Don tapped the top of my head gently.

Marty said, "I don't know. I've never seen anything like that."

Don: "It's the plague. I've seen it. This guy has the plague." Marty went back to work and Don spun the chair around so we were both looking in the mirror. "So how do like workin' at our little radio station, Mr. Barker?"

Dr. Samuel Davis was professor of music at the college. His family lived in a beautiful, well-maintained, classic Craftsman Era bungalow a couple of blocks from Sam's office at the college. We had a number of common interests besides music, including weird bicycles, humor, badminton and fishing. I was often a dinner guest at their house. "Guest" is too formal. If Sam and I were involved in something of an afternoon, Kathrine might walk by and say to me, "You're staying for dinner." It was not a question. Alicia and Jay, their kids, were delightful. Alicia went on to a career in television, on camera. Not sure if I influenced that.

One of Katharine's directives regarding my dinner occurred on a winter Friday evening so I stayed as ordered. Shortly after we had dined, Sam announced that he had to leave abruptly because there was a home basketball game and he needed to lead the pep band. "Do you need a tuba player?" I inquired, expecting a no.

"Yes," Sam said, brightening. "We don't have one."

"Do you have a horn I can play?"

"Of course. Finish your pie and let's get going."

It had been several months since I had played. I wasn't familiar with most of the music but was able to fake my way along after we did a runthrough in the band room before the game.

I got my chops back in shape and became a regular. What Sam hadn't told me was that WMC school spirit was so low that they had to pay the pep band to show up. I got on the payroll, even traveling to a couple of away games. I was holding up the bottom end of Sousa marches, novelty tunes arranged for brass band, and everybody's voice-breaker, The Star Spangled Banner. More fun than a weekly chili cookoff.

Looking at the rest of the Bulldogs' schedule I noticed WMC would be playing Westminster College of Salt Lake City later in the season. I called Coach Steinke. Would he want a little scouting info on the WMC Bulldogs? Of course! I took notes at the games and called the Coach back.

When the Parsons came to play I was in the gym playing music to gin up the home team, got paid three dollars (doughnut fund!) for doing it, and witnessed the visitors beat the locals convincingly. Afterward the team bought me a steak dinner at Skeet's Cafe. Sam was thoroughly amused. Spycraft and fine art take the win over athletics.

One beautiful summer evening Sam and I were fishing the Beaverhead River, a Blue Ribbon Trout Stream, and as twilight dimmed it was time to head back to the car and dump the river water out of our waders. We crested a hillock just off the riparian zone and stopped, stunned: Hundreds of dancing dots of light cut through the gloaming. I thought it was something extraterrestrial. The seconds were as heavy as the silence.

Sam: "What?" Lee: "I dunno." Big pause. The "no" had two syllables: "no....ooh." Sam, flatly: "Fireflies."

I hadn't seen any since my first five years of life in Wisconsin. Haven't seen any in the west since. My current research shows sightings of Photinus pyralis well distributed in the eastern half of the U.S. There are 13 western states, Alaska excluded, where there are *none*. Another strange mystery of time and space. (Cue the theremin theme.)

In my high school years I saw a picture of a homebuilt highbike. I built one.

I still had the bike in Dillon. Sam built a buckin' bike. This required one donor bicycle frame, two wheels from a smaller bike, and many spokes. He dismantled the wheels and relaced them with varying lengths of spokes so the axles were eccentric.

If you're with me so far you are likely imagining that, as you ride, the bike goes up and down, smoothly. True, but that would continue *only if the eccentric wheels were identical.* They weren't. So you might start off in UP down UP down mode but quickly you'd be updownupdownupdown as the frame went down with the front wheel and up with the back, simultaneously until that synchronicity would decay and you'd be headed back toward UP down UP down.

When we'd ride around our quiet little town of a summer evening the reactions from kids were predictable. They'd see mine first: "It's a circus!" Then Sam's, and silence. Then hilarious laughter. "Mom, come and look!"

The highest and best use of our creations was to take them up to Poindexter street which allowed us a view of the northbound highway traffic where it entered town (as highways used to do). Cars were traveling slowly at this point because of a curve. We'd launch ourselves to cross Atlantic Street in front of a car. We'd be deadpan, staring straight ahead, never acknowledging the car. You think of doing this kind of stuff in a small town when the weather's nice and there's not much else to do on a Sunday afternoon in a sleepy, isolated town in Southwestern Montana.

THE RECIPE:

- 2 pieces of pipe 24" long
- 1 regular size single speed donor bicycle

1. Remove wheels. Remove the crank and put it back in the other way around.
2. Remove the front fork and put it back in the other way around. Do not install the gooseneck.
3. Replace the wheels.
4. Now you have a sort of normal-looking bike frame except the crank is where the seat was.
5. Weld one pipe onto the crank housing and attach the seat to it.
6. Attach the other pipe to the fork and attach the gooseneck to the other end of the pipe.
7. Install handlebars. Climb up on something to get on the bike and ride it around wondering how you're going to get off.

Wednesday morning, June 5, 1968: I arrived at the station about 5:45 and switched power to the transmitter. This triggered the network feed from ABC which was carrying live the events following Sirhan Sirhan's firing the bullets that killed Robert Kennedy in Los Angeles. Likely I was the first person in Dillon to learn of that tragedy.

VI

One of the conveniences of my Dillon years was proximity to my parents. Shortly after they had moved to Butte, my dad was diagnosed with colorectal cancer. That started a steady downhill medical journey marked by many surgeries. Some were "exploratory" (a word we seldom hear now) and some were resectioning of the intestine. All unpleasant, all extending his time and prolonging the unending demands on my mom, without much regard for the quality of both their lives.

I was thankful I could be there to visit on my one day off and be a little bit of a distraction for them but it was painful and unsettling to witness his physical decline. Sometimes the trip was healthful for me not to listen to the radio and just enjoy the silence on the road, pondering the impossible image of life without my dad.

He died in 1968 just a few months after I had moved to Salem, Oregon to take the evening shift at KSLM. By then he was completely bedridden. I knew when I said goodbye to him that that was the last one. I couldn't say it but I knew it.

I was grateful for his support during my student years—he sent me $35 a month—but there was no obligation to stick with any specific course of study, spoken or implied. The parental reins had been loosened early and were long since gone.

From a cursory description of the change in my life from college textbooks, essays in blue books and puny meals prepared in my basement apartment in Salt Lake City to salaried radio station employee, there had been sweeping changes. Slightly below the surface things were the same: puny meals, focused effort to learn as much as possible every day, and nothing in the bank to fall back on. And so we start out, young, optimistic, energetic. I could claim no skills or experience specific to my job, which had a picture-window public aspect. I made mistakes and there was no hiding them. Critics would call me on the phone and say unkind things and hang up. It would take an hour or two for the acid in my gut to subside. What to do? Press on!

My mother saved a note from those years. *"Dear Mr. Oliphant: I want to express my gratitude for your announcer Lee Barker. We do so <u>enjoy</u> listening to him—his humor in the morning is exactly what I need to start the day. His "Classic Corner" is wonderfully refreshing after hearing pop music. We feel he is really a highly professional announcer and our personal rating of your station has raised a thousand per cent since Lee Barker's arrival. Sincerely, Mr. and Mrs. Clay Anders."* I can't remember anyone by that name.

I was enchanted with my lot in life overall and celebrated the friends I made in Dillon. There was a palpable sense of caring in that community. No homeless people. A small hospital. Weekly newspaper. Not many trinket or cutesy stores, just places where you could buy what you need. News could be passed along the back fence, at the farmer's co-op or in the barber shop. One wood-frame roadhouse where there was regular live music: He played guitar and she stood beside him, behind a tall drum on legs. A foot pedal below it allowed her to play the bass drum beats and she used brushes on the drumhead. They both sang the yawky and grim lyrics of early country music interwoven with Patsy Cline ballads. It was called The Royal Inn.

In one of his remembrances of these years, Glenn Larum quotes Montana novelist Thomas Savage: "Dillon is a place where people treated you well and when you go back, they will again." It's tough to leave a place like that. Memories put me at the dinner table with the Grahams, the Wiebers, the Simmondses, the Greenes, the Davises. Feeling like I'm in a Norman Rockwell painting, comfortable in the same atmosphere I knew as a kid in Big Timber, but restless for more. Giving in to that intoxication would involve grieving for the lost simplicity of Dillon as well as the death of the most profound male influence on my life, my father E. Brentwood Barker, who died November 25, 1968. He was fifty-three.

I flew to Butte for the memorial service and after I returned to Salem I got a call from the KDBM guy who was on the air when he heard this IMN headline in the introduction to the news: "Two Prominent Montanans die." He just wanted me to know.

THREE

KSLM 1968 - 1971

I

Salem is a beautiful city, especially if you're approaching from the southeast on Highway 22. The road settles down a gentle slope, bears slightly left, passing emerald-green fields and subdivisions both sides. Enter the city on Mission Street near Willamette University. You'll find the capitol in all its art deco cubicity, topped by the fluted "upside down cupcake" on which stands the gold-plated pioneer. If the sun is shining, it is a dramatic moment. Loren and Barbara Donaldson, college friends, were living in Salem, and had helped me identify KSLM as a station where I would fit. They welcomed me warmly.

I had no time for reminiscing or sightseeing.

I rented a furnished apartment on Hyde Court, halfway between Mission Street and State Street, and went to work. KSLM's studio and transmitter were in a rambling, flat-roofed stucco edifice, top of a hill across the Willamette River in West Salem. Right off the entry was a large office room with separate desks for the shirt-and-tie sales force and a private office for the manager. Closest to the door was Esther's desk. She was the office harridan and, I was informed, a person who had easy access to the station owner. Best to stay on her good side.

Away from that center of steak-and-sizzle sales energy was the heart of the diurnal broadcast operation, the control room; small, central to this wing of the building, and windowed on two sides. It faced another glass-walled booth from which the news director would bring the big local newscasts of the day: early morning, noon, and 5pm. Next to the control room: the newsroom, replete with clacking teletype and a large drafting-table like surface for laying out the typewritten elements of a news cast. Nearby those windowed rooms was an alcove that held the coffee pot, a fridge, and a day bed.

The transmitter was in a windowed area across a wide hall from the control room and newsroom. The production room was down a hall and around a corner, in what was originally a bomb shelter.

A few evening shifts learning the station protocols from Ron Manches, a part timer whose day job was selling annuals to high schools, and I was on my own six to midnight, alone in the building. Oh, and Sunday afternoons, eight hours on the air. Our air staff, and most across the nation, needed a union.

Musically this was a big change. Instead of the block programming in Dillon, KSLM's playlist was consistent throughout the day. Everything was from albums which were rotated into and out of the control room weekly. The rule was to alternate the tempo from one tune to the next.

Bob McCarl, the program director, was a stickler for front- and back-announcing each record. This was a little dated to me; the cool guys elsewhere just back-announced. But doing both had a smoothing effect on the overall product. It was conversational.

I was not thrilled with the middle-of-the-road music at KSLM but it was workable. It was good stuff, well done, free of distorted guitar solos and simplistic chord changes. And certainly more variety than one could typically expect from adult stations in similar-sized markets. But it was dated, and we were slow to introduce new material unless it was newly-done old stuff.

From a list of the top one hundred singles of 1968 the only tune we played was "Love is Blue," the haunting minor-key instrumental by Paul Mauriat's band. At least twenty on that list would be played by any other MOR station of the time. There were lots of albums by the female balladeers of the time—Jo Stafford, Rosemary Clooney, Dinah Shore, and the more energetic Barbra Streisand, Shirley Bassey and Keely Smith. The A Team was the male vocalists including Sinatra, Martin, Davis Jr., Eckstine, Munro (Matt, not Burt) and the more Broadwayish brood like Robert Goulet. Vocal groups were from Ray Coniff, Johnny Mann, Gordon Jenkins and Anita Kerr. Lots of albums of instrumental covers done by Percy Faith, Bert Kaempfert, James Last, as well as nameless bands fronted by Al Hirt, Acker Bilk, Ray Anthony.

During my tenure we pared away some of the stuff that smelled of mothballs and added artists like Roger Whittaker, Free Design, the Carpenters, Cashman and West, and the Gerald Wilson Orchestra, but we were still way south of Hip.

The Carpenters. "Goody Four-Shoes," as some wit of the time wrote. We played all they did but, had "Goodbye to Love" with its raucous, fuzz-tone, screechy guitar solo come along then, it wouldn't have been acceptable. Too jarring.

On the air for a month or so I was getting calls around ten pm from a woman. Just friendly "enjoying your show" stuff at first, then a little more intentional. She was interested in my understanding and appreciating how pretty she was. She alluded to a 'screen test' and I was supposed to be impressed. I was curious but suspicious.

One night she said, a little huffily, "I can tell you don't believe a word I'm saying. I'm coming right up there to the radio station to see you. Right now!" And she did, and I let her in, perfume trailing like dust behind a pickup on a Montana summer back road. Hair the color of straw in the late afternoon sunshine, held in place by some member of the varnish family of shiny, sticky coatings. Hardly sylph-like, she followed me to the control room and came inside. Standing room only, fortunately. I was nervous, unsure that letting her in was wise. She pulled a large manila envelope out of her oversized vinyl purse and flopped it down. I segued from the ending record to another and suggested it was time that she leave and she did. Later I looked at the pictures.

I didn't know what exactly a screen test was but I was looking at some very flattering black and white 8x10s which were a little creased on the corners, not fresh. They might have been a decade old. I left them on my McCarl's desk when I shut everything down at midnight.

"So you got to meet Charlene!" McCarl said when I walked in the next afternoon. "I knew it was a matter of weeks before she showed up. Like clockwork. You didn't leave anything on the casting couch, did you?" he said, winking. I felt properly, and safely, initiated into the brotherhood. All the on-air guys knew about Charlene. And like any sophomore, I looked forward to the next newbie who came on staff. I had inside information.

One evening Bruce Kerr, the station manager, called to tell me that the station owner was in town and she and her friend were entertaining Robert Goulet. Would I please play lots of Robert? Like five or six an hour? There was no refusing the manager, who was speaking for the owner, so I complied. It was difficult to frame any kind of program around that much treacle profundo. Next night, back to normal.

Bob McCarl was a short guy who carried a slight limp from a childhood bout with polio. He tipped his head to one side when he spoke. He had a cute grin that occasionally slipped to a smirk if the subject encouraged it (Charlene a sterling example). His desk and mine were against different walls so when we conversed, we had both pivoted around face to face. He often smoothed his tie between two fingers, speeding up the movement at the end of the tie so the tip of it would flip and make a little *snap*.

II

This was a unique station. McCarl was the program director, meaning he was responsible for whatever went on the air, news and music, and dealt with the personnel stuff necessary to make all that happen. He had been a big deal in Portland radio at the height of its Golden Age of DeeJays. He and a handful of other guys had the city in their hands. It was, he told me, "A time of babes and convertibles." Rather than stay there and experience an inevitable time of decline, he chose to move forty-five miles to the south and still be a big fish but in a smaller pond of his own shaping. KSLM was a rock solid business owned by Mrs. Paulus, whom we rarely saw. It thrived under good management on the sales side and McCarl's crafty programming.

McCarl had given a lot of thought to the evolution of American entertainment. Radio, he said, was at its best when it paid attention to Vaudeville, which was the pinnacle of American entertainment evolution. Superficially we know Vaudeville as a variety show with a master of ceremonies ("interlocutor" in those days) but it was much more. It wrestled itself away from coarser forms of entertainment, built elaborate and ornate theaters in convenient downtown locations and even, in some cases, went to continuous entertainment for twelve hours. Courteous behavior by the audiences was expected and those who did not comply might be visited by ushers or management and removed from the "palace."

The interlocutor's job was to concretize the audience's enjoyment and appreciation of the entertainment. Upon the completion of an act he would make comments to insure that the art just rendered was fully appreciated. He might interject a few jokes—a technique still used by educators and conference speakers—and then, skillfully, create anticipation for an act to come. Not the next act, no, but several acts hence. This is the heart of that perfected art.

For just a second there, having heard that you are not only going to hear the finest female vocalist this side of the Mississippi (plus other frilly qualifiers) *but also see the amazing Dancing Cansino Family*, you are eased into believing you are getting double the value of your ticket price. (This anticipation technique lives on at this writing with announcers at classical music radio stations and hour-long "news" programs on television.) The successful interlocutor knew how to become your trusted friend early in the show and you would rely on him to deliver what he promised.

Vaudeville lived on into radio's early variety-show years. Consider programs like Jack Benny, Bob Hope, and the Phil Harris and Alice Faye show. They had resident orchestras and vocal ensembles and usually a "special guest" singer. Note that the special guest had the next to the last act, followed by a "family reunion" bit with all the stars. This is pure Vaudeville.

There were many times during my years there when the station was completely sold out—no more commercial time available at any price. The listeners were responding to the advertisers. A refined operation, solid and consistent. If an on-air guy kept his skills sharp and his feet on the ground, he could work here a long time.

When I arrived the morning person was a bland but dependable guy who shortly went on to a colorful career driving a bread truck. Radio work was not for everybody. McCarl was very excited to have hired Martin Doerfler, who had been at a station in Grants Pass, Oregon. That was a two-station market, Martin told me later. When he learned that his competition played a Hymn of the Day, Martin started playing a Her of the Day. He was excited not only about KSLM but also moving back to the area where he grew up, an agricultural setting on the hoopskirts of Salem.

He was a guy of demonstrated raw talent attached to a charming voice. His upbeat viewpoints and slightly naughtyish chuckle brought transformative energy to our crew. McCarl was the station's acknowledged top dog on the air but Martin's pace and easy, natural humor set the tone for the rest of us. Two of Martin's gems: "...alternate months that end in the letter J." "Pornography isn't the problem; all we need to do is get rid of the pornographs they play them on."

Frank Woodman, noon to six, looked like a suspicious character from Eastern Europe, especially when he put on his wool topcoat. Average height, round face, glasses, mustache. His head tipped a little bit forward like he was waiting for you to say something. About

THE SCHEDULE:

- 5am sign on
- 5-7 the Morning Person (eventually Martin)
- 7-9 Bob McCarl
- 9-12 the Morning Person (eventually Martin)
- 12-6pm Frank Woodman (eventually Lee)
- 6-midnight Lee Barker (eventually Tom Etaoin Shrdlu)
- Midnight sign off

the time you're thinking you're watching a black and white spy film, his smile would widen across his face and you'd see his charm. The complexity here was strictly visual. Unlike many on-air types in the radio business, he was not a class clown. He would be the quiet guy in the back row, little to say, not getting into trouble, just observing keenly. Totally likable and did his job with subtle humor.

Frank's voice which had the timbre and authority of a formal network announcer. One day he did a bit about the size of women's breasts, based on some study he was citing. The researchers' conclusion: the ideal breast would fit in a larger-size martini glass. This went on through several breaks and the kicker was that I—the same Lee Barker who would be on the air at six tonight—would be available to conduct test fittings. I had never heard anything this racy on the radio! But hey, if he's going to promote my show, sure!

In a few months Frank quit KSLM and moved to Corvallis to be on the staff at KOAC, the public radio station at Oregon State University. He worked there until his retirement. I could not understand why he would want to leave the vibrant energy of commercial radio in exchange for what to me was the plodding regularity of the block programming on a station such as KOAC. "Retirement," was his reason for the change. I was twenty-five; he was about twelve years older. He had a longer view of life which I could not yet grasp. Makes perfect sense to me now.

With Frank gone I was bumped up to afternoons and the fun began. There was way more vitality in the station atmosphere than I felt at night. I got to hear more of Martin (I'd come in at ten) and could bounce off his stuff when I went on the air after noon. McCarl cross promoted our shows and off the air encouraged us to let our creative juices flow (so long as we didn't threaten his place at the top of the pyramid). He had his Dirty Old Men's Club (unimaginable today but then, ho hum) and Martin and I were able to relax and stretch out. Things got looser and smoother as we found our way.

We partied together and shot pool at a scruffy North Salem bar called "The Burrough." We were so well known there that one night the owner took Martin and me into the back room and showed us a window, up high and beyond reach, which, he announced with a gush of pride, "I have never washed."

III

The longest and deepest thread that runs through Martin's life is propulsion by internal combustion, mostly motorcycles, beginning his high school years. He worked in motorcycle shops. He built, restored, tinkered with, and raced two wheelers. When he wasn't competing, he was in demand as a motorcycle race announcer.

After his stint at KSLM he went to work in a motorcycle shop in Salem, then to various radio gigs in Portland, some personality, some news. He bounced back to Salem where he worked his microphonal magic at a country station "until the checks started to bounce." From then to retirement he sold advertising and did audio work for The Capital Press, an agricultural newspaper. As for spare time pursuits, later in his life the idea of going really fast in a straight line caught his fancy and the result was a Bonneville Salt Flats record: 115.081mph in the 500cc special construction pushrod gas class motorcycle. He was sixty-eight at the time.

KSLM had an aging teletype machine which clattered out news both local and larger, sports stories and scores, and an occasional feature. It was a significant tool for a station with a single-person news staff. Our newsman, the turbo-powered, crew-cut T. L. Fuller, is most easily remembered grabbing his sport coat and sprinting toward the door of the station, headed to a presser at the capitol. He drove, at times quite briskly, a yellow Buick coupe, black top. Perfect. He was the polar opposite of Les Nessman, the laconic, milquetoast "five-time winner of the prestigious Buckeye Newshawk Award" on the contemporaneous TV sitcom "WKRP."

Our sales manager, "Loganberry Lou" (he was fond of fruity wines), was a doppelganger of Herb Tarlek, the slick-haired, slightly stocky, brightly dressed parody of a used-car salesman on WKRP. Same way of talking, same swagger. Uncanny resemblance.

I was feeling at home at the station and in Salem, which I began to view as the town you went through on your way to Portland.

Salem had the feel of a small town; none of the vitality of city. A little slow, like an old clock.

As a kid reading Popular Mechanics I yearned to build a car and be in the Soap Box Derby. My cobbled go kart in Big Timber was no match for the sleek, knife-pointed, tapered-back, slick-painted gravity racers that could take you clear to the finals in Akron, Ohio if you were good enough. All those images came back the first time I saw Salem's permanent derby track at Bush Park. I had no idea that in a few months I'd find myself sitting in a vehicle at the top of that paved downhill run, yellow lane lines painted bright.

Through some machinations by Bruce Kerr, Martin and I were to be in a head-to-head grudge match at that very track. We'd be racing between the official Soap Box Derby qualifying heats and the finals on the big day. Bruce wisely saw all this as a win for everyone: The Derby got a lot of mentions on KSLM in the weeks leading up to the race and Martin and I had the luxury of an ongoing promotion which would wrap up with a tidy conclusion. And the winner would be able to lord it over the loser.

Hundreds if not thousands of people were there on the glorious, blue-skied race day. Derby cars were up on simple sawhorses while eager drivers and their pit crews busied themselves spinning the wheels, using a length of rag held taut between their hands, to warm up the ball bearings. About twenty-five gravity racers. Experienced Derby officials had clipboards and walkie-talkies. The crowd moved fluidly from up in the pits (the lawn) to down to the finish line. It was vintage, colorful Americana worthy of a Norman Rockwell Saturday Evening Post cover.

Martin's entry was a tricycle affair which started with a bicycle frame and three bike wheels. Ape-hanger handlebars stuck up like antennae. He sat on the bike saddle but there the bikeness ended. High above the wide back axle a stub axle was attached, pointing backwards. A full size actual wooden airplane propeller spun freely on this shaft, on ball bearings. This tricyclic biginormous insectoid was all speed and spindly steel and a terrific visual surprise. The propeller was a brilliant, er, prop.

I modeled my gravity racer after the archetypal slingshot dragster: Front axle way far out front on two parallel wooden rails. I sat in a repurposed wicker baby carriage and steered by a flywheel from an old sewing machine with cables that went out to the center-pivoted front axle. I was operating on the theory that the vehicle was so long that the heavy part, over the back axle, would still be coming down the hill, therefore accelerating, while the front axle went over the finish line for the spectacular win. The checkered flag was mine, mine, mine!

As we were waiting at the starting line for the barricades to drop to allow our creations to begin their downward journey, Martin's dad stood behind, ready to give the prop a hearty spin. And off we went, Martin quickly in the lead. As his velocity increased and the prop's revs did the same, there was an unanticipated delivery of torque to the centerline of the vehicle which promptly lifted one of the rear wheels off the ground and kept it there until the end of the race. Martin was traveling on two wheels, which were not in alignment with one another, and one of them steered. This wasn't steering as we know it. With sheer force of will and considerable body English he was able to make the projectile loom in one direction or another. His experience riding motorcycles and his acquiring his pilot's license both contributed to his victory.

Subsequently my vehicle, which I insist should be shown in the record books as coming in second while Martin's came in next to the last, was on display at Handyman Hardware which had donated some metal bits and the lumber for the frame. The store burned down and the car with it. I went through the ashes and found the sewing machine steering wheel, still mounted in the block of wood that had been screwed to the floor of the car.

IV

There is seldom snow in Salem. It just rains, all winter. Apologists rationalize "You don't have to shovel the rain." It's "liquid sunshine." On balance, the summers were glorious, temperate, and given to easy livin'. I had purchased a red Datsun 1600 roadster and the top was down and I. Was. Cool.

I fell in love. Her name was Diana and we were living in the same neighborhood. She was pretty and ambitious. She had two jobs and was going to school part time. Eventually we were married and bought a house and got a dog. She was very good at her job—administrative assistant to the director of the Oregon School for the Blind—and was well liked. I was still driving up the hill in West Salem six days a week.

We went on a vacation the next summer and when I was back on the air I promoted a report of our trip on my show "in a few days" I had an old time push-button light switch that made a two-part *snick...clack* sound like you hear from a slide projector between slides. I just made up narrations of pictures I imagined, leaving enough out of the description to trigger some inclusion from the listener's mind. Bruce remembered that bit thirty-five years later when we sat down in Salem to reminisce.

When Bruce walked into any room in the station, the energy indicator rose. He wasn't loud, just joyful. Fun to be around. He stood an easy six feet, muscular, as ready to move quickly as to lay out a belly laugh observation. He like to walk into our area at the end of his day out selling and try to make the guy on the air laugh while he was attempting to deliver a piece of live advertising copy.

Just how the Merritt Davis School of Commerce Carnivores came to life at KSLM is a cipher. We didn't ask, we just did it. Merritt Davis was a secretarial school which also offered accounting classes, mostly female students. We made them part of an imaginary local "Six Man Women's Football League" and took them on as "our home team." Martin, McCarl, and I

THE OPPONENTS:

- Salem Meter Maid Citations
- Cinderella School of Modeling and Self Improvement Playtex Pouncers
- Western Baptist Euphorics
- Modern Beauty College Strippers and Teasers
- Rickreall Fire Department Pole Sliders
- Miss Oregon Finalists
- Salem Area Chamber of Commerce Maids

gathered one evening in the production room and recorded some interviews and play-by-play clips.

Folks at Merritt Davis heard our bits and got some castoff football equipment and took pictures of six of their students in ragtag pads and helmets. When we got that image, things picked up speed. We printed posters with the picture of the costumed players and the full schedule including locations and halftime shows. Everyone at the station, including the sales staff, had fun with this.

One punchline to this story: a fall Saturday, early afternoon, someone called the station, apparently serious, and said they had been down under the Ferry Street Bridge but couldn't find the game that was scheduled for that day. Had it been canceled, or were they playing somewhere else?

V

After Martin was hired and I had been promoted to afternoons, McCarl shared with me his delight at our talent lineup, how he and Martin and I were going to "sing." He understood the chemistry thing. Given the ego profiles of people who will end up on the air, it is a rare experience when they all are performing at their peak *and* contributing to each other, creating something larger than the sum of the parts.

We had that and it was like floating free. Everything was better. Day after day, eager to get to work.

Although on the surface I had a secure future with KSLM, I felt a growing sense of rejection of the consumer values that stare you in the ears every day in that job. I was part of the Establishment. This was in contrast to married couple weekend projects creating tie-dyed jackets and reading Stewart Brand's Whole Earth Catalog. I felt pressure from my generation to reject the status quo; it was a time of personal turmoil.

My high school years were in an Air Force Base town and I had respect for military institutions and an adolescent understanding of the Cold War. Now, with quite different ears, I was hearing multiple daily network news reports about the Vietnam war, pretty certain it was a big mistake.

I was not in a uniform because of two major episodes of rheumatic fever at ages five and eleven.

Parallel to this, tension developed between McCarl and me. In memory, I felt less valued and less important than before. I didn't have the communication tools to sit down with McCarl and discuss it. I just let it build while I did my job.

I talked at home about quitting. Diana was secure in her position at the Oregon School for the Blind. We could live for a short while without my income if I left KSLM. Alternatively, more money and stay at KSLM might be a temporary fix. So, into Bruce's office to make my case for a raise.

I wanted a hundred dollars more a month. I hadn't seen any ratings results, but Bruce knew I was pulling my own weight. He pondered it for a nervous while and said he couldn't do it. "Fine," I said. "Then this is my two week notice."

Bruce was taken aback. But he made no counter offer on the salary.

VI

My dreams of eventually being a major market radio personality were assessed, stamped "probably not good enough to accomplish this" and set aside while I regrouped at home. How about becoming a state employee? I scanned the lists, visited offices, submitted applications. I got close to landing a position on the team that certified homes for foster care kids. The leader had interviewed me twice and was ready to ignore the prior applicants and offer me the job but that was not allowed, state hiring regulations. I was back on the street.

In a bit of foreshadowing I was making wooden toy cars in my tiny garage workshop. I had a hand held Black and Decker jigsaw (the cheapest model) and an electric drill (the old fashioned kind which you plug in). I made wheels, bought dowels for axles, and cranked out a couple dozen unique designs. We displayed our wares at the Saturday Farmer's Market in our neighborhood and sold a few. Two went to Bob Straub, secretary of state and eventual governor of Oregon. We spent the money at other booths, for fruits and vegetables. Perhaps all of life is an exercise in discovering what won't work.

Because of Diana's inside information I signed a ninety-day contract at the Oregon School for the Blind, a state residential facility in Salem. I was a teachers aide, working with multiply-handicapped kids (that was the language of the time). In a classroom setting I helped students learn life skills that would contribute to their future independence. I also participated in field trips and campouts. Combining my photography and writing interests I sold a newspaper feature about one of the multiple-day camps at Wallowa Lake. That ended on its schedule, not mine.

We had made friends with an interesting couple—John and Elana Hatch—and John worked for U.S. Plywood as a timber cruiser. He was involved in a tree planting project with the company and would I, being "between engagements," want to come to work as a tree planter? "Sure."

The eight months I had spent in bed with rheumatic fever had taken a bite out of my social interactions as a fifth grader but I didn't lose any school progress. The Big Timber Lions Club purchased an intercom system which connected me with the classroom so I could be present electronically for some classes. My math teacher sent homework with my sister Bernie. What was stunted, as a result of all this, was my sense of my physical ability. Our very conservative family doctor and my hovering mom combined to keep me from pushing myself physically. As an adult I assumed I could do only limited physical activities, and was limited to a sedentary career. I treated my persistent heart murmur as a limiter rather than an artifact of my health history.

VII

As Rinker Buck says in <u>The Oregon Trail</u>, "Naiveté is the mother of adventure." I thought planting trees would just be a lot of walking.

No. Trees grow really well in western Oregon but rarely on flat ground. Trees grow well because it rains a lot. Forty-two inches of rain per year in Salem, but up in the Cascade Mountains where we planted, sixty-six. Up and down hills, in the mud.

We replanted clearcuts, climbing over downed cedars which were felled and left, plowing through salmonberries and ferns, tying off tags of bright orange survey ribbon up hills and down into valleys, to keep our spacing and columns true.

The work was interesting and athletic. Typical tree planting is accomplished with a soft bag of moist bare root trees, usually about 2 years old, and a digging tool of some type. The key to success of the tree is to get the roots into the hole straight up and down, not curled up at the bottom end. That condition, called J-root, will likely lead to death of the tree. Scientists rooted around in the lab to find a better way to plant.

The result was a block of styrofoam about twelve by twenty-four inches and eight inches deep. It was peppered with depressions that looked like they had been formed around test tubes. Into each of these depressions a seed was placed, in a nutritious mix of peat moss and vermiculite. Hundreds of these blocks, laid flat, were watered by overhead sprinklers which served up a liquid fertilizer cocktail. These trees were younger than two years and hardy enough to plant.

The planter carried a dibble, a half-length shovel handle with a foot pedal and a steel end just the shape of the holes in the styrofoam. Stomp the dibble's foot pedal down and pull it back out. Grasp the next tree by its skinny but woody stem and pull it out of the styrofoam (the root wad kept that test-tube shape) and slide it right into the hole the dibble had made. Give that planted "plug" a gentle sideways kick with your booted foot. Done! Quicker to plant, better chance of survival.

We planted on Thomas Creek in the Cascades and then Slick Rock Creek in the Coast Range, off Highway 18 near Rose Lodge, to complete the project. We were the Elite Dibblers of U.S. Plywood, responsible for thousands of promising young seedlings in Oregon's forests, and I enjoyed the physicality of the work. But not the wet.

As I gained calendar distance from personality radio I appreciated what goes into it, what happens underneath, part of a textbook artistic journey to find my authentic self. What I did best at KSLM was elicit a warm, inward smile from the listener. My self guide to what kind of mental framework would facilitate authenticity and consistent quality:

1. Never say, "I don't know" when you should know. No need to lie, just don't let yourself get there.

2. There are good guys and bad guys. In everything. Be selective so that no single group is always bad guys.

3. Never knock the music. It's part of your persona, so the negative message would be confusing.

4. Always refer to the listener in the singular. That's how we're listened to. "They" aren't a giant multi-eared organism sitting in an auditorium. At any given moment someone is taking a radio into the bathroom to listen to you, maybe even with bubble bath. "All you people out there" blows radio magic to smithereens. Connection broken.

5. Radio is theater of the mind. It doesn't happen here, it happens there. So let it.

There are pitfalls in all of these notions. That only affirms that we're talking about art and, in the end, one must do what pleases him as an artist and remember to listen to the voice on his other shoulder, the one which says, in a gentle parental tone, "It's time to drop this topic and move on to something else. Start the record!"

All this analysis was interesting but clearly a dead end. "I am done selling Buicks and Pepsi," I said, flatly. Let go of radio! Grieve the loss and move on! Look back at the trees you just planted!

Yep, done with broadcasting. I was a tree planter. I could do it physically, and the optimism of youth convinced me that, one day, something else would come along. Exactly what, was a delicious mystery.

And then Bruce Bell called from Salt Lake City.

FOUR

KALL 1971 - 1975

I

While still employed at KSLM in Salem and before my disenchantment with radio in general, I had sent an audition tape to KALL in Salt Lake City. Wrapped in audacity sealed with egotism. I was nowhere near the caliber of the talent there, the hippest station in the seventy-third largest city in the country. So I forgot about it.

I was a professional tree planter. This day I'd been up in the rainy Cascade Mountains compressing sequential sole-shaped layers of mud onto my boots until, when I got home, I was tall enough to play center for the Celtics or change the light bulbs in an auditorium.

The phone rang, interrupting the evening. "This is Bruce Bell at KALL in Salt Lake City."

He offered me the evening slot. You could have knocked me over with a dibble. I turned him down. I was done with radio. Done.

The next evening, a call from Tom Barberi, KALL's morning personality, inviting me to "come on over." He talked about the freedom he had and how much fun it was and what a great guy Bruce was to work for. Still no. Still Done.

Next it was Bennie Williams, the sales manager, calling to raise the ante. The money got my attention, but still no. Diana was ambivalent. She was up for the adventure but could as easily stay in Oregon, her home state. The calls stopped.

Several days later I was lugging my box of baby trees up on Thomas Creek on a drizzlin' drippy highly humid day. We were ascending a gentle slope recently clearcut and cleaned of slash. What was left was the wet, knee-deep understory flora including salmonberry, which is a member of the rose family (ooh) and classified as a bramble (ouch). I was dibbling distractedly along, minding my seedling spacing when I encountered a large cedar tree which had been felled and left because it wasn't a Douglas fir. Three to four feet diameter at the butt. Right in my way. Too long to go around. I scrabbled up on top of it and took two steps uphill on the slippery bark looking for a likely place to jump to on the other side. I lost my footing and fell on my nose, spread-eagled over the scabrous tree-husk, dropped my dibble on the uphill side, and my box of trees down the other side, where I'd just been. Rolled off the tree and fell into the chlorophylled silence.

Lying on my back in the wet vegetation on the forest floor, I reached out and touched that spiritual cedar. There came a compelling vision of a cozy warm radio studio with a large window facing South Temple Street in downtown Salt Lake City. A powerful, epiphanic moment. That night I called Bruce Bell and told him I'd changed my mind.

Bruce was open to my pleading. He had since made arrangements for the evening shift but he didn't think it would last. He promised he would keep in touch. I took the initiative to call him every few weeks to remind him of my name. Summer months passed.

August. Brrrrrrring! "Barker? This is Bruce Bell. Sell your house and get down here!" So we did.

We loaded our stuff into a U-Haul truck, the last item being Tilman Kreft's BMW motorcycle, and Tillie drove the load and Diana and I followed in the Datsun 1600. When we got to Salt Lake City, we offloaded the Beemer and said goodbye to Tillie, who had done us a terrific favor. He headed back home to Salem, taking the circuitous and scenic route through Klamath Falls. (Later, in my motorcycle years, son Joel and I did the same type of trip for a Redmond school teacher who moved to Merrill, Oregon. Just payin' it forward.)

II

At four pm my first day at work at 312 East South Temple Street, I presented myself in Bruce Bell's office. He stood six three, authentically athletic, and moved with intention and anticipation. I sat there, nervous as a kid standing next to a flaming incinerator into which he had just thrown an empty spray can whose subsequent explosion had brought three neighbors into his back yard.

Immediately I felt that I was the most important person on the staff and he had been looking forward to meeting me since our first phone conversation months before. And that was Bruce. Imagine working for a supervisor whose first word of a sentence was often an explosive, "HAH!" That, too, was Bruce.

What a beautiful, awe-inspiring building on a busy street on the edge of downtown Salt Lake: Two floors plus a basement. Down below were the printing facility, the music library, the engineers' office and the desks for the air staff. Main floor was control rooms, news, and programming secretarial offices where the daily logs were created. Upstairs, the sales and management offices. I was getting the tour of the flagship of the Intermountain Network as well as an ABC Radio Network affiliate. And, in some corner of my little-boy mind, I was inside the castle on the hill of dreams where I'd first met Jack Bogut. Dreams I had dared not share.

As I stood in that control room my first night alone I had a textbook Pinch Me! moment. All the radio I had listened to those months of childhood confinement, the sound effects story in my grade school reading book, the Webcor tape recorder my dad bought and let me play with, listening to Wayne and Schuster, Stan Freberg, Bob and Ray, Steve Allen, Spike Jones, and Irwin Corey, were planks in the subfloor where I stood. I was twenty-seven years old, the youngest on-air person on the staff, and overwhelmed, intimidated, juiced, and eager to prove myself. In my life there has been no other moment so weighty, except holding my newborn sons.

III

In the control room facing the control board, I could look over it through a window into Master Control which was the on-duty engineer's bailiwick. He was shunting IMN feeds around the region, monitoring the performance of our AM transmitter and doing engineerish things which were beyond my ken. To the left, across South Temple Street, the Cathedral of the Madeline, a lofty Gothic Roman Catholic edifice dating to 1909.

That window was large and triple-glazed with the interior pane tilted at a slight angle. These are common in both broadcasting settings as well as sound recording. There's no magic to the angle. It just allows the center pane to be a different vertical dimension from the other two so that it doesn't vibrate sympathetically with them. If it weren't there, sound would radiate easily both directions. And that's why studios have an extra pane in the glass.

I thrived on the music. It was fresh, compared to KSLM, and felt just right.

Middle of the Road (MOR) music as a radio format had bridged the awkward time when some well-done, not excessive rock tunes were bumping up against Frank Sinatra (remember "Summer Wind"?) and had

THE WEEKDAY SCHEDULE:

- 6-10 Tom Barberi
- 10-2 Dan Tyler
- 2-6 Will Lucas
- 6-11 Lee Barker
- 11-Midnight "The 11th Hour" with Paul Engmann (prerecorded)
- Midnight-6 a.m. Dale Etaoin Shrdlu who could sleep during long songs and wake up before they ended. Dale had another job plus he was an officer in the National Guard. One morning he left his all-night radio job in his dusty light blue Ford Pinto and was found parked three blocks away, idled into a traffic sign on a median, the exhausted driver deep in peaceful sleep. No harm, no foul, except for the front of the Pinto.

come into its own. The jazzy end was Sergio Mendes and Brasil PickaNumber. We played Fifth Dimension and Neil Diamond and Gladys Knight and Peter Yarrow and Linda Ronstadt and Norman Greenbaum and Olivia Newton-John and had concrete hopes that Rikki wouldn't lose that number when Steely Dan came 'round the rotation. Jim Croce was a stalwart. Hamid Hamilton Camp and the Skymonters had a bit of a hit with "Gypsy" which was an engaging invitation to a female to "...come on with me, for a while our home's out on the highway."

I often played "Alice Adams" from the same album:

"Alice Adams lived in Provo Utah / with two kids and a husband name of Joe / They'd been married eight years come October / life in Provo Utah's kinda slow /"

Alice had edited "the paper and the mag" in college, but had to give that all up. Then the walls began to close in. So one day she whispers her goodbye and, with just her "suitcase and some books," hits the high road, destination Big Apple.

"Don't look back now, keep on moving / You'll be in New York by Monday, / Steal away, steal away..."

After that tune ended one night the phone rang. "KALL Radio" I said.

"YAY ALICE!" An animated female voice. We laughed together and she hung up. The joy of connection.

July 4, big summer celebration. I went to work as usual. On-air types even in this size market didn't get holidays off. I thought about others who were working and listening. What could I do for that person? I put on a long song and went back to the production room—not far away—and flipped my way through the sound effects albums and found the Official Proof of Performance recordings.

The FCC at the time required periodic testing of a station's equipment: proof of performance. One of those sequences involved playing various pitches on the turntables and comparing them to FCC standard frequencies to determine if the turntables were running exactly at 33.33 or 45 rpm. The listener never hears this testing because the station, at some wee hour, is off the air, "for transmitter maintenance."

I started a recording tape and set the needle on a random track on the tone record. Immediately I took the turntable out of gear, which permitted the beautifully balanced wheel to slow down at a consistent rate. Now I had a recording of a tone that got lower and lower. Reversing the tape gave me the opposite of the turntable out of gear—the pitch started low and ascended, a perfect audio recreation of the firework from launch to apogee. (I was doing this during records which were getting cursory attention on the air, moving quickly between studios.) Next was sound effects. Odd things, like burps and boings, trumpet fanfares and water gushing. I recorded a bunch.

I went back to being present on the air and casually mentioned that we would be enjoying a private fireworks display later in the evening.

Occasionally, even during a song, I'd start the recording of the ascending tone and stop it...wait a second...then play one of the boings or trumpet tunes or explosions.

I'd do a few, applause track after each one, and on to the next record or whatever Better than beer and brats and apple pie in the back yard with kids running amok with sparklers.

IV

Will Lucas had been the morning guy on KALL years ago, for years. He was pure talent, creative, wise, smooth and funny. One of his regular features in that period was to read the daily Peanuts strip on the air with lively music interstitial to the dialog in the balloons. (My inspiration for reading Rick O"Shay on KDBM, you'll doubtless recall.) People hung on it. And that led to one of his great public stunts. Every Yule, the Salt Lake Tribune, the city's largest newspaper, would erect an ostentatious Christmas tree downtown. Across the street Will would place his Charlie Brown Christmas tree. Small, scraggly, formless, with one ornament dangling precariously.

Will was widely and deeply loved while he was on the air. He was short and stocky, craggy-faced. His voice was unique in its timbre but better noted for how he could draw sounds out for emphasis without appearing affected. One one commercial recording he said "polymerrrs" and it sounded mystical and magical, high-science and important. He could load up his language and make it compelling in a style he owned. I heard ambitious junior varsity disc jockeys on lesser stations in Salt Lake City trying to emulate Will. Didn't work.

Midday was owned by Dan Tyler (his radio name), a solid guy with a great voice. We don't use the word "housewives" much anymore but that's the term for the market he served, and he knew it. Dan was on the coasting side of his career and his authoritative voicing of commercials was a great asset. Dan was stocky like Will, oval-faced with a quick, kind of diagonal smile, and always on his way to somewhere. That might be a recording studio in the city to do commercials or voiceovers for an ad agency.

Tom Barberi was the star of the station but no prima donna. He'd been recruited from a successful stint in San Jose, California. Football was his passion. The University of Utah was a Western Athletic Conference school at the time so there was plenty of rich local sports material to inspire his creative mind.

His on-air shtick included a bicycle horn and a bell which were used to emphasize his discovery of something funny. He often played comedy bits off records—something I chose not to do—and it worked for him. Tom was a big-chest type guy, black haired, always looking for the corners of things so he could break them off and talk about what he saw. His was not a typical radio voice but when you're as talented as he, nobody cares. Tom worked Salt Lake radio until his retirement.

Ongoing, every show, Ophir State University. Ophir was a ghost town about fifty miles west of Salt Lake. An imaginary institution offers a broad landscape on which to build imaginative stuff on the radio.

He started with music, a master tape of Tijuana Brass-type tunes which were played perfectly except for the second trumpet part which had been overdubbed and was hilariously inept. Out of tune, off time, rushed, dragging, every grade school band teacher's worst nightmare was realized on these cuts. Tom would play a couple a shift. It was the Ophir State Marching Band and he knew how to use it in creative ways.

Just before I arrived at KALL Bruce had spearheaded making an album from this master tape. The shipments of freshly-pressed vinyl arrived with the records inserted in blank sleeves. For the album art a bunch of the staff acquired fragments of musical instruments and spent a couple hours doing a photo shoot at a local dump. Bruce created a two-color montage—yellow and black—for the cover and he and Tom concocted the liner notes with the tune names and other absurdities.

The name Bucknell was an integral part of Tom's Ophir schema. A friend played the part of Swanee Bucknell, coach of the imaginary Ophir State teams. Tom would call Swanee on the air and just wing it. There were times when Swanee would tell Tom that things were so bad he didn't want to talk to him and just hang up with a clunk. That, with Tom's handling of it, could be as funny as five minutes of unscripted insanity with Swanee.

V

"Have you heard about Lee Barker?" was the theme of several spots airing on KALL before I started there. We had heard a couple of these on the AM radio as we negotiated I-15 approaching our new home.

It was a homecoming for me. People I had known from college days were still there. Some had heard the promotional spots on KALL, stuff that I had had no part in creating. Linda Hanson must have been one of those.

I had introduced myself to her, a freshman; I, a senior, because Mrs. Booth, one of my English professors, insisted. Her concern for my having a balanced life (read: girlfriend) extended beyond an assurance that I understood all the images in Edward Arlington Robinson's richly textured poem called, "Mr. Flood's Party." Through the years she had nominated several interesting female candidates and pointed them out to me. My response had been pure tepid shyness. But this time she was adamant—it was my last year—and I reluctantly agreed. Meet Linda Hanson. Right. OK. Check.

I was stunned and I stuttered. I was standing before a strikingly beautiful girl with a wide smile and a coy style. Her picture would be a perfect Webster's illustration beside the "Nordic Beauty" entry.

We fell stupidly in love. We would cut class to sit opposite in the student union and stare at each other and laugh. It was the freefloating film sequence from "A Thousand Clowns" where Murray (Jason Robards) and Sandra (Barbara Harris) swing and swirl through New York City to a simple ukelele version of 'Yes, Sir, That's My Baby.' We were a twitterpated twosome who mindlessly reshaped their temporal lives to share the mystic oneness of pure limerence.

When Christmastide came 'round that year I was away from home for the first time. My commitment to playing in a band, the leader of which depended on employment to support his wife and daughters, precluded any absences. Classmates were gone, daylight was short and I was shuttered in my bleak basement apartment. But there was Linda, who lived with her family a few miles away. So I went to see her. This was going to be a great Christmas Break!

I was met at the door by her father, a large guy. I introduced myself. "She does not want to see you again," he said flatly. Whaaaaaat?

I was stunned. I had no response. I backed down the concrete steps and made my dejected way to my '51 Ford and drove slowly away, hollowed out. I searched my memory for some clue I had missed, some sideways glance whose off-key head-tilt was a harbinger. Nothing.

Instantly the days were even shorter, my apartment darker, my life one large black circular void that I would walk around during the day and, after distractedly playing four hours of music for drinkers of beer or bringers of booze each night, I'd fall in.

School resumed in January. I avoided her, languishing in the pain of rejection. Our schedules didn't intersect much and I didn't want to be reminded of that awful message and the way it was delivered. No explanation. Possibly her dad found out I was a musician. And she couldn't persuade him I was not one of *those* musicians. Maybe it was that I lived alone in an apartment. Perhaps they were Mormons and I, being a Gentile, was unacceptable. She disappeared from my world.

I had been on the air a few evenings and was getting my sea legs with the equipment and the flow of things. Aware of some movement to my left, I turned and looked out the window to the well-lighted sidewalk. There she was. *Linda Hanson.* Radiant, smiling, stunning as ever. Our eyes met; she moved closer to the window. There were two stairstep tow-headed boys next to her and a third, toddler-size, on her hip. The longest second in the world; then another. "I love you," she mouthed. I mouthed it in response, and had to turn and tend to my job. When I looked back, she and the three little boys were gone.

VI

OTHER MOMENTS FROM THE LEE BARKER SHOW:

- I interviewed Desi Arnaz. Just kidding, partly. I interviewed Desi Arnaz *Junior*. Completely forgettable, as was the interview with the stunt guy from the movie "The Seven Ups." Oh, and a representative from the company that makes Sharpies. Hindsight, I wished I had done something like, "These are special markers that only work on radio. Here, hand me one of the colored ones. (make squeaky noise) Hear that? These are *actual special radio felt-tip markers* available at your stationery store." I had little warning about these things, which were probably sent downstairs from a salesman who was doing a favor for a client or a client's client. I just did them.

- I played a PSA (Public Service Announcement) for some charity which was hosting Rose Kennedy one evening. I had to play it right after her limousine passed the station. It reminded me of the Evening of Excessive Robert Goulet at KSLM. Both were unfun.

- Outside utility work required some deep excavation just in front of the window to the control room. Utilizing tools from my Christmas toolbox and my modest woodworking skills, I built a box at home. About the size of two shoeboxes. I asked for contributions to our time capsule. I got a bunch, but only one remains in my memory: A sequin from Eugene Jelesnik's jacket. Jelesnik was a Salt Lake institution and his life—after escaping from Ukraine as a toddler with his mother and aunt to avoid the Bolshevik Revolution—was show business. For nearly fifty years, "Eugene Jelesnik's Talent Showcase" presented little girls dancing and twirling batons, and young boys squeezing out "Lady of Spain" on the accordion. The sequin was perfect: silly, yes, but also acknowledging a local character of historical significance. The KALL listeners loved to respond to stuff like this.

- Halloween Day around 5 pm I was puttering about and saw two creatures walk in the station's front door: Wolfman and Frankenstein's Monster. The latter was clicking and clattering as he walked because, as I learned later in an entirely different work environment, he was wearing drywaller stilts. He had to duck through doorways. They went right into the control room and picked up Willie and carried him out the back door. I finished Willie's shift. He came in later that evening, and I chatted with him on the air. He complained that his abductors had forced upon him "...some sort of strange beverage that had an unusual effect on my mind and my limbs."

- Was handed a record of "Sweet Grass County Montana" sung by Phil Everly. Big Timber is the county seat of that very place. It was a fine tune with driving rhythm and a flimsy story line hung on clichés. Came and went, like records do.

- I called on an ad in The New Yorker advertising a writer in Bournemouth, England who would take your idea and turn it into a book or a story or whatever you wanted. "I have an idea," I said. "I'm thinking about an Albino ship captain, mid nineteenth century, who becomes obsessed with a whale which has a wooden fin. What do you think? Could this be a worthwhile project for us to work together on?" He was funny and a good sport.

- I was streaked! University of Utah women, I theorized. Must have been a half dozen of them, strung in a line, jogging past my window. They were laughing and screaming so much I could hear them through the three panes of glass. The ratio of hilarity to lasciviousness was about a billion to one. I commented on the air to increase their enjoyment of the whole adventure, of course, but that was it. I took it as a compliment.

- Made up and aired some late-night advertisements to "learn to cut hair at home in your spare time." Your first tuition payment covers "two sets of clippers, a spray bottle and that jar of blue stuff to keep your combs in, a detailed workbook with lessons and templates, as well as 10 pre-addressed, postage paid envelopes." You were to study a lesson and then try it on someone, sweep up the cut hair, place it in the envelope and send it in. You'd get a letter back with an "encouraging critique" of your progress so far. Shades of Jack Levitan and the Columbia School of Broadcasting.

VII

The Ophir State Marching Band record and Tom's love of silliness inspired me one night, after I finished up at eleven, to step into the production room and record off-key falsetto singing along with Johnny Nash on "I Can See Clearly Now." Entirely by accident my "singing" was similar in timbre to Nash's. Could have been the last take of a session when they let the guy who delivered the pizza and beer join in with the artist for one last shot at the lyrics.

It was an unplanned vocal parallel to the Ophir State Marching Band record. I stuck a label on it—Emma Bucknell audition—and put it in Tom's mailbox. He played it on his show and that started something. Bruce: "Hah! Let's make another record!"

The Bucknell Sisters: Emma, Erma and Floyd. I found an instrumental-only version of "My Skies Were Black (But You Made Them Blue Again)" and gave that to Emma to solo. In my darkroom I created a superimposition of the three um, er, artists, all me. Diana took the photos. Strep Throat: A Sock Hopera was ready to be pressed.

Bruce and Tom wrote all the liner notes for Strep Throat. My name appears nowhere on the cover or the record label, which identifies it as a KALL Radio recording.

In the text Emma is described as "swept up in her search for her real identity by a big mouth shovel at the local landfill." Erma is "Cousin to the main character and steady date to Sherman Scentless, the department's chief scout." Floyd: "An itinerant housefly trainer whose brace of attack flies has just been wiped out by an unseasonal July snowfall.

"Listeners to the disc will be mistreated to such titles as:

I Can See Clearly Now

My Skies Were Black (But You Made Them Blue Again)

Ain't Misbehavin'

Back Roads

Uptown Girl

Hey Jude"

We pressed five hundred discs and sold them for $2 out of the front office. Then another five hundred. At this writing, you can occasionally find one on the web, perhaps noted as a "Deejay ego project from KALL in Salt Lake City." During this writing I found one for sale in Italy, 135USD.

Two big releases, blockbusters in both sales and our complete disregard for copyright laws. Hah! We weren't looking for a third album to complete the trilogy, but it found us. A little later.

VIII

Because of their passion for sports in general, Bruce and Tom made sure that KALL reached out to sports fans. The station carried the Utah Stars basketball games when the American Basketball Association was flourishing and flaunting the three-point shot, which it originated.For games scheduled when I was not at work, I could always get free tickets. We saw a lot of basketball those years.

We had a softball team called "The KALL No-Stars" which practiced shenanigans and then went bigtime playing the wives of the Salt Lake Angels, the local triple A baseball team. It was a beautiful summer night and Tom made it more beautiful by landing a nice base hit into short right field whereupon he ran to third base. From the batter's box.

In yet another foreshadowing of vocational menopause I had acquired a softball bat and, with careful sawing and drilling a hole for a dowel pivot pin, created a hinge about 16" from the big end.

The hip of the hinge was cut an an angle so it would remain straight if I held it in a certain orientation. I put it on my shoulder and carried it to the batter's box and prepared to hit. Upon the delivery of the sphere I rotated my wrists just a little and the bat, still over my shoulder, bent into an L shape, pointed down. I had thought it might be funny but the crowd found it hilarious. Next pitch, I did it again; more laughter. I could not risk hitting the ball with that laugh-getter bat. The game would have to be called on account of kindling. Got another bat, got a hit, and was thrown out at first. Not out of the game! I would have missed the chili cookoff.

I was invited to play at a Saturday morning tennis exhibition featuring aspiring boys ten to twelve years old. I saw a chance to have a little fun and get an audience to laugh. A guy who sends his stuff out into the silent ether and never really hears a laugh coming back, craves the occasional live venue. I miscalculated the whole scenario.

I doctored tennis balls. I injected various amounts of water into several, sealing the hole with Duco cement from the tube. Unbalanced a ball with a glob of glue. Another I cut along the figure eight lines and loosened flaps of the ball. It wouldn't go far and made a "blappety blappety" sound until it landed.

I snipped and removed all the racket stringing and replaced it with white elastic from a sewing notions store. I expected the racket would receive the tennis ball, stretch to its limit and then launch the tennis ball back, but no. There was too much velocity on the ball and too much freedom for the lines of elastic to move out of the ball's way. The result was a real-looking racket with which you could stroke a beautiful forehand shot *and the ball would go right through it and the racket would instantly return to looking normal.* It was amazing and simultaneously disturbing. Better than I had hoped for!

The boys, my opponents, didn't find any of it funny. Tennis was a way of life, not a way to get a little fresh air, and their faces faithfully conveyed that my humor was falling fully flat. Ever the trouper, I soldiered on, spacing out the faulty balls and switching back to the Oral Roberts Autographed Super Healing Racket from time to time just to nudge them out of their Tennis-Is-Everything state of mind. The parents were mostly quiet after the event, only a few acknowledging my contribution. I was not invited back, a good thing. Otherwise, it was a nice morning in a park in Salt Lake City.

IX

When I was hired at KALL, the evening sports news was presented by Bill Marcroft, a TV sports guy who worked at Channel 2, under the same ownership as KALL. When that talent-sharing arrangement ended, Bruce asked me to leap into the breech and what, do a sports news show? Me? I was reluctant. I had an acquaintance with sports but could hardly be called a fan. Bruce demurred and leaned me into the gig. It got easier. I rewrote sports copy off the teletype, and always had a press release "just in" with some flak about the local professional teams, which included the aforementioned Bees as well as the Salt Lake Golden Eagles, of the Western Hockey League. And always something about the Utah Stars, even in the off season when trades happened.

Every Stars game had a "sponsor," which involved some complex mix of mentions on the PA system at the game and giveaways for the attenders and all that. Thus this line on my sports program: "The Utah Stars meet the Memphis Tams tonight at the Salt Palace. The game is sponsored by the United States Marine Corps, a good arrangement since both the Marines and the Stars are currently looking for a few good men." (Context: This was the current recruiting slogan for the Corps, and the Stars were not shining brightly at the time).

X

Evening newsmen (a gender-specific term of accuracy of the time) came and went at KALL. Of special mention would be Dan Breinholt. Tall, long legged and athletic, he was a gentle soul in a world of guys in a hurry brandishing sharp edges to help them get where they were going and do incisive reporting. Dan was more of a plodder, but thorough. He had an unnewsmanlike voice but when he spoke it was with such sincerity and guy-next-door directness you just had to trust him. He was an example of an early observation I had made about radio voices: If one tries to change his voice, it will always sound not quite right. Plus there's the risk of forgetting to adjust your adenoids before pontificating and accidentally sounding normal, therefore silly. Dan was easy to work with and always poked his head into the control room to say goodbye when he left for the evening, usually around eight.

At the other stations where I had worked, the amplified sound we heard on the monitor speakers in the control room was exactly what was broadcast, taken from the downstream end of the transmitter. There was a practical reason: If something failed electrically or electronically, the person on the air—perhaps the only person in the building—would know immediately and could address the problem. It was different at KALL because we had a remote transmitter on a hill outside of the city and the engineers monitored that program signal. So the sound we heard throughout the building's various speakers was *not* what was broadcast, it was program *on its way* to the transmitter.

Afternoon drive time with Will Lucas, Dan Breinholt in the newsroom. Something failed electronically in the remote transmitter and we went off the air. Protocol is to keep the programming going if it is a minor problem, but the phone call came back from the engineers, just to Willie, that it was going to take some time to repair it. Willie kept rolling along, right up to the news as if everything were normal. Dan, unaware that an audience of zero awaited his newscast, stepped into the booth, facing Willie's back, and commenced the 5 pm report with headlines and a cue to Willie for the recorded commercial, which aired as usual. Back live, Dan read the important lead story. Willie left his mic open and was shuffling stuff around. From Dan's perspective, Willie had just forgotten about the mic switch. As Dan got to the end of the story, Willie said, "Wow. No kidding." Just the kind of comment one would make out loud to himself but to Dan's ear this was *in his broadcast and he could do nothing about it*. He gulped and went to the next story. Still shuffling papers, Willie added, "Aw, that's a shame!" Dan was distracted but forged on nobly in his endeavor to deliver the latest. Next story, Willie dropped his incendiary bomb:

"NO SHIT! THAT'S INEXCUSABLE! Why would somebody do something like *that*?" Dan was blanching now, beads of sweat, voice wavering a little. Willie didn't overplay his hand, just kept his mic open. Dan closed out the news; Willie went straight to music. Now pale and rattled, Dan stepped quickly across the hall into the newsroom, put his newscast in the proper bin and blasted out the back door. I had watched all this from inside the newsroom.

As we later learned, Dan went home to his apartment and sat down, still pale, at the table. "Honey, what's the matter?" his young wife inquired.

"Oh, you wouldn't believe it," he said.

"I know," she countered. "You've been off the air! I haven't heard a thing on my radio for an hour!"

Dan went on to TV news and anchor positions in Salt Lake as well as Illinois, did a stint on a cable network and then went into real estate in southern Utah.

XI

MORE SNAPSHOTS FROM KALL:

- I was invited to a family reunion. A Mormon family. I had become so familiar to the young lady who called me (maybe in her twenties, just a guess) and her sister that they thought I would fit right in. I begged off; it sounded like an afternoon of complete awkwardness. I saw the thing in black and white: Go or don't go. In retrospect I could have done the courteous thing of agreeing, showing up, meeting a whole bunch of nice people, and then leaving. She deserved better treatment than my refusal.

- We advertised for and went to a Saturday morning doughnut eating contest presented by a local doughnut house. It was in a bleak multipurpose room and Tom, Bruce and I were what, judges or something? It was poorly planned and proceeded without help from us. The amateurish host of this apparent attempt to sell doughnuts would badger two entrants to get up on the stage and stand on opposing sides of a table on which were two piles of deep-fried, unfrosted toroids. The whistle signaled the start. When a second whistle announced the end, the competitors would be shoulder to shoulder, leaning over a garbage can and vomiting. What a salutary way to promote your product! We just stood around and kept our distance while Bruce took pictures that made us look involved.

- The next week Bruce was writing a story about it for KALL Playback, the house organ (distributed by the sales staff to advertisers and prospects) and he couldn't remember the name of the winner. He asked around; none of us could. So we made one up. Glenn Cutler. Well done! Tough competition! Congratulations Glenn!

- Remember "Let's Spend the Night Together" by the sultry song-whisperer Claudine Longet? Well. I got a small package from "her" when that song was current. The promoters of the recording realized their best advocates would be evening radio announcers in major markets. Brilliant! I eagerly unpacked the small reel of tape and was distressed when I read the misspellacious label: "Let's spend the night together with Lee Balker on KALL." Aw. Disappointment. I couldn't use it if she mispronounced my name! Turns out it was fine. "Ziss izz Claudine Lonzhey...less spend zeh night togezzer wiz Lee Balker on KALL," (music up with the breathy chorus).With her French accent that spelling and the correct one sound the same. Roll it!

XII

Bruce nicknamed him"Blueline" and it stuck. Colin Thomas, a diminutive guy with a round face and hair the color of fresh rust, was our skilled advertising copywriter. You couldn't know him without knowing his passions—The Yankees, Cheryl Tiegs, hockey, and golf.

He became the voice of Dr. Golf on my program. It was material I stole from a book of the same name, written by William Price Fox, the format of which was letters from people with golf problems followed by Dr. Golf's responses. I lifted five-minute sections and adjusted wording. Sometimes absurd, sometimes laugh-out-loud funny.

Blueline would phone me from the chaos of the Salt Palace lobby after Salt Lake Golden Eagles games and recount the scores and the great assists and standings. He was good! Excitement and passion made for superb on-scene sports reporting.

I cadged hockey tickets and Diana and I would bring infant son Guy along in his curvy plastic baby tote. Evidently there was no specific imprinting on the young boy's psyche because he could take or leave the skating sport. The roar of the crowd made its mark, however, because he likes, and follows, baseball, football and basketball.

XIII

Bruce asked me to host an evening movie. Sure! A late-night screening of the cult classic "Barbarella" at a downtown theater. We pushed tickets on the air. The timing was perfect: The film was released in 1968 so in the early seventies it was still present in a lot of minds, especially male, because of the opening credit sequence in which a callipygian Jane Fonda, at the lingering peak of her feminine pulchritude, lugubriously removes her multipiece spacesuit *while weightless!* At the climax of this sequence there are no clothes, no gravity, just Jane.

Lights up in the theater, I stood down in front, back to the proscenium, and welcomed the film buffs to the nearly-full house. I waved to the projectionist to roll the film. We saw Jane, but not enough of her, because of the randomly-occurring vertical green streaks which were teeth-gnashingly distracting. I held my breath. If this was the condition of the entire film, I was the lightning rod about to receive a whole lot of static and grief. What I anticipated would be a fun evening could be turning genuinely bad.

The green streaks went away as the story started and I realized what had happened. We got a film copy which some projectionist had had rerun—well, just that good part—multiple, maybe hundreds of times, enough to sear scratches in it.

Ninety minutes later, as the pertinacious Barbarella's search through the weird worlds for the elusive Duran Duran ground to a close, nobody remembered the green streaks. The smiling crowd emptied into the quiet streets of downtown Salt Lake City, unaware of my sighs of relief.

XIV

Jeff Gray called me periodically. He was enchanted with radio. He came to visit a couple of evenings. He was late high school, strangely funny, leaning a bit toward Andy Kaufman in his unselfconsciousness. And he wanted to be on my show.

"You've got to have something, do something, in order to be on. What is your talent? What can you do?" I queried.

"Well, I play the drums."

"Good," I said. "And sing too?"

"Sing? Um, sure, sing."

So He brought his elaborate drumset into the control room. He performed live. Totally absurd. He came in days later and I set him up in the production room and rolled the recording tape; he played the drums and sang.

"Hah!" exclaimed Bruce. "We're making another record!" We loaded up Jeff's percussive paraphernalia and hauled it out to the wreckage that was once Saltair, the one-time dance hall glitter spot miles west of Salt Lake City. On the lake, and sometimes in it.

Tom and I wrote separate comments for the liner notes.

FROM JEFF'S ECLECTIC REPERTOIRE

- Strangers in the Night
- Downtown
- Jimmy Crack Corn
- Doggie in the Window
- Mack the Knife
- Blues in the Night
- She'll be Comin' Round the Mountain
- Medley: Dashing Through the Indian Love Call Wearing Jingle Bells

Self: *"Jeff has a rare talent, that magic spark, for doing the dumbest thing at the worst possible time. I see his creative genius as a giant Caterpillar Tractor perched at the top of a huge hill. It could sit there forever."*

Tom: *"...climb on board our musical chain letter and whisk yourself beyond the bounds of reason. 'Four Leaf Clover' is Jeff's salute to St. Patrick's Day which Jeff celebrates by covering himself with guacamole and running all over town yelling, 'I'm a dip, I'm a dip, I'm a dip.'"*

Loyal KALL listeners bought this trilogic completor. A lost media archive on the web reports that one sold at $161.96.

XV

This narrative of one man's nine-year stint in the waning years of radio's Golden Age of Personality leaves us wondering, "What the hell?"

What is personality radio? What is it that a radio personality does, or rather did? And why are there two questions when it first sounded like there was just one?

"Tune in tomorrow" was a common imperative invoked by the announcer at the end of a Golden Age of Radio type program. It's also the title of a fictional accounting of a project to bring back personality radio to—ahem—a small Oregon town called Redmond. The siting is no coincidence. The author is Bruce Bell, who has visited us in Redmond numerous times.

In his introduction he reflects on his management philosophy as program director at KALL Radio, Salt Lake City:

The team building exercises in my radio experience covered a wide range of human characteristics. Ego and status, real and imagined, were always part of the mix. Among the staff members you could find strains of the gregarious, the introspective, the studious, the street smart: each one spontaneous and the one or two who were self-destructive. And they were all blessed with an innate curiosity. To this the on air talent lent their own slanted, entertaining views. Those views and styles ran from country cousin humor to satiric barbs against the pompous. My assignment was to embrace, boost or tone down these talented, overdeveloped egos as I saw fit. This task to assume control, as I learned from other 'talent wranglers' of the era, was an exercise in self-delusion. What could be accomplished was to support all of them in ways that they could use to do a good show on a daily basis, and a great show once or twice a month that provided an idea or theme that could be turned into a recurring concept. What they were all doing is taking daily risks without benefit of a safety net or a risk management consultant.

So there you stand. What you were hearing on the monitor speaker ends. You open the mic and words come out. It happened just like this yesterday, and you remember what you said then, and *you cannot say the same thing again.* Your brain is scrambling like a crawling infant trying to get across a slippery floor to get a dropped peanut butter sandwich before the labradoodle shows up. You feel like the quantum mechanic looking at a particle at which time it's not a particle it's a wave, and when she looks away, it's a particle again. And you remember that newspaper article you clipped last week, the one about the lady who found a shark in her freezer, no, discard that...

And you do *something*, and maybe it's good and maybe it leads nowhere but at the moment just before decision you are one with all humanity. Everybody's looking for what to do next. Great place to start.

We are in human, ecological, climatic, governmental, community and family history, and the Dodgers, the NASDAQ, the Beatles, Volkswagen, Betty Crocker, AIDS, the Hadron Super Collider and the ski report are leaning forward at this very moment. And what about the Solstice? There is a town in Utah, Vernal. Are the high school teams called the Vernal Equinox? Or Equinockers? I'll call the school!

Bruce is right. Twice a month. Take the risk.

If it's good, stuff happens inside the head of the listener. Do we dare try to quantify that, to hold it up to Don Sherwood at KSFO or Jack Bogut at KDKA? We're faced with a measuring question best handled by the National Bureau of Standards but right now they're busy working on the exact size of a jelly glass and the absolute maximum duration of a chili cookoff. Leave them to it. Just pursue context and, from time to time, get a glimmer of where the core of truth nestles and how the thread of consistency weaves through it.

Such is personality radio.

Why did it die? The short answer is, new rules which allowed entities to own multiple stations in multiple markets. No longer was a station encouraged to be of service to its community (and thereby be successful in it). Instead, everything was homogenized into a one-size-fits-all package whose singular goal was to enrich the owners. Given the evolution of how people get news, information, entertainment, and companionship, it will never return.

RECOMMENDED READING:

- **Don Sherwood: The Life and Times of "The World's Greatest Disc Jockey"** by Laurie Harper

- **Truly Records is my Middle Name** by John Landecker and Rick Kaempfer

- **Tune in Tomorrow** by Bruce Bell

- **Life in Double Time: Confessions of an American Drummer** by Mike Lankford

- **Wounds to Bind: A Memoir of the Folk-Rock Revolution** by Jerry Burgan

Play the Star Spangled Banner.

FIVE

Student of Carpentry

I

Salt Lake City, February, 1975. Life was good for the Barker family. Guy Brentwood (Pete) was seventeen months old when his brother, Joel Byron, was born January sixteenth. We knew we would be cramped in our two-bedroom brick bungalow so we purchased a five-bedroom rambler on Phylden Drive in Holladay, farther south from downtown and my place of work but only a couple miles from freeway access.

The house and yard were well-suited to our family and I was especially fond of the fully-electrified stand-alone single-car-garage-sized cinder block building in the back yard. I had a Sears electric drill, an $8.88 Black and Decker jigsaw and a small, underpowered tablesaw, a gift from my father-in-law. My seventies edition of a primordial man cave workshop. I could savor the silence, a healthful escape from the listening demands of my radio job. I built little things, like a rack for the wedding gift set of Acock kitchen knives (still in use at this writing). Mostly I just puttered.

Just as at my previous radio gigs, I was the designated trainer of future on-air persons at KALL. There was always a need for Casual Talent—folks who could come in and cover a shift now and then. My most striking trainee was Rick Barnes. Striking in the first two minutes you met him: He stood 6'7". Add shoes and hair, and you've got more height than a typical doorway. When he spoke his voice rumbled out like distant thunder across the fertile undulating Palouse of eastern Washington. By day Rick and a partner framed houses in the Provo area, forty-five miles south of Salt Lake City.

Rick and radio never connected, however, in spite of his active sense of humor and keen grasp of irony. On the air his voice was squeezed a little with anxiety, which a listener could sense. The Ether was not his bailiwick. But good for him for trying. We became great friends.

Rick had had a promising basketball career in college until a grisly ankle injury blew the final whistle. For me he was a valuable companion at Utah Stars games where, because of his inside sense of the game, I learned a lot of basketball strategy and playmaking.

At our home, Rick and I insulated the raised ceiling in the living/dining area. I was watching myself take orders from the expert, carefully climbing my stepladder as he climbed his, four hands carrying a four-by-eight sheet of half-inch thick paneling up to nail on the exposed 4x6 rafters. Following that project he encouraged me to tackle little remodel tasks that seemed way beyond my ability. He boosted my confidence to where I was willing, though not always comfortable, to just start something and solve the problems as they arose. Invaluable inspiration for one stepping into a new career, midlife.

Our Phylden Drive neighborhood was a mix of single family dwellings and apartments peopled by a high percentage of short persons—kids, kids, kids. Our street was just a block long, up a slight incline where it teed with a cross street. Just across that street, in line with ours, was a driveway in which a large Mercury station wagon resided. One afternoon gravity overcame the forces of parking-brake friction that had been keeping it on that sloped driveway and that Mercury came down the hill, tailgate first, accelerating just like Sir Isaac Newton said it would.

It backed down the street forty yards then curved to the south, gaining momentum. By the time it got to our house it was on our side of the street, across the curbless margin, backed over our rural-type mailbox on a steel post and went on to complete the U-turn and destroy the row of mailboxes on the other side of the street. They had been mounted on a section of flimsy fence. The car stopped because (a) those impacts stole a lot of its momentum, and (2) the U-turn had forced it back uphill a little. That it was on lawn, and there were mailbox fragments scattered about, kept it there, pointed downhill, scarcely scratched. There were no kids outside at the time—a tragedy averted.

With counsel from Rick I built new structures for our single and the multiple mailboxes for the fourplex across the street. I toiled in my spare time in my cozy little shop, loving every minute of the process and the aroma of fresh-cut wood. I installed new bases and replaced the crushed mailboxes, restoring the neighbors' to its original look and tarting up mine with some fancy diagonal redwood cosmetics. I contacted the two involved insurance companies and got checks. What a concept! I was astonished I could do something that much fun and get money. True, I had been paid for writing and photography during my vocational menopause in Salem, but this project got me in touch with something internal, fiercely magnetic, even hormonal. This was just right.

But that nod toward the future was ignored because I was solidly in place at KALL and active in the media world of Salt Lake. I was doing occasional voice-overs for a few ad agencies, I had recorded a narration for a short educational film and was an on-call extra voice for two guys who were creating a daily 5 minute radio show of snippets of U. S. history which was designed for a 12 month run, ending on the bicentennial July 4. All these gigs were extra money and easy to schedule since my KALL workday started at 4 pm for my six-to-eleven show.

The two babies were fun and Diana was finding friendships with young mothers. We were getting by, making house payments, knowing that one day, given KALL's history, there would be a daytime slot open up and I would move into it. All was well in my world.

II

Except for one thing: Bruce Bell had been fired in January. Everyone on our floor was blindsided and baffled. The station was perking right along, sales were fine, our position in the array across the AM radio dial was enviable, what the hell is this? And to make it even worse, his replacement, a recycled radio guy of no particular credentials who had bubbled up in our market occasionally over the last few years, was inept and everyone knew it. Mousy, not likable, bobbled when he walked and rarely looked you in the eye. I couldn't envision a future with him in it but I lacked the maturity to realize that all I had to do was hunker down, stay off his radar, and do my job. I might have outlasted him. Instead I was testy and directed my displaced anger and uneasiness at him. Much like an adolescent, I talked thoughtlessly and spent no time considering what might be the consequences of my behaviors.

Valentine's Day, afternoon drive time: I was subbing for Will Lucas. That day I had picked up on a rumor that someone was going to be fired soon, probably Tom Barberi, the morning guy. So when Bennie Williams, the sales manager, stuck his head into the control room just before six and asked me to pop up to his office after I was off the air, it occurred to me that, what, wait, *I was going to get the morning shift? What else could it be?*

That was absurd, of course, but ego was filling my wheelhouse like a big balloon in a small shoebox, so I went upstairs at 6:02 and, nervously attempting casualness, took a chair facing Bennie's desk.

"How long have you worked here?" he inquired. I noticed the sign on his wall that said, "Big Ben Has Time For Sale." The air was strange. Bennie wore after shave. I hadn't been in this office before. His words echoed in my head, like a movie scene where the fuzzy big guy is leaning over you and speaking very loudly only it sounds soft and the colors are merging into an adjectiveless gray. No morning show was mentioned.

I was fired. Ousted. Canned. Farbined. Shown the Door. The new Program Director's buddy was to take my place. Bennie handed me my check, which had a few hundred bucks added to soothe my wounded soul. Stunned, I walked out of his office, numbly negotiating a flight of steps down to the main floor and again to my basement office.

Called Diana and told her. I was in shock. She was optimistic: "We'll make it just fine," she said. I found a cardboard box and filled it with once-important ironic and unusual clippings from magazines and newspapers and the detritus of paper clips and scissors from the center drawer. I drove home, the car a horse who knew his way to the barn. The street lights flickered on as dusk passed through that February evening. Happy Valentine's Day.

Bennie had mentioned that he had talked to the manager of another radio station, all talk and no music, who was interested in talking to me. I never responded to that. I had no aspirations to become a talk jock and I couldn't see myself at any other Salt Lake station. I was angry and hurt, and it took months to get through it. (Years later I read On Death and Dying by Elizabeth Kubler-Ross and discovered that this was my first life experience of grief. In my rearview mirror I could see all five stages—denial, anger, guilt, bargaining, and acceptance.

I struggled my anger. My family of origin did not allow that emotion to be expressed. We kids were told "not to feel that way. It's wrong." Fixing that has been an ongoing project.

Salt Lake Friends offered ample consolation and some even wrote letters to the radio station, which became part of its permanent file per FCC rules. Their heartfelt efforts did nothing to affect my being fired. I stayed fired. Ten thousand well-written letters would have about as much leverage as a toothpick trying to tip over a John Deere tractor. Around home I was emotionally distant and withdrawn for a good deal of time, stewing my acid batch of bile.

III

A radio personality is an actor of sorts. Whatever ideas you have, whatever emotion you want to share, has to be made to fit through the tiny pipeline of a microphone. In any given hour you have a few minutes to stuff something into your end of the tube and hope—because you may never know—it registers in an ear somewhere and converts to a human response. In order to put forth this daily effort you have to believe that you're doing it successfully. It's easiest and most efficient to keep that belief pulsing with life all the time. You can have a normal existence outside the studio but somewhere just below the surface that slurry of self confidence and self delusion bubbles. Get fired and it drains out like hot ten-dubya-thirty from the busted oilpan of a Chevy pickup pulled over on the Interstate. Time...will...pass before it gets fixed.

Bruce and I had conversations as we both dealt with our surprise futures. He was working toward launching an advertising agency with a partner. He encouraged me to think about how I could fit in as a freelancer in the Salt Lake advertising world and I put my energies toward that. It wouldn't be enough income, and without being on the air daily I was bound to fade from the conspicuity I had had in the broadcasting community. Still it was something.

At home we tightened our belts and Diana continued her part time transcription work. The second baby isn't near the out-of-pocket cash guzzler the first is, but when their nap clocks are non-synchronous the days can be long for the stay-at-home parent. I could help.

Out of the blue, probably due to Bruce Bell's influence, I was offered a ninety day contract at a local ad agency whose specialty was print ads in the mining industry. Ross Clay, the owner, wanted to explore the five-minute syndicated daily radio show concept that would work on any station in any market. This could be nicely profitable: After you have sold enough stations to pay for the production, each additional station required only the costs of duplicating and postage. The rest, gravy.

I became a nine-to-five commuting guy. We were a casual staff of five, including Ross. I parked my red Volvo PV544 in the lot adjacent to the office building five days a week. And sometimes on Friday afternoon we'd all head off to a downtown tavern and knock back a few three-point-two beers.

We landed on a series about automotive history, USA. We got enough episodes in the can to roll the concept out to potential customers and Ross got right on it. He reported serious interest from a regional car dealer organization and about that time the guy who was funding the project—a friend of Ross's—decided to pull the plug. We tidied up the loose ends, I cleaned out my desk, and was back on the street. I did get a gig doing a TV spot for a men's clothing outfit. Sport coat, flashy tie, nice shirt, no pants. Another as a window washer on a skyscraper. I wasn't the guy hanging on the side of the building in the outside shot, but you thought I was. The recording part was fun but the ad runs didn't jumpstart my TV career, *quelle surprise*! My devilishly masculine good looks and finely chiseled features were clearly much better suited to radio. Or perhaps darkroom work. Maybe cleanup after a chili cookoff.

IV

I eased into constructing things. I bought a used leather tool belt. Used, because it was cheaper, but more important, it made me look more experienced.

I was using the sixteen ounce True Temper Rocket hammer my father had given me on my sixteenth birthday. And while he firmly believed that his three kids should have college educations—and we all do—he also regularly asserted that I—male breadwinning archetype—should "have a trade to fall back on." This was common counsel from the generation that struggled through the Great Depression, and it kept me from feeling that this transition was a step down from white-collar pursuits. Most intoxicating was the empirical nature of the work accomplished. At the end of the day I could see and touch what I had done, and the smile that generated could last the entire evening.

I was sad that I couldn't talk to my dad about it. And thank him.

Starting in my neighborhood, I had remodeled several basements for growing Mormon families, and done an architect-designed family room added under a roof already over a patio. Then this: a neighborhood couple that owned a duplex, and lived in half, hired me to take out the middle wall and create a single family dwelling. "Sure," I said. They sent the renters packing. This was a heady project for a rookie carpenter with a slowly-growing collection of tools.

And now I had a truck. Ford, vintage 1959, originally property of the U.S. Army. Straight six in the power barn, four with granny gear on the floor. Exterior color a repaint to a brighter green; inside, original olive drab. Stenciled on the dashboard: "MAX SPEED 55." That was a bit optimistic. Best part was the truck's back half, a sturdy steel utility box with locking tool boxes, both sides. Later saw Max and my toolbelt as fulfillment of my childhood enchantment with olive drab telephone trucks and workmen with tools.

Several days into the duplex project I backed Max up to the door of the empty unit, sashayed into the vacant living room and, with my True Temper Rocket, busted out a hole in the drywall to start ripping it off the studs. This would all have to go to the dump.

My face went slack with shock when I discovered that, between the stud walls in the two mirror-image living rooms, there was a *full-height, full width, fully mortared cinder block wall staring right back at me and my puny little hammer*! Eventually all the cinder block chunks and sheet rock shards went to the dump in a truck driven by a guy who was much smarter than the week before. Every remodeler has adventures like this and while at the moment of discovery there are two lungs desperately seeking oxygen, we become better investigators and wiser predictors of what's slightly out of sight before we say yes to a job.

V

The kids were a year older and I felt a tug to return to Oregon where our sons had three grand- and five great-grandparents, Diana's side, living. Diana was reluctant—she had made good friends in Salt Lake—but we agreed that school life there can be needlessly difficult for non-Mormon kids. After much discussion we made plans to move and then, in an eerie replay of the KALL call in my tree-planting phase, I got an offer for an attractive radio job. A good station in Tri-Cities,

Washington. Their long-time news director, Mike Berriochoa, was a high school mate, a year younger. He knew what I was up to and I trusted him completely in describing the gig. Diana and I gave the opportunity serious consideration but we never got as close as a drive up to Richland to check it out.

At the final whistle of the contest, it was grandparents and greenness and, we hoped, eventual self employment in the construction trades, for the win. The ego ride on the radio became a dry page of my resumé, dusty and cracked around the edges.

Diana's uncle was building houses in Redmond and he offered me a job. I would be a hammer slammer and I was ready. With Rick Barne's counsel I had moved up to a Vaughn twenty-ounce wooden-handled beauty. "You can do a lot of framing with a twenty," he said. He was likely using a thirty-two at the time. For now it was clear that I was intoxicated with learning my new trade and crazy with the fun of building stuff that was real and sturdy and plumb and square. The Phylden house went on the market and sold. We were moving back to Oregon, but not to the rain. To the dry side, east of the Cascade Mountains.

VI

Disregarding speed and with a heavy emphasis on low maintenance and insurance costs, I decided this truck was worth taking to Oregon. I loaded all my tools in it and lashed it behind our longest-of-all U-Haul moving van which was up to the gunnels with household chattels. Some of that was really ugly stuff I had built, the exception being a pine rocking cradle I had crafted for Guy, then submitted for Joel's roadtesting for functionality and durability. It eventually rocked as infant bunkage for numerous babies of friends and family. It's still around at this writing.

We were on the road, Utah receding in the mirror and Oregon Or Bust painted on our imaginary flag. Rick's wife Karen rode with Diana and the boys in our Volvo 122s station wagon. Immediately dropping behind their freeway speeds, Rick and I drove the plodding big truck pulling the twenty year old little truck, rolling north through the desolate expanse of southern Idaho.

Our goal for the day was Ontario, Oregon, just over the state line, where friends Irv and Sherril Smith expected us to stay overnight. The crepuscular light faded to night.

About ten miles south of Ontario we blew a front tire. Rick nobly rassled the rig to the side of the freeway, tight to the curb and the guard rail. A kindly passing motorist in an imported pickup not designed with Rick in mind gave us a lift to the Smith house in town. I called the 800 number for U-Haul and the local guy said he would head right out there right now if I wanted, but we could also go out tomorrow morning, a Sunday. The better option. We met him out there. It was me, Rick, the Volvo, and the U-Haul guy in his service truck. No traffic. Quiet.

No orange and cream slab-sided chattel truck. No five-eighths ton Max. Our stuff was gone. Everything.

In my adult life I had never felt lighter, even giddy. My fresh start got fresher. I didn't think about the process of replacing what was gone; this was how starting over ought to be. Clean slate.

But that was short-lived. We found the truck in Ontario right where the Highway Patrol had impounded it because it was a "safety hazard."

We bought a house in Bend, a comfortable twenty miles away from other family drama. I went to work for Jim McCaul, Diana's uncle, rolling the commute to Redmond daily, Max proudly singing at the top of his six-cylinder lungs.

Jim did his own foundations, framing, and finish work, so I got some good housebuilding carpentry education. During that time he opened a main-street office where he displayed, and sold, custom-sized replacement windows. People were becoming acutely aware of heating costs and how leaky, single-pane windows contributed to their financial pain. Second, the office was between the telephone company and the power company offices, same side of the street. In those days people would walk downtown, maybe go shopping at Sprouse-Reitz and Mode-O-Day, and stop at these utility offices to pay their monthly bills. Inevitably they would walk past the display in the front window of McCaul Construction and see these new, energy-saving double pane windows.

Jim's other employee, Jack Charlton, became a good friend and we worked together on numerous projects over the years. My time with Uncle Jim was about ten months.

The next was to partner with my brother-in-law, Rob Trout, an accomplished and precise carpenter. We framed a bunch of houses as subs for several contractors for less than a year. I learned how to do things better than Jim usually did them and that confidence nurtured my goal of business independence. When it was time to move on, Great Ned! Construction popped up on June 3, 1977, the name from an obscure exclamation synonymous with "ohmygosh" or "wow."

State of Oregon Construction Contractor's Board License #17771. I kept that license active for twenty-nine years.

We had a building boom in Central Oregon. Max was gassed up and ready to roll and I had a fistful of business cards in one hand and my twenty-ounce, master's degree-equivalent hammer in the other.

VII

Working summers on the grounds crew at Westminster College, I met Ern Pedler, carpenter, hired to do carpentry. Actually that was a side; his main gig was cowboy. Authentic, weathered skin, slow-talkin' cowboy. But while he was doing repairs on campus buildings, Parke Miller and I enjoyed his company. Ern left public school at age sixteen, preferred being outdoors where nobody else was, rode Morgan horses, chased and caught wild Mustangs in Utah, *and wrote about it*. This literary cowboy carpenter published a book, The Big Lonely Horse, and authored many short stories.

After Diana and I moved to Salt Lake City, I reconnected with Ern and his wife. The four of us enjoyed several evenings at their house on the edge of Alpine, Utah, population less than a thousand. "Someone shot out a street light in town," Ern said, laconically. "It was a crime wave." All his sentences were bracketed between pauses.

Ern, feeling the effects of too many horse wrecks, went to work for the state Department of Corrections. I asked about this desk job, and how it compared to his carpentry work. "I much preferred the carpentry," he said.

"Why?" I asked.

"Because when I drove a nail in, I knew it would stay drove. You don't get that feelin' workin' with people."

You don't get that feelin' workin' in radio either, Ern.

House construction hit all the right flavor notes for me, including a nice woody aftertaste. Good solid physical labor, geometry, transforming a patch of ground to a habitation, working with lumber. I threw myself at it and savored the learning.

My Oregon contractor's license, along with bond and insurance, enabled me to hire out as a subcontractor and though I had learned enough about finish carpentry from Uncle Jim and Bro-in-law Rob to take that specialty on, I preferred the outdoor air and brute physicality of framing.

It was easy to find a likeminded licensed guy to partner up with. A package of two licensed framers, working as subs, was more attractive to a general contractor than hiring two employees and futzing with their attendant paperwork. This partnering arrangement did not comply with state law. Technically, as soon as a second party took orders from the first and used the first's tools, there should have been wages reported, insurance, all that stuff.

But we didn't care. If Cash and Haggard and Kristofferson and Willie could be Outlaws touring the glamorous country music concert venues and having that much fun, why should we let a few minor regulations get in the way of doing good work, driving a truck with a lumber rack on the back, and bringing home money? Central Oregon had a healthy streak of take-care-of-our-own attitude delivered with a keep-your-rules-and-regulations-in-Salem sneer in those days.

The partnership arrangement was loose and unwritten but we all knew that the longer we worked together the more efficient we got and that meant more money for both of us. Upon completion of a typical house, we'd deduct the expenses for nails and caulking and split the remainder fifty-fifty. In the interest of keeping a partner as long as I could, I would submit the bid, work out the schedule, and furnish the ladders, compressor, and nailguns. I was the boss of the crew, which was a democracy except that I had two votes. Or however many were needed to get my way.

When we'd roll onto the jobsite, the concrete foundation was done. We'd build subfloor, floor, walls, exterior siding, and the roof, sheathed with plywood and ready for the shingle slingers.

An increase in home values in California usually generates a migration of families who leave the stresses of city life in favor of a lower cost of living and a closer-to-nature, small-townish domicile in the attractive state to their north. Such was the case in the late 70s when Tom McCall was governor and Oregon was becoming synonymous with livability and environmental conscience. Our state had the bottle bill, land-use planning, the beach bill, cleaned-up rivers, all that stuff. He famously said, repeatedly, "Visit us again and again, but for heaven's sake don't stay" and everyone knew the words were pointedly aimed due south. In spite of bemused press coverage, well-marketed "Ungreeting Cards from Oregon" and clever bumper stickers ("Don't Californicate Oregon"), the Golden Staters still came.

They came in spite of the James G. Blaine society, a non-organization whose slouchy, hoody-eyed namesake ran for U. S. President in 1884 and visited every state in the union except Oregon. This hilarious bit of history faithfully reflects the fun of being an Oregonian in that era.

When a new home belonging to a Californian was coming out of the mud (had a poured foundation) and we were the framers, we could find ourselves in an awkward place.

Some of these people gave not only California but also humankind a bad name. Their conversations around us concerned the ghastly deprivations they were experiencing in rural Oregon and how much better things were where they came from. We had to work beyond that glaring philosophical inconsistency and focus on the job, all the while remaining on their good side. They were, after all, providing us with work, even though we weren't eager to welcome them into our community.

I had a young family. The need for money won out over being a one-man vigilante gang trying to discourage the asphalted flatlanders from invading our sweepingly scenic High Desert home.

The Dry Canyon
Filharmonhick 1984-1988

Leroy Newport went to the City Shops of Redmond and borrowed some barricades with which he blocked off the street in front of his house on July 1, 1984. He invited neighbors and his co-workers from the Redmond School District to a Fourth of July party. Beer from a keg and macaroni salad and chips. And music: Leroy and his banjo and others who stepped up. There were two guys playing guitar: Mike Sutherland and Joe Elliott. The bassist, who was struggling nobly, was Sandra, a teacher whom I recognized. I asked her if I could sit in and was declined on the grounds that she was playing a "school instrument" and she couldn't let me play it. After she left, Mike sheepishly pointed behind the bass amplifier and said, "Hey, there's a bass back here. Plug it in!" And off we went.

Silly, wide-eyed fun. When the party sputtered and muttered to a close, we cased the instruments. Let's do this again, and soon! We invited Jim Erickson, high school teacher and musician, who said, "Sure!"

But what were we? Leroy's banjo, which can't help but be front and center in a group that size, wasn't very good for lullabies and sad country songs. Mike could play nearly anything, having been a professional player in Portland for over two decades. Joe tended the bluegrass flame while Jim fancied an earthy strain of Americana peppered with early Beatles and Dylan served with a side of Lovin'

Spoonful. I wasn't too choosy about repertoire, I just wanted to play the bass and feel it through the soles of my feet.

The Dry Canyon Filharmonhick. Initially Jim wore tails and sometimes red Converse shoes. Mike had a red Eagle Claw gimme cap; I stuck to my $8.88 corduroy sport coat with a blue engineer's cap. Leroy favored his white broadbrimmed fedora. Joe showed up wearing whatever he was wearing that day.

There was magic in this fivesome. When we traveled it took two vehicles, any distribution of personnel made for great conversation and plenty of laughs per car. If we were playing for folks who didn't know the band, we'd let them try to tag the profession on the player. Leroy was the business manager for the school district, Mike a headhunter

Dry Canyon Filharmonhick | 1984
Jim, Mike, Leroy, Self, Joe

for sales personnel in a niche medical machine arena, Joe worked with kids who had made a few mistakes and needed a little guidance in life. Jim taught social studies and coached track and, while in our midst, was named the Oregon Teacher of the Year.

Leroy: "Having a banjo in the band is like trying to stuff five pounds of shit into a four pound bag." Leroy was a lover of life, an easy friend to anyone. His was a wide open face with "a genuine #8 smile." He loved the banjo and practiced with diligence.

Mike's guitar was musical bedrock for us; his playing was full and rhythmical. He was modest and unassuming about his playing but it was good, way better than any of the rest of us. He stood as the tallest, sang harmonies effortlessly, and imagined arrangements best. He was a gentle soul with an impish smile.

Joe took up the mandolin which added chunky afterbeats and sweet trilly solos from his end of the line. Joe was animated offstage but when we played, he was focused and intense. He was wiry, thin and the perfect iteration of a Central Oregon Quiet Beatle. Except when, rarely, after playing a very familiar song that was well received, he'd shout, "WE WROTE THAT."

Jim was well respected in Redmond for his devotion to education. Instrumentally he played harmonica and Dobro but certain tunes shone best when his rhythm guitar drove them. Our lead singer. He learned lyrics by the cubic yard and never complained.

We liked to say that it all added up to a group that constantly pushed the boundaries of mediocrity. From the beginning we did not take ourselves seriously. Nope.

We played often at the Inn of the Seventh Mountain, booked by the convention coordinator when a conference or retreat needed a band. Elsewhere we played parties of all kinds, a garage sale, business events. Even a

OUR BOOK WAS NOW OVER FIFTY TUNES, INCLUDING

- Rollin' in my Sweet Baby's Arms
- Amarillo by Morning
- The Cuckoo
- King of the Road
- City of New Orleans
- Route 66
- Hot Rod Lincoln
- Pancho and Lefty
- Juniper Berries (an original about the birds who get drunk on said fruits)
- Silhouettes (medley with Blue Moon and ShBoom)
- Mountain Dew
- Grandma's Feather Bed
- Born to be With You

calf branding where Jim, always in the spirit of things, fried the Rocky Mountain Oysters for all, well, not quite all, to enjoy. Being in this band was so much more than grueling rehearsals and hello before a gig and goodbye after.

T-shirts: "Dry Canyon Filharmonhick World Tour, 1984 —. We had played every town in Central Oregon and always were booked for at least two sets at the Deschutes County Fair.

The summer of 1988 we played that fair and headed east the next day for Ontario, Oregon on the Idaho border. We played a couple of sets on a rickety stage there "between the siphon tube setting competition and the swine unit," according to Mike. We came home, added our golf clubs and fishing tackle to the luggage and headed south and west to Roseburg, home of the Douglas County Fair.

We played five days, three sets a day, and still found time to fish and play golf. Between our sets the Oregon Jazz Band played, a bunch of old and very accomplished guys who played Dixie jazz splendidly.

And every gig we chose Joe as our Champagne Lady to sing our only operatic number, "Summertime" from Gerschwin's Porgy and Bess.

People were drawn to us by the variety and stayed because of the energy and fun.

Items gleaned from a contemporaneous journal of our road trip to Douglas County: One of our uniforms of the time was old timey polyester suits, purchased at thrift stores. In preparation for an evening set Mike had donned his, replete with a slightly ruffled shirt. He stopped at a McDonald's for a snack and was eyed for a while by two women who alternately glanced and spoke tête-à-tête. Finally one stepped over courageously and asked, "Are you with Paul Revere and the Raiders?"

As we were setting up, a man stopped me and said, "I saw you guys on Fire on the Mountain," an obscure TV show that showcased bluegrass groups. I thanked him graciously but we never were.

Later that year it all fell apart.

FROM OUR PROMOTIONAL PACKET

MIKE SUTHERLAND, GUITARIST:

"All of us have to work full time to supplement our music income."

JOE ELLIOTT, BLUEGRASS WARRIOR:

"Some of this material has been around a hundred years and some of it isn't."

LEROY NEWPORT:

"If the Beatles had only had a banjo player, they would have been REALLY popular."

JIM ERICKSON:

"If I had anything more fun than this band, I'd do it too."

LEE BARKER:
"I am just a bass player trapped in a cabinetmaker's body."

Hiatus 1989

I had let my entertainment ego expand unchecked while the other four, unbeknownst to me, decided that playing music was their priority, not humorous presentations. While I thought I was successfully entertaining the audience and simultaneously giving my colleagues a brief respite in a performance, they were standing and stewing.

I went to a scheduled practice and got out my bass and tuned it and only then noticed that no one else had an instrument. I was ambushed. They fired me. I argued, which didn't help any. Jim spoke up for me and lobbied hard for finding a working resolution. He seemed to think things could be salvaged. I certainly was willing to change my style in order to stay in the band, but other minds were made up. Had there been some history of ironing out smaller wrinkles as they occurred, this could have been just another laundry day, but we had done well together for years without disagreements. It was our first tiff. I took this hard.

We played at each other's parties. Our families were friends. The band had been a real anchor for me as I flopped around trying to figure out my life as a divorced father with physical custody of two pre-teen sons. Being able to call myself a musician had been a bit of sheen on my dull self-concept of a financially struggling hands-on blue collar guy.

They auditioned and hired another bassist, Dave Warren, who brought his own set of gifts to the band. They added others players here and there and continued for a couple years.

Finding a replacement creative outlet was a slow process. I made a proposal for a regular column in the Redmond Spokesman, our weekly newspaper, and it was accepted. That writing discipline filled the creative void where once I rehearsed and laughed with those four amazing and humorous talents.

In one sense I had a perfect musical performance record: I had been in two bands and each one had a kind, understanding, patient guitar player who helped me along. By now, with Mike's help, I had refined my ability to keep good time and learned some more about note selection.

Foreshadow: I had built a warm and dazzling walnut and alder body for a bass guitar and transferred the rest of the parts from a Fender bass I owned. It worked! That was the instrument in the early photos of the DCF. Later I bought an Epiphone Rivoli bass, a short-scale semi-hollow body blond beauty which was easy to play. It sounded OK to my contemporaneous ears and I liked its stage presence.

One small but bright spot in this transition time was a call from a Bend musician who worked in a downtown music store. He played mandolin and he had a dream of a top-tier bluegrass band which didn't slog the bog of gigs here and there, we would just get ten tunes that were exquisite, complex arrangements and do appearances like, but better than, a chili cookoff. He singled me out as the bass player. I immediately was on board but the idea never took solid form. It felt good to have my name was on his A List, even if it was written in pencil.

Five years of being divorced ended and everything changed when Linda and I got married in 1991. We blended families. There were three teenage boys, one away at college, and a daughter on her own. Music seemed a distant part of my past with no referent on the horizon.

Linda and I began to socialize a bit with Mike and his wife Sandy and their circle of friends. One evening we were doing a lot of damage to a large bowl of chips and a satellite of salsa when a third friend, Dan Schmitke, said to Mike and me, "Hey! Why don't you get the ol' band back together?" We looked at each other, eyes widening, and said, "Sure!"

SIX

Mistakes Were Made

GROWTH RINGS

The house was small, L-shaped, and had low ceilings. You can find homes like this sprinkled around the historic center of Redmond, many without foundations. Built way before building codes.

Jack Charlton and I, of McCaul Construction, were there to replace the front window. Not a big deal. Uncle Jim had assumed that the old window would come out as a unit and, with dimensions he had inferred from it, the new one would slip right in. The wall thickness, hard to measure, seemed typical.

We removed the old window, expecting to see an opening in the wall surrounded by wood framing. Instead we had a wall with no studs. It was made of multiple layers of various materials, applied over many years. There was pine shiplap siding, tar paper, vertical inch-thick pine 1x10 boards, wallpaper, half inch thick Celotex (a fiberboard, sometimes made of sugar cane byproduct, developed around 1925), and an exterior covering of asphalt shingle material which had been stamped to look like bricks. Most recently, exterior shake siding.

You could grasp the sill area in the opening and easily move it back and forth several inches, flexing it—something you could never do with a studded wall. We were inserting a window to give the front wall structure! We made the opening as rigid as we could and installed the new unit.

At this writing the house is still there, with yet newer windows, at 135 NW 10th Street. I feel a kinship with the carpenter who removed the double pane fenestration we put in—aluminum framed—and replaced it with a more modern vinyl-framed window. I suspect he started with the same assumption we made, and was as surprised as we were by the way the house revealed its growth rings.

WHOOMP

Several years later, after I had left Uncle Jim's employ, Kent Bingham and I were framing some houses in Redmond when Jim asked us if we could come over the next day and stand a twenty-four foot long wall on a remodel he was doing. He knew we had wall jacks. "Sure!"

Jim and his helper had framed this wall, inserting the windows and applying the exterior siding on the wall as it lay on the floor. With all that mass it was more than the four of us could lift but if you were armed with wall jacks, no problem.

These jacks were Olympia brand, cast iron, the whole assembly the size of a cowboy boot box. They climb up a 2x4, two inches at a time, using a lever which caused the jack to catch on the wood, release, rise, and catch again.

We were professional, efficient, and a bit puffed up by Jim's overblown description of our skills when he introduced us to the older couple who owned the home.

We set up our jacks. The bottom of the wall hinged on the floor and as the top of the wall moved toward vertical, the jacks would move higher with it. We would be standing on stepladders at this point, pumping jacks in concert.

All was going smoothly. We were in a shady, grassy back yard, earning cash. We were certainly impressed with how impressive we looked. The visiting firemen, the consultants from New York, the animal trainers from Ringling Brothers, The Pros from Dover in the movie M*A*S*H, the hockey coaches from Saskatchewan,

Penn and Teller with a trick Just For You. Yeah, there were studs in that wall but there were studs on the stepladders, too.

Click-chick, click-chick, click-chick, the wall nearly vertical. At that theoretical point it settles onto the flat floor and we would brace and nail it down. But something went wrong and those long 2x4s leaning on the wall with the cast iron jack frames near the top kept exerting outward pressure. Not enough folks holding the wall plumb, no braces getting nailed in place, nobody taking down the jacks promptly. That fully-formed wall, which was about to define a wonderful new living space for the homeowners who were on hand to witness this landmark event, just kept on going right past vertical and on over WHOOMP, landing face-down on the lawn.

Not a window was broken, not a scar on the siding! We sheepishly hauled our wall jacks around to the other side and, in a rerun dripping with forced nonchalance, jacked it back up, backwards. Jim, bless his heart, was busy explaining to the homeowner that this was a "pretty common occurrence" and nothing to worry about.

Mutely we gathered our tools, gratefully accepted Jim's check, shrugged ourselves into the truck, and headed home.

IN THE BACK YARD

Henry hired D.W. Glass and me to frame his new house, a two-story dream home for his family, out on five acres of juniper and scrub west of Redmond. He was a nice guy, in his forties, who worked graveyard for the railroad. His job was putting together freight trains with the cars intentionally grouped so there would be efficiency and timeliness down the high line.

He wasn't a sleep-all-day, work-all-night person though. He had enough energy for three Henries. In the morning he'd be out on the job site helping us and learning when to stay out of our way. He was fun to have around,

Henry had purchased a precut Capp Home, which came on a semi trailer out of Portland. It had been unloaded there on Henry's lot, bundled and labeled, ready for assembly, predating IKEA. The new homeowner gets the complete set of house plans and all the lumber, cut to the necessary length. Henry had hired someone to do the foundation, which looked good. We were eager to work with him and help him realize his dream for his family.

We found a few minor inconsistencies in the bundles of precuts but had solved them as we went.

A few days and we were well into the second floor, deck down, exterior walls up, and working on the upstairs interior walls, when Henry noticed that the master bedroom wasn't as big as he expected it to be. He showed us, on the blueprints, how the master bedroom had a two-foot overhang on the west side. "What happened to that?" he queried. Clearly there was no overhang.

I gestured him over to the west-facing bedroom window where we leaned out the opening. I pointed to the random assortment of 2x12 floor joist pieces, each two feet long, scattered around on the fill dirt. "There it is," I said, chagrined but not cowed by this strange turn of events. This was my mistake but an unlikely one. My mind was racing, trying to understand the error. No theories emerged. We spread out the pages of plans on the floor and the three of us knelt down.

He was right; the plan elevations (side views of the building) showed clearly that overhang. I leafed through several other pages and found the second floor plan. The dimensions were the same as the first floor plan below. We had built the second floor exactly as drawn on the plan, no overhang. The two pages we were looking at disagreed; one showed the bedroom two feet longer than the other did.

The page Henry was referring to was not how we had built the room but it was the one used to determine how long those floor joists should be. He was right and I was right, and the plans were at fault.

Henry shrugged. "Oh well. It's still our dream house and we'll be just as happy this way as that. Let's keep going!" Oh that the world could have more Henries in it! He was as appreciated on our list of good clients as a chili cookoff the day after a blizzard on a weekend in central Iowa would be welcomed.

The Bend subdivision where Kent Bingham and I were framing several successive houses for Ron Schirm in 1980 was about four blocks from where my family lived. Diana was busy being a mom to our sons in their single-digit years, becoming a part of the post-hippie nutrition counterculture food co-op and reconnecting with her Central Oregon family and friends. I was intensely consumed by the demands of my trade. When, one evening, she said, "I went to the dead end of Noe Street in that subdivision and I can't stop imagining the boys riding their tricycles around there. Do you think we could build a house for ourselves? Right there on that dead end?"

We did. She was a skillful handler of money so she managed the purchase of the property. The lot was shaped like a piece of pie, wider at the back than at the front. Because it sloped back quickly, the house had to be quite close to the street so that the driveway could be flat. We engaged Orie Fridley, a local designer who was working for Ron, and he came up with a two-story design that was attractive, basic enough to fit our budget, and a bit quirky. He started with a square garage, since that's rather important. It was parallel to one side of the pie slice. He sited the house over at the other side of the pie slice, parallel to that side, and connected the two. That meant the back wall of the house, which came across the lot and touched the back corner of the garage, was longer than the front wall, which came across the lot and touched the front corner of the garage. He added some exterior design touches that were just right: a sniped roof (also called a Dutch hip) and wide, tudor-like trim framing large areas of the flat siding. We had designed in a large kitchen and overall Diana and I were just enchanted with the whole endeavor.

We poured the foundation in October and started framing in November not realizing we were headed into the coldest winter in Bend in years. Days of freezing temps made excavations for utility hookups impossible. Framing progress was glacial, both in velocity and ambient temperature.

It was a challenge to frame. First, a quarter-turn stairway; second, framing the roof where the two differing sections joined; and finally, the steepness of the roof itself (forty-five degrees or, in framing parlance, twelve/twelve).

So we had a two-story house and a single-story garage and the front roof surfaces meet. The finished view looks simple enough, but the inside structure was not detailed on the plan. Orie trusted me to figure this out. Kent and I stared at the problem, crunched ideas, drew on plywood, and finally decided the only solution was to cut the tops off two roof trusses.

You don't cut trusses. Engineered truss integrity is dependent on their as-designed shape. Our solution, my solution really, was untruss-worthy. Still, I was confident that the results of our problem-solving would be not only acceptable but also properly strong. Hey, my family was going to live there.

The day of the framing inspection Kent and I had done what we could inside in the way of sweeping and cleaning, so we lit up a warming fire in the front yard, talked about what our next job might be, and waited for the inspector. In the back of my mind I was imagining getting the plumber in and the HVAC guys and electrical and insulation and then drywall and paint and...it was all pretty gosh darn exciting!

When the inspector arrived he gratefully took a few minutes to stand with us by the fire. "Well," he said, staring into the crackling of the fir framing cutoffs, "I see you cut a truss." We had thoughtlessly thrown a waste chunk of one of the mutilated trusses, complete with the telltale steel nailing plates, onto the burn pile. He went right upstairs and I followed close.

I got a little lecture, which I didn't mind, and we moved directly into discussing solutions. He drew out on a piece of plywood exactly what he wanted for remediation of the two trusses which I had so callously brought to submission with my Skilsaw. I gladly complied. It took a day's work to accomplish the glued-and-nailed cleats he required and he came back and signed it off.

SEVEN

Moving to Redmond

Our family was living in Bend in our unique custom home designed to fit on our oddly shaped lot. Two stories tall, double garage, stunning kitchen, post-modern hippie rodent-proof bulk food storage closet, recycling center, pre-wired for our fancy component stereo system, even a plumbed hobby photography darkroom off the garage. I had built most of it, weekends and often for a few hours early morning before I went to work framing other people's houses. Diana handled the finish and décor.

Guy and Joel had room to play inside and outside, with interesting yards front and back. Little bikes, powered by former tricycle motors growing up fast, carved up our section of that dead-end street. Pieces of my soul were woven into that building from the rustic siding outside to the intentional built-in bookshelves and unique storage places inside.

Day in and day out I was a vacuum-totin', toilet-scrubbin', babysittin' co-opin', bicycle-repairin' househusband and stay-at-home dad who was slowly mending after the double whammy of an accident as a house framer (a wall jack had fallen on me) and a car crash in a residential area (in a mindless hurry he ran a stop sign).

Diana had earned her Realtor's license, and was in her rookie year selling houses in Redmond where she had spent her middle and high school years. Her dad, George Trout, was a well established and highly respected broker there. (He would be honored as Central Oregon Realtor of the Year in 1983.)

But her commuting from Bend to Redmond was not viable. She wanted to be enmeshed in Redmond's daily life not only as part of her professionalism but also because she is wired for giving back to her community.

Leaving that house would be a wrenching loss for me. But, since she had moved with me to Salt Lake City in support of my radio career, it was right to move to Redmond for hers. After weeks of resistance, processing, and acceptance, I agreed. So we did.

(From this time on, real estate sales has her consistently successful lifetime career. Her volunteer investments in the life of Redmond led to her selection as Citizen of the Year in 2018.)

So we moved from Bend, population 17,263, to Redmond, population 6452.

I was recuperating from my injuries at the time of our move. I was the general contractor for a 6000 square foot lodge at Suttle Lake Camp, a Methodist facility north and west of Sisters, running a crew of four and rarely getting my hands dirty. Wesley Meadow Lodge was dedicated in 1981. With that job completed, and Diana's career dream an ongoing reality, I was waking up in a featureless house I didn't like in a town where I didn't want to live and was physically incapable of doing the level of work that had defined my existence for years. I saw a therapist (who took woodworking in trade for her services) and sorted out the tangled threads.

My first break: Tektronix, a Portland manufacturer of electronic test equipment, set up an assembly plant in Redmond. Their modular work stations were shipped flat to Redmond and I refurbished and reassembled them. Success.

Tek liked my work. They leased larger facilities and eventually employed over 100 people, a source of pride for Redmondites. Through those years there was scarcely a month went by when I didn't build something for them. It might be a small magazine rack for the waiting area in the main office, or twenty fixtures to hold some particular part which was receiving manufacturing attention, or specific tables which were crucial to the production of multiples in the most efficient way possible. They were a terrific company to work for as a vendor. I was building their stuff in a two-car garage, rented from Diana's cousin.

Time for a larger location. They called it the Honey Warehouse because that was its most recent function. It was Redmond's first ice house, on a railroad siding. The Redmond equivalent of the golden spike was driven 150 yards south in 1911, where the track crosses Evergreen Avenue. This little building was likely built shortly thereafter. And it was for sale.

THE ORIGINAL ICE HOUSE

Everything needed paint. The south side of the building had been re-sided but the other three were original boards, battered and warped. The shed roof sagged like old socks on scrawny legs. In all, it looked to be a sidehill fire hazard that had wandered down Evergreen Avenue, turned north along the tracks for a hundred yards, and hunkered up against the tracks. Seven hundred square feet of possible shop space for a fledgling woodworker who nurtured the cockamamie idea that he could earn a living doing his craft in Redmond. I had never heard of a Business Plan.

$3500 would buy the building; the land was leased from the Union Pacific railroad, $45 a month. That lease contract can be summarized in one sentence: If a railroad fire ignited my building, that was my problem; if my building caught on fire and destroyed railroad property, that too was my problem.

We bought it.

I pulled down the large plywood sign that said "Honey" and had a local sign company paint "Great Ned! Woodworks" on the back side. Jack Charlton volunteered some time to help me prepare the inside of the shop and reinstall the sign. After the shop was up and running, he had a key and could use it anytime, evenings and weekends, for his projects. He was respectful of the tools and always left the shop clean.

I was in business. I got a city license to prove it. Started advertising in the Redmond Spokesman.

It was slow going at first. At a low point I seriously considered shutting the door and trying to resell the building. A Madras farmer, whom I had met during the Suttle Lake Camp job, had told me that I could go to work driving combine for him if I needed some cash. I set a deadline; if no work came in by the end of the week, I'd call him. Next day, a lady brought in a broken drawer, and I fixed it for her. And then someone else came in, and then someone else.

I wanted to listen to Oregon Public Broadcasting at work but the signal was weak and distant. I fetched a library book on antennae, calculated what I needed for the low end of the FM band, and built it and mounted it on the roof. Ron Terry, a Toastmaster friend who did electronic stuff at the airport, helped me tune it. I was able to listen to the sepulchral voice of my former KSLM colleague Frank Woodman, who delivered classical music weekday mornings from KOAC in Corvallis.

There was a concert on the large loading dock one summer evening. The band was called Boch, a trio of Seth Erickson, guitar; Will Chisolm, drums; and Guy (Pete) Barker, bass. They did the advance legwork to get a verbal permit from the local police. Boch turned their volume knobs up to eleven and did their thing as Jim Erickson and I, and other proud parents, listened. From a distance.

THE DUCT TAPE PULPIT

When we joined Community Presbyterian Church in 1981, the new building was under construction. With the large octagonal sanctuary anchoring one end and a narrower rectangular section pointed north, it resembled the Starship Enterprise. This was a startlingly contemporary destination for the congregation which had been meeting in the original, white, wood-frame, bell-towered building which looked like it had been plucked from a Whitman 500-piece jigsaw puzzle of a New England autumn scene and set down a block west of Redmond's main street in 1912.

Worship was held in the new multipurpose room, which would eventually become the fellowship hall. Plastic chairs, random folding chairs, just making do until the rest of the building could be completed.

The congregation had made a pay-as-we-go commitment to the project and stuck by it, ceaselessly seeking volunteer labor. The smallness of the membership equaled a dearth of cash and not many tradespeople to offer their skills.

Time passed, progress began to show. Pews were ordered, and a committee was charged with designing and acquiring the chancel furniture. There were two professional woodworkers in the membership: Robert Miller, one of the finest furniture makers in Central Oregon, and your author, an eager, untested rookie. The committee decided that Robert would construct a communion table as well as a large walnut cross which would hang on the reredos. My assignment was the pulpit and lectern.

Bob created a cross about nine feet high, octagonal in section but which included just the two sides and the front three faces. The hollow space within contained fluorescent lighting which reflected onto the reredos in a soft and warm way. The Celtic cross, common to many Presbyterian chancels, has a circle centered on the intersection of the cross elements. Bob used brass-faced plastic laminate for the circle, a stunning contrast with the dark walnut. Everything about his construction—proportion, finish, mounting, lighting—was spot on. He was a master of his craft.

His communion table was three simple boxlike rectangular shapes: the top and two legs. The interior of these shapes, called torsion boxes, made them lightweight and destined to stay flat forever. At the time I could not have completed either of these projects. I did not know how to start, or cut, or clamp the parts while the glue cured. It was wise committee members that divided the work as they did.

I met with the committee to begin the design process for the pulpit. Its general look and size would define the lectern.

We looked at some pictures and chatted about the scale of the project: How big did it need to be? The actual dimensions, or even the sense of size, was relative to the size of the rostrum and the room. While the group wrestled with this, I was constantly reassuring myself that I could do this project successfully. It was a high-visibility piece of furniture.

The real challenge was dealing with the micromanaging from the committee. On the recently completed Suttle Lake Lodge, I had been handed the blueprint and entrusted to deliver the finished product; the details were mine. This was different. We worked through some design stuff which challenged my ability to render sketches on paper. Some people can look at a two dimensional drawing and visualize it in three, while others just can't. The process stretched on for weeks.

General features for the pulpit: It had to have a look of authority. It had to be easily moved to clear the rostrum for programs or dramas or concerts. And roomy and comfortable but not outsized. There must be a place for a Bible to sit, plain sight—a requirement from the Presbyterian Book of Order I was told. Oh, and everybody on the committee had to like it. That was important. Sketches on paper were inadequate.

With cardboard from Wilson's Furniture and Appliance I built a full scale mockup of the pulpit design using duct tape. Now we could see the design in real life.

I hauled tools and the model to the church and set it on the rostrum in the cavernous, pewless sanctuary. The committee members pondered, prodded, and pretended to preach. Due diligence done, they cut some tape, changed some things, and gave me the green light to proceed.

The pulpit shape echoed Bob Miller's octagonal cross. Both the pulpit and lectern were walnut and red oak, matching Bob's communion table. No one complained.

The furniture lasted for over two decades. I was commissioned to do the replacement, a much airier lectern concept with a small footprint.

"I have about a hundred board feet of claro walnut and I want you to make me some furniture with it. May I come by your shop?" The voice was warm, masculine. I didn't know what claro was but I'd look it up before our appointment.

He was already sold on my abilities. I do not know how that could have happened that early in my woodworking career. In the first place he was from Bend, not Redmond. Bend had more than its share of good woodworkers. Redmond had two: master craftsman Robert Miller and me, the greenhorn.

Pete Grisel (rhymes with drizzle) was a blue collar kind of guy of medium height. Black mustache and black hair so dense he wouldn't need a hat in a blizzard. His business was making rifles. I would go to Bend later that week and look at the lumber, stored at his house.

It had been stickered (little boards between the big boards so air can circulate) and stacked and protected from sun and wind. It was gorgeous stuff. I was feeling anxious; This could be a bigger bite than I could get my teeth around. I fought the urge to suggest he go talk to Bob Miller. I listened carefully.

We visited his immaculately clean machine shop on a busy street in the south end of Bend. He had several employees tending compact, clean and complex machines which hummed as they spun off shining skinny spirals of silver steel. The air was heavy with cutting oil, a sulphurous aroma that took me back to childhood and my infatuation with a welding and machine shop in Big Timber.

Pete manufactured exquisite collector firearms. "Most of them never get fired," he confided. The idea of creating a functional object while elevating it to high art seemed a little fluffy to me, a practical realist raised by survivors of the Great Depression. Since then, however, I have learned that the Grisel approach is evident in lots of realms of manufacture and bespoke hand-crafting. I had no idea that I would one day be in that pool, albeit the shallow end.

Pete showed me a room stacked with hundreds of walnut blanks for rifle stocks, chosen because the grain was straight where the fore-end would be and curved slightly downward through the buttstock. My gosh, he was a woodworker too! He indicated he wanted to be involved in the building of "our projects" if he could be. That unnerved me a little, but there was something about Pete that suggested it would be OK.

A machinist came in, wearing the typical denim apron of that trade with the telltale chest-high pocket for calipers. The pocket is not integral to the apron--it is a flat pouch which is stitched onto the apron just at the top of the pouch's back. When the apron-wearer bends down, the pouch hinges at that stitching and stays vertical so the calipers—which may have cost hundreds, even thousands, of dollars—stay put. She showed Pete a small cylindrical rifle part and they discussed changing a dimension a "couple thousandths."

Concrete foundation contractors talk inches, house framers talk quarters, cabinet makers refer to eighths and sixteenths, on occasion a thirty-second, which is thirty-one thousandths (.03125 if you're a machinist). I was in another world and just as fascinated and awestruck as the Big Timber kid who liked to wander around the welding shop. I agreed to take the job.

I built a table for their breakfast nook. Pete turned the tapered legs on his metalworking lathe. They included an offset foot which was created by mounting the leg in two different orientations in the turning process. I did not have the equipment or the knowledge to create these.

He was so excited about it he nudged me to get started on a china cabinet for him. When I completed that, he said I could keep the rest of the claro.

In our process he remarked, "That's why I love you." I was not raised where men said stuff like that and I was taken aback. But I felt the same about him.

He moved to South Dakota in 1986 and, in partnership with Don Allen, established Dakota Arms. There are rifles extant with Pete's name on them and at this writing I found one for sale for over $6000. Pete died in 2017.

"He was the model of what America can be," began his obituary in the Milton Freewater (Oregon) Union Bulletin. "A self-made man, capable of fixing or making anything, building a business from scratch while supporting a family, elevating the community of gun craftsmen with his attention to detail. He could be charming and light on his feet, then determined, gruff and tough as shoe leather." It went on to say that, later in life, he had become an accomplished woodworker.

Claro Walnut Waterfall Table

EIGHT

Four Jobs in a Small Shop

THE WHAT? BOX

He was about my age and came in one afternoon. Out the window I noticed his truck—a raggedy Ford, rusty wheels, spare tire recumbent in back. A working man. "Could you build a box for me?

"Sure!" I needed work. I sounded overeager. We discussed dimensions, about eight inches square and six inches high. A lid with a secure latch; a handle on the top so he could carry it with one hand. Then things got curious. He wanted dividers in the box, leaving sections about an inch square. That would take a little more work. "Will you be needing more than one?" I was already thinking about multiple notched parts and efficient ways to make them.

"No, just one." He seemed a little tense.

"What's this for?" I asked.

"Um, gaffs..."

"What are gaffs?"

"Um, they're like spurs..." And he shifted the subject.

Later I got it. These were weapons for cockfighting. I was building a box for razor-sharp knives which are fastened to the feet of birds to enhance their ability to wound and kill each other. It's a blood sport. My Pollyannish view of raising my sons in Redmond took a hit.

I had never considered that my little business might offer me an opportunity to say no to a job on ethical grounds.

If he had said, up front, "This might not appeal to you, but I need someone to build a box for spurs for cockfighting," I may have declined. But having invested the time with him and come to an agreement, I felt an obligation to produce the box.

And I did. Took the money, which I needed. But I didn't feel real good about it.

HUNDREDS OF BOXES WITH LIDS

I picked up the lime-green dial phone on the wall of the Ice House shop. "Hello, I'm calling from Westinghouse." It was the late eighties.

It was the Westinghouse. They needed someone to build some plywood boxes and crates. They were dismantling parts of some Central Oregon electrical substations, those chain-link fenced, gravel-floored complexities of pipes and insulators and coils one often sees from the highway. Some of what they removed contained PCBs; hence the boxes. I was listening.

This wasn't the woodworking I was hoping for, but I enjoy the challenge of multiples. Physical labor, under your own banner, is its own reward, so I stayed on the phone, asked questions, took notes. This would be the biggest job in my short career. No time for a chili cookoff.

Delivery was by a friend who had a long single-axle trailer. He traveled as far south as La Pine and northeast to Shaniko.

The Westinghouse job totaled 373 Boxes. Some the size of a Coleman cooler; some like a small closet. All those PCBs tucked safely inside.

I never met my contact guy, it was all by phone. I mailed a bill and Westinghouse paid promptly.

JUST TELL ME WHEN

When the lady on the phone identified herself, she was all business. "Hello Mr. Barker, this is Rhonda Spelvin, ON the Ochoco." That would be the Ochoco National Forest, 850,000 acres of "rimrock, canyons, geologic oddities, pine forests, and high desert terrain as well as the North Fork of the Crooked River" according to its USDA. The Forest Service was building a new headquarters in Prineville, a town twenty miles east. Rhonda came to visit me in the Ice House shop. It was 1992.

She was red-haired, crisp, stocky, and well dressed. She exuded confidence and energy. Sentences were staccato. We chatted, she looked over my shop, and handed me a thick manila envelope with the red-string-and-paper-washer closure. I agreed to get back to her promptly. And she was gone.

In our phone conversation she had noted, clearly, that I would not get paid until ninety days after the work was completed. "I know that can be difficult, but that's just the way the government operates." I had no line of credit, little cushion, but still curious.

While the square footage of the reception desk was significant, it was the intricacies of the cabinetry on the non-public side that intimidated me most. In one area, for example, there were two banks of drawers, each locking, and a confusing schedule of locks and master locks. In view of the installation deadline she had presented to me, it was just too much. I called her back.

"Rhonda, I've been through these plans and I'm not going to be able to deliver this on time. I wanted to let you know as soon as possible." I left out the truth about it being over my head. There was a pause. She cleared her throat.

"Mr. Barker," she said, "please go ahead and bid on it and tell me when you will deliver and install it."

Responding to her confidence in me, I agreed. In retrospect,

For delivery I rented the largest U-Haul van, hired the versatile Jack Charlton, and in three days it was, as the Brits say, done and dusted.

The check arrived on time, and my bank account swelled enough to catch up to my confidence.

Arriving at the Ice House on a clear spring morning, I saw a tandem axle trailer backed up to the loading dock. On it were three commercial type cabinets, all clearly used but not trash. Puzzling, but never mind. I have work to do.

Terry called later that day. I told him my name was Lee but from then on I was "Leland." Endearment. Was I available to do some cabinet work for him? It would turn out to be a long-term relationship encompassing commercial projects both stringently constrained by franchisors and wildly freeform when Terry got a certain look in his eye.

He was opening a restaurant in Bend, a franchise called Hudson's. The main décor gimmick was the nose of an actual Hudson automobile of the fifties emerging from high on a brick wall, bricks splayed out from the exit wound as if the rogue car had nudged itself through from the second floor of the adjacent building. Cleverly done.

The rest of the place had a vintage car dealership/garage/ petroliana theme. Those three salvaged cabinets got rebuilt and repurposed at Hudson's by Great Ned! Woodworks, saving Terry money and time.

Terry gave me lots of freedom of design. For a station for the maitre d' and I fancied up with a 55 gallon drum on end, partially cut out, with a work surface on top and a shelf below for menus. To the cut metal edges I added an edging of small rubber hose—actual fuel line purchased from an auto parts store.

I built a ten foot long bar with a curved front, all in plastic laminate.

The south wall of the restaurant, away from where the Hudson emerged, was lovely old red brick but for a wide former doorway, sealed up with visually-jarring gray cinder block. The line of booths against that wall covered the bottom two thirds of the block but the upper part needed to be disguised. Terry said, "Leland, figure out something to fix that."

I constructed what would be the visible upper part of three doors, accurately re-creating the architectural details of a pre-1950 building. Everything stained dark brown. The glass in the doors was obscure frosted. A local sign company installed, in period-perfect gold lettering, signage for the three offices:

SALES • PARTS • MILDRED

Terry loved it. That's what mattered to me. When I've told the story since, no one has found it as hilarious as we did. Surely someone, somewhere, had dealt with an office dragon in a car dealership. Or the opposite: Their Mildred experience was a dear aunt who helped them through the male-infested jungle of buying a first car.

Through his time in Central Oregon Terry built the first four Subway restaurants and fostered the fifth. I enjoyed building all the casework for all of them; I was by then in my larger shop. He built and opened a franchise deli restaurant and favored me with constructing the specialty stuff in it. I always felt challenged, trusted and appreciated when I worked for him. How Terry chose me is lost to history but I am forever thankful he backed his tandem axle trailer up to my loading dock.

AD DENDUM

Small-town weekly newspapers were strong in this era, and the independent Redmond Spokesman was a muscular example. One joke was, "I open it to see if there's a picture of somebody I know." Usually true. The news was local, businesses bought ads, and the publication was the main artery going to Redmond's outsized community pride. The Panthers, of Redmond's only high school, featured large. The police log was often humorous when the humor was harmless and nameless.

When Carl Vertrees, the paper's publisher (and salesperson) got wind of this Great Ned! business, he came to call. The ads would be two columns wide and three or four inches high. The cost fit within my budget.

A few of the ads I ran in the local
news paper, Redmond Spokesman

THE GOALS:

1. To establish my face as familiar
2. To illustrate the variety of things I built
3. To generate a smile
4. To underscore that I was the owner and the craftsman.

Text at the bottom, with address and phone, always the same. What varied: a different picture and caption, every time. Usually it was me in some odd relationship to something I had made. In the caption, "Lee Barker, owner/(something). Somewhere along the way we included the Redmond Hotel memorial coffee cup, which became an homage to the "Highlights for Children" hidden pictures feature.

It worked. Several times I'd get this visit: "We have been planning to move to Redmond and got the paper to learn about the community and here we are. We feel like we know you! Bingo.

Like whipped cream on nutmeggy pumpkin pie: In 1986 the ads won First Place, Best Advertising Series, among Oregon weekly and daily newspapers. In his regular column, Carl wrote, "The previous year in the same competition, the Great Ned! ads won a third place award. We're happy to note that the judgment of the judges is improving."

Absent the fluctuating quality of the humor, the print advertising takehome message is: persistence pays off, and its subtext is dependability.

NINE
"A Few Bad Checks"

He seemed like a nice guy. Pleasant, well groomed, average height, dark hair. Late 30s maybe. We were standing in his woodworking shop on a rough asphalt floor when I noticed that his green Powermatic Model sixty-six tablesaw had adjustable feet added to it to compensate for the unevenness. This building was just a block from my Ice House shop building. "Cabinet Corp" said the sign. In this "call on the new competitor" visit, I learned that he did only Euro cabinetry, something I did none of. In a sense we were not competitors because our products were so dissimilar. In actuality we were, in that somebody upgrading a kitchen or contemplating storage casework in a business would likely want to consider both options, especially as European style cabinetry became more common and accepted. I also learned that he came from a closed business in California where his former partner had absconded with the money and, before leaving, had maladjusted all the machinery just for spite. I felt bad for this guy.

I humorously complimented Blake (not his real first name) on his truck: A Toyota 1-ton dual-wheeled flatbed with stake sides. It was similar vintage and identical to mine, even down to the color. Shoulder shrug. Not much else to say. "Good luck."

"See you around."

There were two brands of tablesaw common in professional shops of that era: The Delta Unisaw and the Powermatic Sixty-Six.

Both were the same physical size, similar weight and power. The Deltas were gray and the Powermatics green. But one significant difference: The Delta blade tilts to the right and the Powermatic to the left. There are loyalists on both sides of this fence. I owned a beautiful Delta, made in the fifties, complete with art deco touches on the design of the base. But I could see advantage of having a Powermatic in its place. Maybe someday. For now, I was holding cash close while I looked for a larger shop building to rent.

I didn't see Blake for months. I learned, however, that his reputation was less than shiny. That came from several sources involved in our trade as well as my regular reading, in Bend's daily Bulletin newspaper, of an infrequent fine print column headed "Deschutes County Circuit Court Judgments." There I read, clipped, and saved notices of three separate judgments against Blake: $1711, $1163, and $16,383. I couldn't imagine (a) owing that much money to someone; and (b) showing my face in public having thus been published in the paper, albeit small print. I was confident that word would get out in our small community and he would fade away like the guy with the tiny sign on the highway.

I grossly underestimated his deceitfulness and total disregard for the law.

In the late summer of 1993 I was busy moving into the Industrial Park building, suspending production for over three weeks while I got my new shop set up. One of the side benefits of the move was the opportunity to have neighbors. The Ice House was isolated and while that did have a positive impact on production, sometimes it was a bit lonely. Now there would be business people coming and going both sides of my unit and pedestrian traffic to and from the group mailbox on the east end of our long building. My office, like all the others, had an aluminum-framed commercial glass door and a window next to it, and from my desk I could see not only the

weather but also human activity. I liked that.

There were seven units in the building. The end and the middle units were 3200 square feet; the remainder, 1600. The five-year-old structure had been built by a Joe Hitch, a non-local contractor who made a big thing of these "incubator" spaces where budding businesses could get a good start. He had an office in the identical building across a small parking lot.

The end unit next to mine was vacant when I moved in. A bright morning a few months later I pulled into the parking space at my front door and noticed a new sign in the window to the east: Cabinet Corp.

I didn't even unlock the shop door. I went from my truck across the parking area right into Mr. Hitch's office. "Joe, when I was considering moving here you made a big thing about the woodworker in *this* building, making sure I knew what he was about and that we weren't competitors, and now, without asking me, you lease *the unit next door to me* to this guy Blake of Cabinet Corp?"

"I don't think he's in competition with you."

"He is," I countered, building a head of steam. "And you must have checked him out. Didn't you know this guys a criminal?"

"He's written a few bad checks, but he's such a nice guy." He grinned at me as if this were immutable logic.

I stormed out, stomach churning like an under-engineered, sheet metal rattly, unmuffled cement mixer overloaded with Central Oregon gravel.

Those visits to Hitch's office continued regularly for over a year, and each time I described a situation in which Blake's presence was having a negative effect on me and my ability to earn a living. My rants were met by condescending smiles and meaningless platitudes. This great new start for Great Ned! Woodworks was thorny.

Weeks later I was returning to the shop in my truck, down a nearby undeveloped street, no curbs or gutters. A large pickup with a contractor's rack came around the corner, aimed at me and forced me off the road onto the sagebrush-scattered grassy desert. The driver got out and stomped over to my door, fists clenched, neck veins bulging. He looked in, leaned back a second and said, "Oh, sorry, wrong guy," and sheepishly returned to his truck. *He thought I was Blake.* Next day I went to a sign company and got my truck's doors adorned with large "GREAT NED!" lettering.

I pulled into my parking spot on a subsequent late summer morning and noticed a pile of small glass shards outside Blake's door. Top and bottom panels in the door were gone, the tempered glass reduced to shiny pea gravel. Police arrived. I kept an eye on things and made sure I was outside when there was an officer I could talk to. We recognized each other. "What happened?" I asked, predictably. He rolled his eyes.

"Your neighbor Blake *says* he was broken into." He tipped his head at the pile of glass on the *outside* of the door. "Says his computer was stolen." It was obvious that the blunt force applied to the glass came from *inside* the door. I heard nothing more about that. Somebody came and repaired the door.

I heard more stories about Blake and his bad checks. Lumber and sheet goods companies all seemed to have their own story, same plot: Blake lies and steals. I learned that the cabinet hardware wholesalers in the Portland area, though competitors, had periodic "credit meetings" where they shared information about deadbeat customers. Blake was notorious, racking up unpaid bills and frequent liar miles.

Weeks later a deputy sheriff showed up at the back side of our building and went inside Blake's shop. Shortly I saw my neighbor in handcuffs, escorted to the cruiser, head pushed down as he was placed in the back seat. I reported this scenario to Hitch, still vainly hoping that if enough nefarious behavior stacked up he'd evict the guy. Later Hitch smilingly told me that Blake had told him that "the sheriff came by yesterday and we went to his office so I could identify the guy who stole my checkbook." Hitch appeared to be entertained by this untruth. I was not only learning about sociopathic criminal behavior, I was also beginning to understand what a spineless landlord looks like. Blake came and went from his shop; rarely were there any sounds or signs of work done.

I read about antisocial behaviors, characteristics of sociopaths. I would have preferred good novels, even books about woodworking. I was becoming obsessed, as victims sometimes do. *"Glibness and superficial charm. Manipulative and conning. They never recognize the rights of others and see their self-serving behaviors as permissible. Pathological lying. Lack of remorse, shame or guilt."*

On a fall afternoon about five a local insurance man came in my office. He was pale and and rattled. "How can I help you?" I asked.

"I just went over to Cabinet Corp and there are no lights on," he said.

"I know. Pacific Power came by this afternoon and shut off his electricity." I couldn't repress a smile.

"But I gave him a deposit! He's supposed to be doing my kitchen cabinets!"

Oh the schadenfreude temptation to offer responses like,

THE BULLETIN, JANUARY 19, 1995: CABINETMAKER ARRESTED IN THEFT, FORGERY CASE

"And did you notice that *my* lights are still on?" or
"I don't recall bidding on your kitchen." or
"Excuse me, I have to go back into the shop to be sure my current customer gets his project on time."

No, I didn't say any of those. I was sympathetic and kind. I never saw him again and I don't know whether he got his kitchen or his money back. But I can guess: No, and no. There were others; same story.

TEN

"Lee Barker's Brother"

THE BULLETIN, JUDGMENTS,
NOVEMBER 1994: $336,421

Things got worse. Mobile phones were just showing up in the business world and a local seller called me. Blake had bought a phone using *my* name and there hadn't been any payments made. His social and persuasive skills must have been awesome, because they knew me—I had done work for them. That sale was a total loss for this small, local company.

A guy who sold copiers, same thing. My name was on the contract, I'd never seen a copier, he'd never seen a payment. This sociopath—my own diagnosis—was affecting our community in vile ways and all I could do was bring timely complaints to Joe Hitch's desk. I wanted this neighbor gone. I did not have the financial resources to move my shop again.

I was still functioning as a professional woodworker but the anger seethed. I had stomach issues, I slept fitfully. I really wanted him gone. He made the air stink. Every damn day.

I severely cut my right hand in an accident one Sunday morning in the shop. While I can't blame Blake (or Hitch) directly for this, it wouldn't have happened had he not been my neighbor.

Blake drove his Toyota flatbed dually over to the only remaining lumber supplier in Oregon who would still do business with him,

Emerson Hardwoods in Portland. He said to the employee on the floor, "I'm Lee Barker's brother; just put this on his account," and loaded up his truck. Somebody upstairs at Emerson found out about this, quickly, and called me. I made it clear they were victims of this bastard's brazen lawlessness and they should call the sheriff, which they did. The pattern was recurring: Blake breaks the law, I get interrupted, nothing much happens.

A local employee at the smoke jumper base, whom I knew vaguely, walked into my shop and asked me the usual questions about Blake. I did my shoulder shrug. He told me Blake had installed "some" cabinets in his kitchen "weeks ago" and he couldn't find him. More shoulder shrugs; he left. He came back days later and asked me to name my price and complete the work. I wanted to; I saw a Shining Knight on a White Horse opportunity to ride in and Save the Day but I declined. I had too much anger stuffed in my gut to do my best work.

Blake was arrested and handcuffed and escorted from a Bend high school where he was installing new cabinetry. Given that I'd never heard or read that he had spent a single night in jail, this information had a tone of sameness to it. I was giving up.

Blake had set up and established checking accounts for three local companies plus several bogus businesses in California. He was an accomplished felonious mover of money and regularly wrote checks on closed accounts in various banks. The article went on to say that an IRS agent participated in the seizure of boxes of Blake's business records. It also noted that Blake "already was being prosecuted on another 15 misdemeanor charges and one felony charge involving similar allegations." The Redmond detective who had taken the lead in the case, my hero of the day, said, "I don't want anyone else to get stung by this guy. He's raked people over the coals wherever he's been."

Five months later, The Bulletin noted two more judgments totaling $2000. The total: $331,307 plus interest and penalties. Considering the cases still in process, this total would approach half a million dollars.

Blake disappeared and I made no effort to keep up with the case. I was not aware of his shop being emptied out; must have been at night. I was breathing deeper; it was a Great New Morning in Oregon for Great Ned! Woodworks. I started mailing my monthly rent check so I wouldn't have to go across the parking lot to Joe Hitch's office. Good self care.

Driving around a corner slowly one subsequent day I saw a notice stapled to a power pole: "PUBLIC AUCTION SALE February 23, 1995." The Department of the Treasury wanted to convert to money some equipment seized from Cabinet Corp! There were 10 lots of cabinetmaking tools and supplies listed, ranging from a couple significant stationary machines to boxes of miscellaneous stuff. I made a note and, a few days later, tucked my business checkbook under my arm, locked up the shop, and went to the auction at a storage unit on the north end of Redmond.

There weren't many people there, and I knew nearly all of them. Mostly colleagues. I picked around through the jumble of items and I could tell that the really good things, big stationary power tools, had been high-graded and were long gone, likely under the cover of darkness. This was the dregs. But there was, in pieces, a green Powermatic Cabinet Saw, Model Sixty-Six. I looked closely. It had adjustable feet welded on; this was the one I had seen the day I introduced myself to him.

Staccato, monotonic auctioneer: "We have here a green tablesaw, whaddyagive, Powermatic, whaddya give for it whaddyabid, Powermatic tablesaw, herewego whaddyabid..." Responses were slow coming. I got in at $500, desire rising in the vacuum where the months of agonizing pain had lived. I heard myself say "Seven Hundred" and then silence. I looked around at the crowd. They were all looking at me. Guys I'd known for years, traded stories with at the lumber yard, borrowed hardware from, they let me have that saw, seven hundred bucks. Street value, assembled, more than double that amount. When the sale concluded, I had lots of help loading the saw onto my flatbed truck.

I put it together the next day and sold the Delta it replaced—a perfectly fine machine—for $1500. At this writing, a quarter-century later, that beautiful Powermatic with the adjustable feet hums along every day at Nedson Woodworks, Redmond, Oregon and Blake is a faded fragment, buried under hundreds of other joyous memories of my years as a professional woodworker.

The Dry Canyon Band 1996 - 2000

Leroy had moved to Beaverton for a new job with the school district there. That left four of us originals. Mike wanted to add a female voice and we found her, too shy to sing at a friend's wedding, but she did record a couple songs on a cassette as a gift for the bride. Mike heard that tape and invited her to sing along with us in his living room.

Linda Buckingham had a solid alto voice with a darkish timbre and edges that were a little smoky. The musicmaking appealed to her—she had daydreamed about it—but she would rather have carried a tureen of hot soup on a tightrope across the Grand Canyon in a gusty wind than sing in front of people. We addressed that with stage plot (the layout that a given band assumes on a stage).

Linda's sound allowed us to add such tunes as "Angel From Montgomery" and "Steel Rails." We were back on the Redmond and Central Oregon music scene and we did it without a banjo or the proverbial accompanying Four-Pound Bag. We were New! And Improved!

New songs, new arrangements as we built our nascent repertoire around the three harmony singers. More musical, more emotional punch, less goofy. This left Joe on the fringe, the bluegrass flame flickering in the freshening zephyrs of new material. But he was a trouper and played his part.

We got gigs. A real estate open house. An event at the college. Then we went large: How about a Dry Canyon Reunion Concert?

That concept got us booked for the Chamber of Commerce summer concert series, Music On The Green.

Leroy agreed to come back over the mountains for the show. There was stage time for everyone who had ever been involved with the band except Dave Warren, the other bassist. He was in Vermont and unable to make the trip. Don Banich and Jo Boozer brought their fiddles. It was well planned and the crowd loved it. From a yellowed clipping of the Redmond Spokesman of the day:

"Barker is calling the concert, 'From Total Obscurity to Limited Stardom and Back Again.'"

Joe Elliott: "What we've always strived to be is a middle-aged garage band. We've almost reached that."

In the interview Mike recalled the time we finished a gig, packed up all our stuff and left Jim. "We just forgot him. It wasn't on purpose. We all thought he was in someone else's car. At our next rehearsal, he handed each of us a Gig Checklist. The last item on it was, 'Remember Jim.'"

This, too, was a good run but Linda and her husband relocated to La Grande, Oregon and Mike was diagnosed with esophageal cancer. Our last appearance was a summertime street event in downtown Redmond. That was all for the Dry Canyon Band. For now.

Mike engaged his battle with cancer and in the early stages of the disease he found a place playing guitar at the Community Presbyterian Church in Redmond. He told me he was having fun there and, "we could use a bass player." I had no idea what this was all about but I said, "Sure!"

ELEVEN

Robert the Great

The employee who was around the longest was Robert (not Bob). He wasn't stuffy, he just wanted to be called Robert. And he nearly wasn't hired. The business was booming and I was ready for a fulltimer so I sorted through the resume folder, and his, being recent, struck me as a good possibility. I liked that he was well-experienced in plastic laminate work. He came in, we chatted. I told Robert I'd contact him in a few days. He seemed shy and unsure of himself.

I called his most recent reference, a commercial cabinet shop in Bend. Talked to Robert's former supervisor. "Oh yeah, he knows how to work. He was all assholes and elbows around here. He gets it done!" I hired Robert.

Robert's apparent reticence in our interview had nothing to do with his skill level and his knowing how to work; It was simply shyness.

In my many years of working by myself I would leave the shop in the evening by walking out—no other rituals—and come in next day and pick up where I left off. Robert asked permission to sweep at the end of the day and tidy up a little. He felt it gave him a better start next morning. Great! Each day, a little before 4:30, he'd get the big broom.

He also had a habit of coming in about 15 minutes early. We'd sip coffee and chat before we unleashed ourselves at whatever woodworking adventures awaited.

About a month into Robert's tenure I was discussing with him some detail that I wanted him to do differently than he was doing. To me it was a simple transaction: The boss knows what he wants and whether that is logical or not he can ask the employee to do it a certain way. Then I noticed Robert was shaking. "What's the matter?" I asked.

"I'm afraid you'll fire me for my mistake," he said.

I paused. "Robert." I looked at him. "If you come in late consistently, or don't show up for work without calling me, or abuse the tools, I will fire you. But I will never fire you for making a mistake. Look how many I make! This is a complicated business and your mind has to be on several things at once in order to get the job done. Mistakes are a part of our days. We can help each other fix any mistake that shows up!"

After that discussion I started joining Robert to sweep together at the end of the day. If I had been working at my desk, I'd come in about 4:20 and grab a broom. We would joke about the imaginary "Sawdust Award." If I had been pushing a pencil around all day I'd make some feeble point about the wood shavings in the pencil sharpener proving how much I had accomplished but, of course, he'd nail the "award." If we had been working in tandem in the shop, we'd discuss who deserved it, arguing in an exaggerated fashion. And during that time, nearly every day, I would point out something he did that was especially good, efficient or innovative. I wouldn't gush, just say it. Over time his confidence grew. No more shaking. We bonded as a team.

A Robert tale: This job we were working on was a big one, and for a week the shop had smelled sweetly of pine and its aromatic resin. Lots of built-in library shelves and a mantel affair for a rustic house at Crooked River Ranch, a large subdivision with serpentine roads, abundant deer and, for a few residents, a stunning view looking down into the Deschutes River canyon. About 25 minutes north of the shop. We loaded the one-ton flatbed truck up with casework and went over our installation tool checklist and headed to the site. It was Friday, just after lunch, and this would be a triumphal way to end the week. An added bonus was that the owner would not be there, making the process more relaxed. It was one of those days when Everything Feels Right.

We remembered everything. Except the house key, which was on the corner of my desk, placed there so I wouldn't forget it. This was distressing. We felt around the top of the door, checked the back door, no go. I was ready to accept the hour delay and drive back into town when Robert said, "Wait a minute." He walked over to the middle of the front yard and stood there for a few seconds, facing the house. He turned to his left and walked a slow arc over to the wellhouse, just a roof over a two foot high set of walls, barely noticeable. In less than a minute he had lifted the roof/lid and taken the front door key off its nail hook. Robert Johnson, Hero of the Day. His slap-happy grin lasted the afternoon.

In his book It's All About the Bike, Robert Penn, who is seeking a bespoke bike of variously-sourced components and travels and shops a lot to get it, decides on Brian Rourke Cycles of Stoke-On-Trent (England) to build his frame. Brian's son, Jason, does the building as Penn observes from a distance: "He worked quickly but there was an ease even in his hastiest movements. His hands appeared to be pre-programmed. They were often completing one job while his mind was clearly attending to the next. I wondered if this was a mark of his artisanship. It was certainly a reflection of his experience: he builds five frames a week." That keen observation fits Robert, too.

Linda took Robert's picture and added EMPLOYEE OF THE MONTH at the top and ROBERT JOHNSON on the lower margin and put it in a no-nonsense frame. It hung in my office from then on. He was the best of the three employees in my work history and he will be quick to tell you that our working together was "The best job I have ever had."

THIRTEEN

Cora Gets Her Money's Worth
& The Case of the Doors

Woodworkers are often introverts. We want a roomful of really cool machines, charming vintage hand tools, a large rack filled with exotic, aromatic, and interesting wood and something to do that involves all of the above. And an ample shop, away from distractions.

In real life, it looks more like this: A leased shop with neighbors, plenty of pavement to permit large tractor-trailer rigs to maneuver and unload, a phone that requires frequent and courteous attention, and interruptive visitors including insurance inspectors, fire suppression equipment maintainers checking little tags, United Way representatives, high school-aged job shadowers and random seekers of employment. Some days feel like wheels spinning in wet clay in a blinding rain.

An inquiry about a project, which also qualifies as an interruption, may not be well timed from the woodworker's point of view, but it's crucial to success. When Cora came in I gave her my usual attention. She was a plain-looking direct person, comfortable in her own skin. She had read the Great Ned! ads in the Redmond Spokesman and here she was. She wanted an open cabinet with fixed shelves and some vertical dividers, about eighty inches tall. As we talked about materials and finish I understood it was for fabric storage. In the back of my head, probably a "one and done" client. Design was simple, nothing fancy to fuss with.

We chatted, she left, I sketched and listed and totaled; I called her, she agreed, sent the deposit; Robert and I built the box.

On delivery day I learned what happens when a professional quilter lives in a basic three bedroom rambler with her husband and second grade daughter. Her business location didn't require the pavement needed for a tractor-trailer rig to pull up and deliver raw material outside but she certainly needed square footage inside. Living room and dining room were devoted to textile storage and production work surfaces. I was impressed.

We were greeted by three small dustmop dogs. Two wanted to help us in any way they could and the third stood back and, in a doggie dialect I understood clearly, kept saying, "HEY, HEY, HEY, HEY, HEY, HEY, HEY." Robert and I carried in case and fastened it to the wall. Cora was aglow with the efficiency she was about to enjoy.

Weeks later she called again. This time she wanted a bed, king size. She came to visit (not an interruption when it is a return customer), gave me the mattress dimensions and brief but specific instructions:. "Build it arts and crafts style with a headboard and a footboard and square spindles. Call me with a price and I'll send you the 50% deposit check." And she left.

I created the design, did the cut list, hand-picked oak at the wood store, and Robert and I dived into the project. When we had it all together, unfinished, she visited, approved, and left. Robert was feeling good about this too. We finished it, delivered it, and carried the components past the quadruped HEY volunteers HEY and HEY their HEY monomaniacal HEY pal, through the Quilt Factory and into the bedroom. It took us over an hour, and Cora left us alone. When we finished, I invited her in to take a look. Again she was delighted with our work and generous in her praise. Robert is a quiet guy, but I could tell his heart was as filled as mine. This is why we do what we do!

As Robert was loading the tools and she was writing the check, I couldn't resist the question: "Cora, we just delivered for you our very best work. We both delighted in building it for you. And the reason it's our very best work is that you let us build from our hearts, without looking over our shoulders even once. You didn't even show us a picture. How did you know to do that?"

"Easy," she said, handing me the final payment. "My best quilts happen when someone says something like, 'Make me one that's mostly light blue.' and then they let me do the rest. I figured you were the same way." That bed was a showpiece. It was in a room of order and refuge compared to the brightly-lit, busy-looking workshop that was the front half of the house. The bed exuded construction quality, balanced design, consistency of grain pattern and the pleasing tactility of the final wax finish. Hands and heart were what really matter. Three craftspeople standing there, a sympatico moment.

Cora called again, months later. There was noticeable music in her voice. "Ever build a hope chest or a blanket chest?" Sure! Glorified box, they are, but they can be fun. Floating panels are always satisfying to do and there is sophisticated hardware that solves all the issues of a heavy lid. Could this be a legacy project for Cora's young daughter Shasta, I wondered? That would be a bonus!

The chest was divided into three equal sections. From the front it was to be three panels across, each panel about sixteen inches high and fourteen inches wide. But the front panels weren't the usual solid wood, they were grilles made of thin strips of oak outlining holes about an inch square. Most important, they were doors which opened from the outside with a touch. The three-bay chest matched the bed perfectly.

Once again Cora got our best work and now you know where her three dogs sleep. But you don't know where the Havloseks found the doors. Yet.

THE CASE OF THE ANTIQUE DOORS

The Havloseks were a delightful couple, early retirement age and vivacious, who moved to Redmond and became part of the community. I met them in 1999 when they told me this story at the shop:

They were living in Chicago years ago when they saw, in a dumpster, a couple of well-aged wooden doors which they extract from that confinement, commuting what would have been a sentence that ends with a loud, sad splintering crush followed by a free diesel-powered trip to the landfill. The couple took the doors home and kept them.

Periodic domestic exchanges might have sounded like this: "Honey, you know those doors? Do you realize how many times we've packed and moved them? Any ideas? "

Answer: "I know, I know. But someday, *someday* we'll do something with them."

Much later: "I've been thinking about those doors you mentioned that we've been hauling around? Maybe we're never going to do anything with them!" Answer: "Me too, but we can't just throw them away. They're *old*, I mean, *really old!*"

And they were. One corner area, front and back of the door, was peppered with tiny pin-sized wormholes—definitely not fake. As remarkable as the old walnut were the hinges: clearly hand forged and had been attached to the original framework via integral sharp, tapered spikes that were pounded into the wood. No screws. Each hinge was fourteen inches long.

Along the way an appraisal of their trophy trashbin treasures marked them as seventeenth century cabinet doors. Inset panels, two per door, separated by a serpentine center rail. The top rail was also ornate. The bottom rails were straight, indicating there had been a drawer below, perhaps a pair of them.

The Havloseks brought a torn-out magazine page which showed an antique armoire bearing doors that were almost identical to the specimens that lay on my work table. They wanted a replica. The picture gave me the proportions to create it.

The armoire originated in Europe, perhaps as early as the twelfth century, and was first a locking case for armaments. Later, ubiquitous clothing and linen storage until closets became an integral part of a house design. Because the armoire's design was firmly established during their popularity in castles, they remained outsized. From my research: "An armoire was considered a sufficient size if it could fit eight small men inside. This was a rule of thumb for craftsmen, and it was often deployed using real men of small stature." Really!

The Havloseks envisioned a television enclosure. Or "audio-video cabinet." Great idea. I could make adjustable shelves and allow for cables and cords.

Robert and I had an executive meeting and agreed that we wouldn't try to match the construction practices that were appropriate to the doors. We had good tools, some that plugged in, and we used them. There was reverence in our diligence to make this the very best it could be; it was a rare opportunity.

It worked; we got it. The Havloseks came by occasionally to see the progress and oohed and aahed.

We stood back and stared. We had honored the craftsman who, without electricity, had created those doors which now would perdure another century. Maybe more. We hauled it carefully to the finisher.

I didn't see it again until it had been placed in its high-ceilinged new home where it stood as the pride of the room. The finish was awesome. Color, patina, sheen, depth, aura, he'd done it all, perfect match to the doors.

Special thanks to whoever put those discards in the dumpster in Chicago. If you hadn't left them sticking out so the Havloseks could see them, there would be no story.

Master Craftsman Robert and the armoire

FOURTEEN

The Underground Tavern
and A Point in Space

The visitor at the shop was a low-key, quiet guy. His clothing was more like that of a weekend gardener than a Carhartt-clad, down-and-dirty, scuffed and frayed, crusty-knuckled workingman. Surely not someone who could pound a nail, finesse a building permit and wrangle or babysit an irresponsible drywall finisher. I was wrong. He could do all those things. I liked Dallas instantly.

His current clients lived in Tumalo and needed a kitchen island replaced. We went out to check the site. Rural setting, through a gate, up the immaculate curving asphalt driveway was the house, imposing and large, high-ceilinged and well-fenestrated. It was a weekend getaway for the clients, Portland residents.

There were new granite countertops on the base cabinets on two parallel walls but the island was old tile and the cabinetry below it was just not adequate for the cocktail party peripherals that needed stored. The general sense of quality was due in part to the depth of the countertops—they were a surprising thirty inches front-to-back instead of the typical twenty-four. Grand and spacious.

The cabinetry was shockingly cheap: Poorly made, under-engineered factory products. The bottoms of the lowers and uppers were quarter-inch plywood instead of the typical three-quarter inch material. You could make them flex with a thumb. To accommodate the deep countertops the lower cabinets were pulled away from the wall six inches and new end panels were applied to cover that gap. I said nothing, carefully concealing my feeling of "Wow, someone actually did this?"

My job was to create a new island that looked like the other casework but had some specific storage features. I didn't have to be concerned with the granite top supplier, scheduling the installation, and all those general contractor details. Dallas would do that part. I submitted the bid, got the job, and built it. The result was a seamless-looking kitchen, adequate for the needs of the household. Dallas was pleased, the clients were happy, and I went on doing other projects for other people.

Months later Dallas called. The lady of the weekend house had taken a photography class and wanted to build a darkroom. Could I do such a thing? Ha! Through the years I had built three for myself, the latter two complete with running water and the last one included a motorized rocker to keep the chemical trays gently agitated. I could build a darkroom.

At this point in my cabinetmaking, the mid-nineties, I was bridging the gap between faceframe cabinetry and European boxes made of scratch-resistant plastic film-coated panels on engineered wood cores. A darkroom was a perfect application of this emerging modular style and I enjoyed the computational and millimetric process of design and the array of sophisticated hinges and other hardware. The budding photographer was excited about being in on the design. Her experience with larger professional darkrooms and mine with smaller ones combined well to make a functional and attractive working spot for her hobby. Another success. Back to other clients, other work.

I was unaware the footloose couple had just returned from Europe, where they had visited an underground tavern. They were enchanted. Now they wanted to recreate this atmospheric scene in their weekend retreat. Dallas went to work with shovel and wheelbarrow.

He was lucky. Everything he pulled out of that room-size excavation was soil, or gravel an inch or less in diameter. The one exception was a football-size rock, which he kept.

Dallas brought me interior photos of the exotic tavern. In the end of the room opposite the door was the centerpiece of the décor: The tapped end of a large keg which protruded about five inches from the plank wall. The spigot was wood. Replicating the end of the cask was no problem and I had found a vintage spigot at a local antique store. Then it got interesting: the client wanted the section of wall which housed the fake keg to open up to reveal a television screen. Dallas had planned for this and provided the framing and rearward support to accept my enclosure.

And then there was the actual door into the room, down concrete steps. Kind of dungeon like, first impression. The Europe photos showed the plank door, round-topped. So I built a Middle Ages-looking door just like it. Jon Smalley, local motorcycle mechanic and metalworker, made the massive lock mechanism for me.

Greg Madesh, a Redmond tile setter, had been engaged to do the stone walls and ceiling in the room. They were stunningly rustic and authentic-looking. He has since expanded to marketing his own inventions to make tile setting easier. Brilliant guy, and fun to be working with simultaneously on the site.

After completion and what must have been an entertaining final inspection, the couple had a party for Dallas and the subcontractors and our wives. We gathered in this cave-like room, enjoyed exotic hors d'oeuvres from the Middle East, wine from way beyond my experience, and interesting conversation. There were fascinating artifacts collected from his years in the petroleum business in Saudi Arabia, beautifully displayed on the (ahem) cleverly built-in display shelves. Stories of the couple's travels were riveting, particularly about their time in Africa.

Later our host complimented each of the craftsmen for our contributions. Greg got appropriate kudos for his stonework. My turn: "Lee, you do excellent work but you are not cheap." I felt pride (all us subs want to be fairly paid, or a little better) mixed with some "aw shucks" humility.

As my career progressed through the nineties I was becoming known as a versatile craftsman who charges more than other people who had had less experience. On reflection I wish I had been better early on at pricing my work at a cleanly profitable point and being confident enough to live with the thumbs up or thumbs down decision at the end of every bidding process. Too often I let fear push me into lowering a bid to increase the likelihood I would get the job. Some of that could be attributed to the general tone of the economics of our small town; we were a largely blue collar community made up of people surviving and helping others do the same.

A POINT IN SPACE

Anticipation of the next delivery of the U. S. Mail started for me in my youth in Big Timber, Montana, where I learned to save the lids from cereal boxes and send them in, along with twenty-five or fifty cents. It would take much longer, but in about a week I'd anxiously await Dad's returning each day with the mail from our box at the downtown U.S. Post Office. It might be the Atlantic States set of Wheaties license plates (just the right size to put on your bike) or the next two medallions of railroad logos. There were tiny submarines and frogmen which, when charged with a bit of baking soda, would emit little bubbles and rise and sink several times in the bathtub. Or Tom Mix Glow-In-The-Dark Spurs. A package in the mail addressed to me!

I felt that same excitement each day in late 1994 as I walked twenty feet to my outside locked mailbox at the Industrial Park shop. I was waiting for my Wooden Boat Catalog of Plans.

My business neighbor Fred had been aboard his large motor cruiser on Lake Billy Chinook, just north of Redmond. Out and away from other boaters, he hit some rocks in a shallow spot and what had been a good day on the water became an uncomfortable and sleepless night. He needed a lifeboat, he said, and I said, "Sure, I can build you one." I sent for the catalog mentioned above.

So here I am with a commission (time and materials) and a plan (Nutshell Pram, designed by Joel White) and that icky feeling I often get after I've said, "Of course I can!" with convincing sincerity. I felt as if had swallowed several toy John Deere farm implements.

I studied the plans and the book of instructions and ordered the wood. I had some vocabulary to learn, too: chine, stations, rubrail, cleat, rocker, painter, moor, and more. Most confounding: where to start? When you built a cabinet, you start from the floor. A light fixture, start from the ceiling. A family-heirloom wall display cabinet, well, you get what I'm sayin'.

For a boat, you start at a point in space. My brain turned to bonfiggus. Then I thought of Lou.

He was a part of a small community of airplane owners who lived on a private airstrip west of town. He was a man of many trades, accomplishments, and shifting interests. He had built his own airplane. He'd built and owned hot rods. He would grasp a subject with the energy and enthusiasm of a terrier, push beyond where most would stop, no compromises, and then, abruptly, clear all of that out of his life and turn to something else, moving on without seeming to look back.

I asked him if he would answer my questions as I built this boat, and he agreed.

He was a wiry guy, a bit shorter than I, with a well-trimmed goatee. His Italian heritage and his chef father had bequeathed him an intensity about cooking. He was as precise in the kitchen as he was when he worked in his shop and that could be aeronautical, motorcyclical, nautical, musical, fiberglassical or fine woodworking.

When I got stuck, I'd call him and he'd come by at his convenience and get me to the next step. His input was remarkable: he would never clog me up with excessive future information. He'd just tell me what I needed and what I would do for the next step, answer my questions, and abruptly turn and leave.

The Nutshell Pram turned out better than I had expected. In the process I had absorbed a lot about careful shaping of curved joints before gluing up. I learned to get loose and relaxed and cut complex parts on the bandsaw. I could stay in that "zone" and sand them to fit exactly. I can now do fiberglass layups with glass fabric and epoxy resin. I became a better sander because (a) there is much to sand when the finish is fiberglass and epoxy and (b) fiberglass and epoxy are tougher than the Unobtainium Lugnuts of Hell and take a long time to sand. I gloried in the process as this little beauty took shape.

I painted the boat white with a line of blue at the top, just under the gunwale. Interior mahogany, varnished. I could lift it alone. Perched on the deck of my client's impressive boat, it was a tangible insurance policy as well as a pleasant addition to his boating days on Billy Chinook. He was as happy to have it as I was to get paid.

Lou and I discovered over time that we had lots in common besides boats and flyfishing. Multiple tracks ran parallel. For a while.

Nutshell Pram

FIFTEEN

The Chamber of Commerce: Plywood Cows and an Oak Box

I n a small town like Redmond in the eighties and nineties, the Chamber of Commerce can be the central point from which the pulse of local business emanates. In our town it's a clearing house for information, the central nervous system for networking, and promoter of annual and one-off events. Follow the blue signs to "visitor information" to know about natural wonders (Smith Rock), wine tasting (fewer than Walla Walla, Washington; more than Nome, Alaska), historical sites (Petersen's Rock Garden), meetings (Kiwanis, Toastmasters), and events (Music on the Green, July 4 parade, Annual Dinner Dance and Auction).

A Chamber of Commerce one-off event in the eighties: The Cows. Imagine a side view of a cow body, nose to tail. The shoulders and legs another piece, the hips and back legs another. These three cow parts, fitted together slot-to-slot much like the cardboard dividers in a box of four bottles of wine, created a cow that stood up and still. Then it was decorated by local individuals and businesses.

I made over thirty cows. Linda painted one, called it "Mootage," and adorned it with parodies of well known painters' works: Edvard Moonch, Vincent van Cow, Henri Mootisse, Edgar DeCow. Decorated cows were displayed on the sidewalks downtown.

The entries were adjudicated by certified cow-art experts and winners won prizes which the Chamber presented. Lots of laughter was, ahem, herd.

Among the Chamber's sources of income is the annual Dinner Dance and Auction. Tickets are sold to attendees, businesses sponsor a table (decorated with their branded swag) and a live auction sells donated merchandise, gift certificates, and services. It's a festive, dressup event which includes a band and a bar. This generates a scenario that stars people who are there to mingle, be noticed, and support an excellent part of a vibrant community. Sprinkle some wine over that and stir in an auction that can get competitive and you've got a recipe for one King Hell Rooster of a fundraiser.

I was never drawn to attend the event but always responded to the request for a donation.

But what exactly does a custom woodworker donate? A cutting board, duh? Fifty bucks off on a kitchen of your choice? A bag of hickory chunks to be soaked and spread to smoke up the spare ribs in your barbecue as part of a chili cookoff? No. I selected some sweetly-grained red oak from my "save for special" rack and built a box. A custom box.

Dimensions: ten by fourteen by three inches deep. I dovetailed the four sides together and glued the bottom on. I gathered some random objects—a few coins, some mysterious hardware gojasters, a marble, keys (both church and house)—to make it responsive when shaken, and stirred them in. A gift certificate from Deschutes Office Products for $12.42 went in. A few dollars in currency. A ball point pen engraved with my company name (free samples came regularly in the mail). I glued the top on which sealed it up, then attended to the most important feature.

I put the box on edge on the tablesaw, set the saw blade up half an inch, and sawed all sides of the box. It looked like it should open, and like it would, but it was solidly shut. It would take a few minutes with a handsaw to cut through the remaining wood to expose the noise (and semi-valuable) contents. I added three coats of hand-rubbed oil finish and savored the feel of a genuine hand-made unopenable Great Ned! box. Time to donate.

Dinner Dance and Auction at Juniper Golf and Country Club: the seating-for-eight round tables were flamboyantly festooned with branded gaudiness, and each place setting offered up freebies enough to make a swag lover swoon. Everybody would go home with something. And for some lucky person, the Grand Prize: tickets for two to fly to Greece for a vacation of a lifetime. The drawing was the last event of the night and you had to be present to win.

Open bar, mingling, music, dinner, desultory conversation, introductory remarks, and the bidding began. With about half the donated prizes gone, the unmarked oak box went on the auction block and aroused significant curiosity as its interior moving parts were jangled and its unopenable mystery was thoroughly marketed. Bidders competed, and it sold!

It was labeled with the winner's name and joined the other loot on a table at the back of the room, ready to be picked up by the new owners on their way out the door.

While the crowd remained focused on the continuing auction, a male person walked past the table of purchased objects, grabbed the oak box and slipped out the door and made his way to the parking lot. In his car he found an appropriate tool—a big screwdriver, perhaps a crowbar—and prized open that prize box, breaking the eighth inch oak barrier that had, so far, prevented its being opened. A dastardly act! In the dusky haze of the lot lights he sifted through the contents and, as near as we can tell, took nothing. He squeezed the two pieces back together and returned the piece to the sold-items table and resumed his participation in the event at hand, muttering his apologies as he reclaimed his vacant chair with his friends at his round table.

He had been seen. The Chamber office staff knew who he was. Yet there was nothing to be done except apologize to the person who had bid successfully on the box and assure them that, since it had been opened, and broken, they needn't pay. They didn't, and Eric Sande, director of the chamber, took the box back to his office. The next week he sheepishly returned the box to me and recounted the events.

"So, all that done, I'm curious, who won the trip to Greece?" I asked. There was a good likelihood that I would know the winners and it would be fun to congratulate them.

"Him," he said. "It was him. The guy who stole the box and busted it open. He won the tickets to Greece."

EPILOGUE

Ten years later I noticed the box up high on a shelf in the shop around the same time I got the letter requesting a donation to the Redmond Chamber of Commerce Annual Dinner Dance and Auction. I refurbished the box, put a similar mix of random stuff in it, glued it back together and did the magic "almost through" table saw cut. And again it sold, fueled by the saga told to the roomful of eager bidders, loyal to the Redmond Chamber of Commerce and all it does for our community. The winning couple did not open it, they kept it on their mantle, a delicious mystery with a colorful history.

SIXTEEN

The Cane, The Grate, and Two Good Neighbors

FREEZING

Duff Young was a beloved man, sweet beyond understanding. He often dressed in light colored clothes and seemed the perfect model for a man in a white seersucker suit, holding at his side a white straw hat with a red hatband, tending to everyone's comfort at some outside summer event on lush green grass with white tables and a band playing ballads in a gazebo while women with parasols strolled about in twos and threes.

In reality, Duff moved slowly, haltingly, carefully, reaching out to steady himself when he could. He had Parkinson's disease.

Duff accepted his disease with grace. His wife, however, was of a different temperament. Lifelong educator, problem solver, advocate and git-er-done personality, that was Margaret. Retired, she got involved with the patients and the people surrounding the affliction.

Duff suffered from 'freezing of gait,' also called FOG. He and Margaret visited me in my office, stood at the service counter. As Margaret talked about Duff's freezing episodes, she paused and turned to her husband. "Duff, walk across to that door, would you?" It was about ten feet. He took half a dozen steps and stopped abruptly. Didn't move. Margaret's words hung in the air: "...and no amount of will power can make his feet move." Duff was still smiling sweetly as she gently guided him back to the counter where he steadied himself.

Margaret: "When a Parkinson's patient is alone, and freezes, they're stuck for some period of time unless they see an object on the floor in front of them." It could be a wadded up handkerchief or a page of coupons from a pizza place. Some unusual connection of neurons in the brain would be stimulated by the sight of what, ironically, could be an impediment. The patient, freed from immobility, would step over the object and continue to walk unhindered.

Duff could have freezing episodes when he got up at night to use the bathroom, or even during the day as he maneuvered about the house. Her solution? The ParkinCane. She had experimented with cobbled together designs and was having good results. She showed me a sketch.

Thirty-six inches long. At the top, if we're thinking of it as a cane, was a piece of the same material attached at right angles. It extended fourteen inches on one side, three on the other. A lopsided T. There were two small diagonal braces which strengthened the joint, one on each side.

Margaret had a half dozen around the house, placed intentionally along Duff's regular routes. When he had a freezing moment, he could reach a cane, grasp the "bottom end" and lay the fourteen-inch handle on the floor in front of his feet. And like magic, he would step over the cane handle, leave the cane by the trailside and continue his journey through the house.

The canes I built were eastern ash, square material so the critical joints could be stronger and construction simpler. Margaret would order eight at a time and I charged her cost. She distributed them through the statewide support group.

I made about forty-five ParkinCanes for Margaret.

No more handcrafted Parkincanes though. Someone came up with the Ultimate ParkinCane: a regular ol' cane with some batteries in it, an on and off button at the handle and, down at the bottom, a laser that lays down a beautiful red beam in front of one's frozen feet, clearly visible day or night, inside or out. I salute its elegance and cling to my own satisfaction in being a part of Margaret's caring for Duff and many other Oregon Parkinson patients during their struggle with FOG episodes.

UPWIND

It was trestle style, big, cherry, two leaves, for a couple who lived in a gated community in Bend. In one of our casual conversations he shared that he had grown up in New York City. I asked him how that came about. "My dad had a business there. He made cast iron grates, the kind that are set in sidewalks. You've seen a picture of one of them." The conversation rolled on briefly until I interjected, "Wait, I've seen one of your dad's grates?"

"Yes, you have. A picture of one. I am sure of it."

"What picture, how do you know?"

"It's the one where Marilyn Monroe is standing on the sidewalk and her skirt is billowing up."

The internet led me to that image. Sure enough, there's the grate. Also on my screen was the iconic calendar pose. The one through the window of the Timber Bar, seen by the kid coasting by in 1954, standing up on the pedals of his bike.

FIRE!

The owner's original business was in Salem, where he cast metal parts and art objects. He fancied one day to move to Central Oregon and he saw the wisdom of using a satellite site as an excuse, or incentive, to keep that dream alive. So he leased the spot next to me, and moved in some big equipment. He would be there for several days each month, puttering, tinkering, doing stuff I didn't understand, occasionally casting something. We'd visit, I'd ask questions. We got to know each other over an occasional lunch.

Don had a machine that ran constantly. It was like a small, stationary cement mixer, and its job was to keep a slurry, which looked like creamy mortar, in constant motion. If it stopped, the gooey stuff would become hard and therefore useless (just like the machine, at that point). The slurry was part of the mold-forming step in his casting process.

I noticed that there was considerable available floor space in Don's shop and I could see the value of doing my finish work there. The place was clean and the machine running did not stir up any dust. So I asked if I could have a key. "Sure," was his instant reply.

Not long after that exchange, while Don was not in Central Oregon, I carried an unfinished tabletop next door and set it on sawhorses and began the several-day process of applying my top secret oil-varnish mixture. I had sanded that beauty to 220 grit and blown the dust off it in my shop and it was ready to go. All was quiet save the purring of the slowly rotating slurry mixer.

Many woodworkers do not enjoy the process of finishing. It is a skill separate, and those who focus on it alone can be a valuable asset to a craftsperson who holds their trust. But farm that out, and you miss that unique moment when the liquid flows and the hand moves it about and the eyes drink in the transformation and tell the brain, "Remember this! A glorious moment! The wood is giving you a reward for your allowing it to come this far!"

And that's right where I was when I saw peripheral annoying flashes and heard an upsetting sound, not rhythmic. The switch box on the slurry mixer was on fire. Flames, even. I scrambled to unplug it from the wall, grabbed a cloth and forced it over the small fire. Then remembered to breathe.

Later that day I called Don and reported the incident. Only then, as we explored the "what might have beens" of the incident, did we realize how much disaster was avoided. Had I not chanced to be there, the sprinkler system would have responded and dumped gallons of water very quickly, inundating everything.

Don encouraged me to continue to use his shop as much as I needed to. We both benefited.

AND RAIN!

On the side opposite of the foundry, in the unit double the size of mine, a local vending company kept their trucks which distributed soft drinks, coffee, candy, and highly-evolved nutritional units like Hostess Ding-Dongs. I liked the manager and the crew of drivers, all friendly guys. They kept a clean shop as well as clean trucks.

Adam was just out of high school and was hired part time to wash the delivery trucks. His diligence and delightful personality supercharged his advance to fulltime work, moving stock up, down, and around with a forklift. And he still washed trucks, weather permitting.

It was a crisp spring day. My overhead door was open and I could hear loud and clear the forklift in gear, so Adam had his door open as well. The forklift engine stopped—nothing unusual about that—but then I heard a new sound, a loud, constant whooshing, mixed with Adam's staccato yelling. I ran over.

A tall load on the forklift had been raised by the operator, hydraulics surging like hormones at a middle school dance, and raised, and raised, until it contacted and broke the sprinkler head of the fire suppression system up against the ceiling. In two inch pipes.

The resulting downward geyser was twelve times what you get out of your garden hose at full blast. Fed from above, the surging water made a shallow pond, expanding toward the racks stacked with product.

I rushed back to my shop and got two sawhorses, the steel-legged kind with wooden top rails. Next trip, a sheet of 4' x 8' plywood. Then a screwgun and a handful of screws. Adam and I looked like the oilfield workers in that John Wayne movie about the legendary guy who puts out oil fires. We got the plywood canted at a 45 degree angle so the downcoming column of water was shooting toward the door, mostly.

And like the Lone Ranger, my job was done; I left to get clean and back to work. Adam had to make his phone call. In gratitude for my help, Dave the manager insisted I come over and pour myself a free French Vanilla latté from their rickety shop vending machine anytime I wanted. And I did.

Church Musician 1999-2014

There were singers, all female, and a piano player named Eric Gleason, who had an engaging "rolling chord" style. He composed praise songs, all excellent, imaginative, and musically interesting. Add Mike's solid guitar playing and we were in a sweet musical pocket.

The tunes were easy, played from lead sheets. We learned several new songs a month and the improvement was constant.

We played good ol' stuff like "Just a Closer Walk," "We Shall Not Be Moved," and "This Little Light of Mine." The rest of the book was mildly aged contemporary Christian music, nothing edgy. We played a sparse but powerful arrangement of "Come Thou Fount of Ev'ry Blessing" and, later, a Christianized lyric to Leonard Cohen's "Hallelujah."

No drummer, so my rhythmic task once again was getting and keeping the groove. Musically I was supporting the vocalists who were leading the worshipers. I looked for ways to get from this chord to the next with a note or two or three. The vocalists had set a high standard of excellence for themselves and toiled doggedly to get the harmonies right. We did well as a leaderless group.

I enjoyed the company of other church instrumentalists through those years. Some were dedicated and diligent, others on the edge of waffish. All were good-hearted. Special memories remain of Jaymee, the keyboardist. She was from a quite different Protestant denomination, but was happy making a joyful noise with us. A rare disease had left her with no feeling in her fingertips so she grew her fingernails long and they, touching the keys, gave her physical feedback of contact. Jaymee and I did some duo and ensemble one-off gigs outside the church setting. She was an encouraging and respectful collaborator with stage charm and poise. She refers to that part of her past as "the Camelot Years."

Under Karen Sipes, the church's third music director (and by far the best), the choir aspired to bigger works at Christmas and Easter: Cantatas, medium-length works for chorus, soloists, orchestra and narrator. The assembled ensembles varied from six to more than a dozen players and the choir continued to improve as we performed the cantatas through the years. Karen was an encouraging and patient leader. We made big music.

The church gig lasted fourteen years. It was a rich experience to be of service to the worshipers and to have so much fun, especially in rehearsals. As in any music making, there were mountaintop moments when it all came together, vocal and instrumental, and the joy rolled out like an everflowing stream.

Karen was involved in the greater music and drama community in Central Oregon. Her friend John Haverly, who had performed with her for years on the Crooked River Dinner Train, asked her to recommend a bass player. Boom I'm in the orchestra for local performances of a Broadway show titled "Always, Patsy Cline," with a pianist, percussionist, fiddler, guitarist (John) and me.

We were not a pit orchestra, we were in costume and on stage the whole show. The "Bodacious Bobcats." Again I was stretched. The show included about a dozen songs that Patsy had made popular. Sherrie Neff, the star, looked and sounded like Patsy. It was a rich story told with pathos and humor. And there was interaction with the band, too. We played multiple performances to excellent ticket sales, wishing we could have booked the venue for another weekend. After the show run we spun off a popup band, adding Rex Gatton, with Sherrie and her costar from the show as front vocalists, and got booked for the local summer Music on the Green series.

SEVENTEEN

The Purple Prototype, 2003

The bass was a whopping two inches thick, three layers of solid oak, heavy like railroad iron. The solution to the weight issue was simple: Cut some wood out of the middle layer next time. Later I discovered I was thereby creating a "chambered" instrument, a serendipitous sonic improvement. The vibrations in the thinner wood contributed to the tone of the instrument. Boy howdy. But for now, we had proof of concept.

As a bass player, I brought little to this exploration other than the ability to road test a new model and formulate an opinion about variables that I had changed. In all my years of holding up the low end I had not really thought about how an electric bass works. Now I was messing with ironclad norms sintered after Leo Fender's realized brilliance.

Later, in the rearview mirror of writing this memoir, I appreciated the intersection of three lines in my life: bass player, an idea for a unique instrument, and the skills and tools to make the idea real. At this stage of my working life, tinkering with this idea for a few hours a week required no outside capital. If the boss noticed, he didn't say anything.

There was no thoughtful analysis, no Venn diagram, no Critical Path paperwork. It was try, fail, learn; repeat, repeat.

The second bass sounded significantly better and was easier to play. The tonality had more bottom end, a richer sound. I had gigged with it and my bandmates hadn't sent me out to the parking lot to change a tire on the van while they finished the set. I took that as a plus.

Robert was working four-day weeks and I was devoting most Fridays at the shop to bass stuff.

One of Redmond's emerging entrepreneurs in the nascent Internet Age was Ian Blackie, a native of New Zealand, owner of Adweb Communications. I got to know Ian and his wife Maxine through our association with the Chamber of Commerce. I asked Ian questions, looked at "Web sites" as I learned they were called, and noted that the ones Ian had created had some subtle qualities that I liked. His electronic portfolio showed an eye for color relationships, page arrangement and user-friendliness.

In what would seem an odd qualifier, Ian was a world-class bagpiper. All bagpipe jokes aside, he had a critical ear for music. When he got wind of what I was up to, Ian, man of few words but a shy, warm smile, wanted to know more.

I invited Ian to a Dry Canyon Band rehearsal at our house so he could hear the bass in context. Prior to that night I would have said that Ian did not emote much, but his enthusiasm for what he was hearing was evident. Ian became Barker Musical Instruments' webmaster, another new term to my ears, and from the moment the site went live, we received compliments on it. Linda suggested we record the Barker Bass, solo, that would play when a seeker arrived at the site. Ian concurred, I recorded, and positive comments about that eight-note ditty were common thereafter. Ian recently said, "Out of the seventy-five sites I created, Barker Bass was in the top fifteen."

I built the third bass and played it in the praise team. Good.

The Great Ned! ride was ending. I'd watched Redmond's population more than double, and grown with it. By all measures my woodworking career was a success, though it was neither a smooth road nor a straight upward-tilting line on a graph.

There was not a certain day when the Great Ned! Sign came down and I disconnected my landline and let my rememberable phone number—923-0808—slip away. It was a process. This ad, the same size as all the Great Ned! ads, appeared in the Redmond Spokesman:

> *Friends of Great Ned! Woodworks:*
>
> *After 22 years of custom woodworking and cabinetmaking in Redmond, Great Ned! Is closed.*
>
> *It has been a wonderful journey. The people of Redmond have been kind, gamely tolerating the off-the-wall humor of a woodworker who's about a half bubble out of plumb. Where else on the planet could a business with such a silly name last this long?*
>
> *To my clients and suppliers, my deepest appreciation. Without you there would have been less wood to work and a whole lot less fun.*
>
> *-Lee Barker*

New sign: **BARKER MUSICAL INSTRUMENTS**

Lou Brochetti, the impulsive, opinionated craftsman who had helped me find the point in space to build a boat from, got interested in what was happening. Started showing up a little more frequently.

His intensity took him quickly and deeply into any construction endeavor he chose. His first job as a youth sprang from his hanging around a hot rod shop in Southern California. Starting with a push broom on the bottom rung of the ladder, he learned the art of painting cars and internalized the high threshold of perfection held by that trade. Subsequently he embraced flying and built his own kit airplane, a Pietenpol, powered by a Chevrolet Corvair engine. He flew it from California to Oshkosh, Wisconsin, for the big annual homebuilt fly-in there. In his boatbuilding period he continued to inculcate those high standards of quality and precision.

Lou excelled at everything he tried, in part because of that intensity and decidedly because his curious mind could take in a lot of information and organize it efficiently. And he'd try most anything. Add fly fishing and its attendant handwork, aircraft maintenance, guitar playing, and restoring vintage Cushman motor scooters. If it interested him, he would take it on, full bore, tachometer at the redline. When he was done, he would sweep the floor so clean that the forensics team would shake their heads, pack up their empty plastic bags and tweezers, and go tweeze somewhere else, maybe a chili cookoff.

Lou had significant inputs on process and construction techniques. He wasn't interested in bass playing or bass design—he was a blues guitar guy—but the newness of it hooked him. His headstrong adherence to making a plan and following it was a virtue and helped me realize that codifying the component parts and construction details of the instrument was necessary to ensure consistency of quality and to reduce the cost of construction. Lou's rigidity, while helpful for me at this development stage of the instrument, allowed little room for human idiosyncrasies in his friends. His was a world of black and white. Character quirks and all, Lou was to play a large part in the early years of Barker Musical Instruments.

Was the woodworking income stream for the Barker family suffering through this period of playing around with a radical idea for a musical instrument? Yes, some, but it was an erratic drip, not a clinical hemorrhage. With Robert, my loyal and highly accomplished employee, lots of work was going through the shop. I could do the front end sales, design stuff and hand off cutlists and sketches to him and know that things would get done with a minimum of my involvement. When two pairs of hands were needed, the shop work was a priority. When I could leave it up to him, I'd sit in the office at my new shop computer and learn bass vocabulary and get glimpses of a world I was about to enter: boutique luthiery. Or, more comfortably, bassmaking by bassmakers.

These bass craftsmen—all males it appears—were making instruments that looked just like what Leo Fender had created in 1951. In over fifty years there had not been a single basic improvement that had stuck. A brand new Fender Precision Bass looks *exactly* like a model from the first year. Even some of the colors, paint identical to that on GM cars of the era, persist.

Nine years into Fender Bass production, Leo added a second model, the Jazz Bass, which differed. The neck was slightly narrower, there were two magnetic pickups instead of one, and the body shape was less chunky and a bit more curvaceous. And it, too, is today exactly the same as those which predate it by a half century.

The upright bass and the electric bass have always been worlds apart. Though there are many players who play both ("double" is the term), a composer or record producer will specify one or the other for a given musical assignment. They are not interchangeable sonically. And optically, one may be better than the other. Yet both instruments typically have four strings tuned E, A, D and G.

Many bass luthiers have successfully reduced the size of the orchestral bass, added electronics to compensate for the lack of the large resonating body, and created, marketed, and sold their EUBs (Electric Upright Bass). But they *all* have a thick neck, no frets, and a bowable bridge. That is, an arched bridge that lets each string be prominent enough to be played singly with a bow, as they are played in orchestras. On all these violin-family instruments the left hand and the right hand are employed in ways completely different from those on an electric bass.

To successfully create an electric stringed instrument whose range of notes equaled an orchestral bass, Leo Fender did four things:

1. Shortened the scale (string length) from forty-two inches to thirty-four. (For comparison, an electric guitar scale is about twenty-five inches.)
2. Put frets on the neck. (Hence, "Precision Bass." There's no guesswork; the note is true.).
3. Installed steel-wrapped strings and onboard magnetic pickups.
4. Put it in a guitar shape.

I stayed with his first three ideas and ignored the fourth.

I wondered how new was my idea. Gibson in 1953 released an electric bass guitar, the EB-1, which included a telescoping endpin to allow it to be played vertically. It was produced in small numbers and never caught on

I stumbled on Bill Cayley's website. We had had the same idea at the same time: Put the scale, frets and electronics of a bass guitar into a vertical format. Bill and I had a cordial phone conversation about it. I sensed that Bill was onto other things in his life and lacked the time, will, and maybe the resources to take his product to market. The bodies of his three basses were more round than tall, lacking in grace. I felt I could say in my marketing that "No one else is doing this" without shaving the truth. At this writing his website has disappeared and I have never heard a mention of his instrument since I spoke with him.

It was decision time. I went home to Linda and said, "I think we've got something here and I don't want to die saying I had a good idea and didn't do anything about it."

"Let's go for it!" she said.

There would be times when I wished she hadn't been so enthusiastic. But her statement was genuine; she is a person who likes adventure, does not shy away from risk, and knows how to partner. We agree that the adventure was well worth the costs.

I was joyous, frightened, fired up, and eager. I'd just received a $16,000 settlement for a motorcycle accident that was not my fault so I figured we had enough to launch this enterprise and be up and running, black ink all the way. The optimism was heady and without it I could not have thrown myself at the challenges that seemed to arise several times a week. About the money, I was wrong. That icy reality would come later, after some adventures in a world I knew nothing about.

Next task: Build Serial Number One.

EIGHTEEN

Serial Number One

The Barker Bass would be "hand-made." There was no capital to invest in a lot of computer-controlled machinery, the space to put it in, and the personnel to operate it. I was confident I could create and feed the image of a craftsman out in Oregon's hinterland, laying his hand to well-worn tools to hew out a unique bass just for you. I did not know what percentage of customers that might influence, nor where they were.

The short view was to create a replicable working model, serial number one, run a print ad in BassPlayer magazine, see what happens. The up-front costs, which included website and ad creation, seemed manageable. The shop would shift shape a little. The implicit fallback plan to woodworking was comforting but I thought little about it.

Important decision, made after consulting with a few trusted friends: make the Barker Bass special, make it expensive. If someone has the chutzpah to copy you, they'll likely rely on a lower price to get attention. Barker Musical Instruments would then play the "original and still the best" card and push the "handmade" image more firmly.

The electronic components included Seymour Duncan pickups, a well-known name that would give the buyer comfort in light of the radical design of the instrument they were considering. Chrome hardware—knobs and tuning machines and bridge—is standard issue on most electric basses. Black hardware suggests a boutique instrument. It costs only a little more. Definitely black hardware.

Cherry for the front. While it's not commonly used on electric instruments, it is a good choice sonically. Another reason: Its warm color is suggestive of the tops of vintage, and even modern, orchestral cellos and basses. They are typically spruce, a light-colored wood, but tradition has them stained darker.

Leo Fender chose alder for his electric guitar and bass bodies. He puttied the defects and painted the instruments solid colors. The premium alder instruments got two- or three-toned "sunburst" paint jobs with a dark brown or black rim fading to a lighter, translucent shade in the center.

Alder, native to the Pacific Northwest and lighter and less expensive than cherry, was a natural for the back. It later became the standard front and back for the downscale Brio.

I would make three or four instruments at a time. Someday, I hoped, we would have a Custom Shop Division staffed by eccentric, long-haired, vegan artisans who would proudly whisk their Prius past a chili cookoff on their way to gleaning for echinacea. Meantime, I had to keep my hands busy working out production challenges. Lots to learn.

I purchased bass necks rather than build my own. It would take two years to learn enough to build necks that were dependably precise and failures would be rare. Necks are mostly wood and, in spite of their steel spine, called the "tension rod," they can occasionally twist or bend enough to make an instrument unplayable. My intuition was correct: in my nine bass building years I had about two percent failure in my purchased necks.

Linda designed the Barker full-name logo, which was laser-engraved on the maple headstocks. Most other manufacturers used decals or medallions.

On the Barker Bass there are two homages to its ancestors in the violin family: the tailpiece and the edge detail. The tailpiece on an orchestral bass is about fourteen inches long. One end attaches to the lowest point of the body on the front of the instrument and the lower

Linda's iconic logo

ends of the strings are attached to the upper end. From there the strings stretch over the bridge, run the length of the neck, over the individual notches in the nut, and finally are wound around the geared tuning machines. Originally these violin family tailpieces were ebony; now they are often synthetic materials but keep the soft charcoal-black sheen of the traditional (now endangered) African wood.

The tailpieces on all these acoustic instruments are more than just a structural beam; they are an important link in the creation of complex tone.

Guitar and violin bodies are described as upper bout, waist, and lower bout.

The body needed something vertical and visually strong on the lower bout. I tried a straight-sided, flat-front interpretation of the traditional organically-shaped tailpiece from the violin family, and it worked. That design feature never varied through the production of over 100 Barker Basses.

The tailpieces quickly evolved to hardrock maple, sanded to 320 grit (extra fine), colored with black leather dye and finished with Johnson's Paste Wax for Floors. Even up close, you'd bet your second to the last dime it was ebony.

Bob and Teri Bender's small business included laser engraving. They had scanned Linda's stunning monogram for the prototype tailpiece and etched it on a cameo-shaped black plastic glue-on part. A serendipitous discovery of one more way to plant our uniqueness on the instrument.

Serial numbers are important on boutique instruments, to both customers and the makers at the moment. And, we hope, to historians in the future (think Antiques Roadshow). Bob and Teri's design included my signature as well as the number, all engraved on a small plastic spear-point shape that covers the truss-rod access just below the headstock.

I was in a whirlwind of joy and energy, eager to get this example instrument done and played. But another voice was urging me to slow down, focus on quality, savor the experience and keep my feet on the ground. Sleep was sometimes adversely affected and I am sure my attention to my supportive wife and blended family LiAndra, Guy (later Peter), Joel, and Joe was suboptimal. There were days when this great adventure was frayed around the edges because my work was not in balance with family life. Women can multitask. Men, not so well. Lee, worst of the men. Despite that, my family encouraged me.

The other homage to the violin family was subtle: the edge detail on the Barker Bass. The violin's top and bottom overlap the edge a little bit. Any attempt to copy this would have been not only impractical but also obtuse. I already owned a cabinetmaker's router bit called the "flush trim vee groove" which would trim the front and back veneers flush with the core piece at the same time it would cut a slight vee-groove right at the glue line between the veneer and the core. It quietly affirmed the Barker Bass's connection to the DNA of her gut-stringed relatives.

That's the tech story so far, featuring the wood crafter, his abundant tools, and his rapidly evolving product which he was preparing for market. The narrative would end here if it weren't for the people who came alongside and helped him carry it outside into the sunlight.

Like Lou Brochetti had appeared when I was about to launch my boatbuilding period, here was another literal walkon: Steve Anderson, who showed up at church and offered to add his guitar playing to our praise team. He was a powerful and confident player, lots of rhythm, and a voice as solid as the lava rock just underneath almost everything in our high desert country. At work he was the sales manager at Breedlove Guitars, a Central Oregon manufacturer of high-end acoustic instruments known throughout the world. Steve educated me in the stratospheric finishing standards required for a quality instrument to justify its premium price. Priceless information. There is a segment of the guitar and bass buying public that buys instruments for their collections, not as tools for making musical art. This is more prevalent in the guitar world but Steve assured me that some of the bass-buying market was going to respond the same way. He was right.

Why is this aesthetic standard so high? It has nothing to do with the sonic quality of the instrument, nor does it impart any additional protection for wooden parts beyond a few coats of paint or clearcoat.

The Barker Theory of Shiny Lutes takes us back to the kings in the Middle Ages. These potentates were a highly competitive lot, happiest when they could send their swordsmen, archers, and mounted knights to sally forth, conquer other kingdoms, and steal jeweled crowns. During the off-season, they would have two-a-day practices for their knights and every now and then, just to keep the testosterone quotient up, they'd host a day of competitive jousting. Colorful flags would go "blip, blip" in the breeze as the neighbors showed up for the precursor for the regional chili cookoff. Vendors hawked chitlins next to a couple of oxcarts burdened with multiple flagons of the region's best artisanal IPA.

And the king would invite a neighboring, friendly king to bring his warriors, just to compete. It's a guy thing. Helmets and chain mail do not suppress testosterone, they enable it.

On the surface it would seem that winning was strictly up to the performance of the competitors. But, as in all individual sports, there are plenty of important people on the sidelines. To win, a given king would have to have the best farrier, the best blacksmith (who would hammer out solutions to problems that arose when something arrived broken in the mail), the best fletcher of arrows, the best vexillographer, and so on.

And then one day the queen protested: "How come, your highness, do you get the best of all these tradesmen to do all this excellent work for you and I get nothing? Look at my poor lute player, trying to set a mood with that cheap-looking instrument with strings that buzz and bouts asplintering! Show me you love me: get me the best luthier in the land!"

So the king, being a pretty smart guy, honored her majesty's suggestion and found the best luthier in the whole flat world and brought him home. The successful hire settled in and made great lutes.

The king and the queen lived together happily ever after. And that, boys and girls, is why everyone expects a good musical instrument to be completely free of any cosmetic imperfections, all shiny and perfect. That's the way they were, and that's the way they are.

Prior to this music adventure, I had made and finished lots of furniture, including tabletops, and had developed my materials, techniques, and standards which I thought would translate directly to instruments. Now I was internalizing new information from both Lou and Steve: What I thought was good enough is *not good enough for Barker Basses!*

It was Lou who showed me. Little nicks in the wood I had not noticed before. A horizontal light would reveal sanding scratches (that's what sandpaper does, even the very finest grits of it) that would show up later in the finishing when the surface was held just so in a cruelly bright incandescence. I installed a high-wattage adjustable lamp on the end of my sanding table and kept a large magnifying glass at hand.

For clearcoat we went with waterborne polyurethane because of the lack of fumes. Lou spoke with the owner of the company that made the product, and they worked out a protocol for the application process and the sanding between coats. The end result could stand proudly in the world of boutique musical instruments. I could not have made that step up without Lou.

I put that first bass together. Hoooo! I felt elevated. I wanted to show the world. Lou sprayed the finish and installed the electronic circuits and knobs at his place and did the setup, which entailed stringing up the instrument, getting the string heights and lengths correct at the adjustable bridge, adjusting the pickup heights, establishing

Serial Number One
Image by Kevin Kubota

the arc of the four strings one to another and, finally, tuning and testing. All of these steps were beyond my understanding and I was extremely grateful knowing that Lou's intensity and precision would guarantee that each instrument would be done right.

There it stood, *Serial Number One*, ready for the launch and some serious ongoing marketing. Enter JD Grinnell and Kevin Kubota, two people without whom the launch would have been as fumble-thumbed as a wine cask warehouseman performing an appendectomy with plastic picnic flatware on a lemming in the dark.

Kevin is a brilliant photographer with a worldwide reputation, as well as a pioneer in teaching other professionals how to use the newest digital software. I was humbled to have him focused on getting me the best possible images of Number One.

JD Grinnell and I had met when we were both under contract to a gung-ho local coffee company which was in the Central Oregon forefront of the national trend perking toward arabica and looking for grounds for divorce from robusta. He was doing their graphic art and Great Ned! Woodworks was building the grocery store fixtures which displayed the beans so enticingly that you were destined to grind and bag your very own coffee right there in the hot beverage aisle. Something clicked when JD and I brainstormed how his ideas for point-of-sale promotion would best be realized in the coffee cabinetry I was building, and we became friends. I called him.

JD had his own Bend advertising agency, Marketing Ink. He had worked for Gillette in New York City. While that might seem to be experience that wouldn't apply to Redmond's fledgling luthiery, not so. The questions are the same: Who is going to buy the product and what do they need to know to get to yes and how do we reach them so they do?

JD designed a trifold brochure, using the same colors Ian Blackie had selected for the Web site. He hired a female model to pose as a singer in dusky profile, wireless microphone in hand, with the bass face-on in the foreground. It is a stunning arrangement of images. Kevin persuaded light to illumine the rim of the bass body while Linda's artful logo anchors the visuals and answers the inevitable question: *"What is that beautiful instrument?"*

Great Ned! Woodworks was still in business, though reduced in scope. And just as improbable as the assembly of the Barker Bass Dream Team, three skilled and trusted subcontractors upon whom I had depended for years just faded away.

My cabinet installer, Dennis, who was so good that clients would call me after he left and sing his praises; Daniel, who worked for a nearby cabinetmaker and did my lacquer work in that shop with his boss's blessing; and Chris, my doormaker, who packed up and moved to Costa Rica. All three gone, no replacements in view.

Was I destined to become a maker of basses? Or was I being watched by an amused omniscient observer who smiles and shrugs at coincidence? Never mind this obtuse exercise, I thought to myself (which is how I usually do it). Let's get going!

Dry Canyon Band (II)

One of the walkons in the praise team years was a fantastically talented musician. Eric was mainly a guitar player but he could figure out any instrument. He sang lead or harmony. He was tall and blond and had a charming, coy smile. Twice through and he had a song's structure memorized. Rarely looked at a lead sheet. He didn't use a guitar pick. Or his fingers. He played the six strings with his thumb, upstrokes and downstrokes. Unorthodox and lightning fast.

I suggested to Jim that, with Eric, we might have the start of yet another Dry Canyon Band. We auditioned each other and Jim was ecstatic. Eric could bring songs that we'd never done. I lobbied successfully for a fourth member. We played a couple gigs with Bonnie Grace Day, an accomplished singer/guitar player from Bend. She loved playing with us but she was planning to move to the Southwest.

The search resumed and it was tedious. We auditioned four guys. One was musically inadequate, one was gone a lot. The third was easy to get along with but he had no grasp of commitment. His purpose in life was to collect guitars and he'd bring a different one to each practice and hold it up at different angles to stare at it. His way of saying, 'hey fellas, this isn't working for me' was to cease coming to practice.

The fourth seemed like a really good fit. He brought some musical experience, was roughly our age, and seemed eager to belong until he wrote a dramatic "I Quit!" letter and took copies to Jim and me but not to Eric, with whom he was evidently having an issue. He had no compunction about abruptly abandoning the band which had been booked by folks who expected a four piece group. Our grief must have lasted about ten minutes, maybe less.

We did a few gigs as a threesome, which was fine, but we were aware that our musical programs lacked the variety we were accustomed to. The idea of a fourth still hovered until someone said, "Hey, what about Rex Gatton?" Well, of course!

I had done some musical stuff with Rex over the years. He was mostly a solo artist—guitar and vocals—which got him gigs but did not feed his joy in singing harmony. He was the perfect attentive player to create space for Eric to do his soaring and engaging solos. Jim was cooking on the Dobro and had become a journeyman songwriter. The Barker Bass got stares wherever we went. Jim was writing songs in wide variety and we tried them all. We were a band again.

We played the county fair, of course, we almost always did, and the cancer Relay for Life at a high school track. I helped build the stage at a pizza joint where we played several times. And the local Senior Center.

I had lifted a crowd-pleaser a cappella novelty tune from the Limeliters' album "Until We Get It Right" (2000). Bill Zorn performed "Folk Rap" written by O. J. Anderson. We'd wear baseball caps backward and over a background of rap sounds and movements by the others, I rapped the lyric that included such lines as "...Peter Paul and Mary now just to name three" and "..."we used to make a lot of cash on Prairie Home Companion." I drove a lot of energy into it, often jumping off the front of the stage to get closer to the audience. It fit with the other "talkies" I was doing and the singers appreciated the small break. It was successful programming to follow this with a plaintive, thoughtful, even melancholy tune like Jim's waltz, "I Know You're Gone."

Rex's euphonious baritone lent itself Clapton's "You Look Wonderful Tonight," Morrison's "Brown Eyed Girl" and folk tunes like Tim Hardin's "Reason to Believe."

Then Rex announced he was moving up to the Tri Cities in Washington. It was a job opportunity he and his wife Sharon couldn't pass up. Meantime Jim had been in on the birth of a new other band called Bellavia. He was playing bass in that group and enthusiastic about the human dynamics and the level of talent he was interacting with.

Eric and I couldn't envision a future so we hung up the sweatsocks. No more Dry Canyon Anything. More than twenty years, off and on, three different lineups, all including Jim and me. What a ride!

TWENTY

Michael Dempsey and The Cure

I n 2003 the Barker Bass was brand new and I was eager to share with anyone the story which started with wrist pain and moved through subsequent iterations of my idea until I had a product and a company. My marketing plan was a penciled list, neither well thought out nor detailed.

Multiple times I heard, "Well, you just gotta get one into the right hands and it will take off." Easy to say. Not sure how to do it.

An endorsement is a player's actual, or figurative, signature on the product, which could be as small as a guitar pick or as large as a refrigerator-sized bass speaker cabinet.

Forget about George Foreman's Grill. That's his product. Forget about the Nascar driver dropping his helmet and putting on a baseball cap with "Vice Grip Garage Sparkolator Spark Plugs" embroidered on it. That's sponsorship. Endorsement is, "I play a Barker Bass because..." And that message is transmitted to other bass players by print or video.

Put simply, it's a contract between two parties in which the manufacturer agrees to give (or sell at reduced price) a product to an artist and in return the artist agrees to use *and promote* the product. The agreement can range from a handshake to an elaborate, signed contract.

Most of the artists looking for such an arrangement aren't prominent enough to deliver meaningful results. Ironically, the fledgling companies they approach often have unrealistic expectations of how an endorsement will translate to sales. I was that naive, hapless entrepreneur because so many people had repeated the "get one in the right hands" bromide that I believed it to be true.

June, 2003. Michael Dempsey, calling from Florida. He said he was the bass player with The Cure in the seventies. He had just found out about the Barker Bass and thought it would be an ideal instrument for him to have at this point in his career.

I checked out this bit of history with my sons Guy and Joel, and it fit. Michael Dempsey was indeed that bass player. This was legit, and I leaped at the possibilities even though it wasn't the genre of music I had envisioned. Stuff by The Cure was dark, nihilistic, gothic rock. But hey, if it sells basses, let's get one into Michael Dempsey's hands! This guy was a good communicator, had some stature, *and liked the instrument and had called me!*

Dempsey said he had toured lately with Carole King and was currently involved in a commitment to Gloria Estefan, but right now he was preparing for The Cure Reunion Tour. I sent him a simple one-page contract which obligated him to provide me with photos of at least 300dpi of him playing the bass, "...especially but not limited to on stage." He would also furnish meaningful testimonial text. He enthusiastically agreed with the terms and returned the signed document, dated 7/4/2003. I was pretty damn smug.

I had several phone conversations with Dempsey as he prepared to head to the U.K. to start rehearsals. I sent him a bass, serial number 003.

There were instant returns on this investment even though there were no sales yet. Dempsey spoke at length about the other products he was endorsing, including innovative bass instrument speaker enclosures made by Accugroove in Cupertino, California. From these conversations I got to know Mark Wright, the owner. Mark, a bassist, was curious about what I was up to. Our products were similar in their novelty. We spoke several times a month, which, I learned, is how the bass playing community stays in touch.

Dempsey called from England. "They are giving me a lot of money, plus a cell phone, so I'll be able to keep you updated." Unfortunately, he added, the reunion idea looked like it was going to implode. This was disappointing to me, but believable; bands often have tempestuous histories.

He called within the week and said as he left rehearsal that day he met Damien Rice, an Irish singer/songwriter who was using the studio next door. Rice invited Dempsey to sit in with his group, just a piano and violin. Dempsey reported that they loved the Barker Bass. My excitement was bubbling now. Next day he called to report that Rice's management had asked him to be the bassist on their tour. "Less money," he said, "but we'll be touring all over the place. And in November we're booked on Good Morning America."

Wow. This guy Dempsey was enthusiastic. He was aggressive, opportunistic, and a versatile professional. Michael Dempsey and I could be a team! We were on our way to the Barker Bass becoming— dare I say it—*internationally known!*

August 5, 2003, the phone again. Not Dempsey. The caller was from another manufacturer who had furnished some products to Michael Dempsey and he was checking to see if I fit in that category. Yes. "Better sit down then, Lee." I was already sitting. "Lee," he said, "Michael Dempsey is a fake." Suddenly there was no oxygen in my office. Shock. Confusion. Bad, icy feeling in my gut. What? This had all been so good! How could this be fake?

The news hit me hard. The money. I had sent him an instrument priced at $2995 and I immediately doubted I would ever see it again. A substantial dollar loss to the company. How to protect myself from this in the future?

Enter Sergeant Robert R. Hart of the Pinellas County (Florida) Sheriff's Office. My belief in the goodness of people was restored. Sgt. Hart had been assigned the case when one of the affected music companies filed an official complaint against Mr. Dempsey.

We had a good conversation after which I faxed him a copy of my agreement with Dempsey. Sgt. Hart said he had contacted a spokesperson for The Cure who affirmed that Michael Dempsey was indeed an early bassist for the band but the spokesperson was convinced that *this* Michael Dempsey was an imposter. Sgt. Hart was familiar with Dempsey's claims about playing for Gloria Estefan, the Fifth Dimension, and others. He had a list of the companies which had given Dempsey products, and he was aggressively pursuing the case.

Hart said some of the listed items had been pawned but the whereabouts of the rest of the stuff was unknown. Dempsey had just moved to a different apartment. Hart said he would do a "knock and talk" to ascertain if Dempsey had the products.

Aha! So two Michael Dempseys. Our interest was the crook who happened to be a musician, or at least could talk the game, and who could con people into giving him valuable musical equipment. And, astutely, he had targeted small, naive companies with innovative products.

Later that day, the Florida Dempsey called, spinning more stories. I did my best to respond as enthusiastically as I had before. He said he had returned to Florida and was on his way "to a gig on the tenth floor of the Holiday Inn in St. Petersburg." He reaffirmed that he'd be on Good Morning America, November twenty-third.

Next day I called Hart and left a summary of that conversation on his voice mail.

Dempsey called later that day, desperate, voice pitched higher, talking fast. He said that two policemen were there. He mentioned Damien Rice and GMA. He begged me to tell Sgt. Hart that he, Dempsey, could keep the instrument. I just kept repeating, "Give him the instrument, give him the instrument." He pleaded with me to tell Sgt. Hart that he and I had had a friendly conversation last night. I was steadfast. He was unaware that Sgt. Hart and I had talked.

Within the hour Sgt. Hart called and said he had confiscated the instrument and he would be making arrangements to ship it back to Oregon. The simplicity of all this was as profound as Dempsey was dishonest. I report the missing instrument, policeman finds it, gets it, and sends it back. I would send Sgt. Hart a shipping box and pay the freight both ways. Gladly.

Dempsey had defrauded companies out of ten musical performance products, mostly amplification and instruments. Total value $22,590. Two of the instruments had been pawned and sold and were not recovered. The rest were in Dempsey's possession when Sgt. Hart "knocked and talked."

There are postscripts to this crime narrative.

Those who con others are audacious, and Dempsey was certainly that. But it would take hyper-audacity for him to do this: he contacted another bass player and asked him to take over Dempsey's commitments with Gloria Estefan. *In actuality Dempsey had no such responsibilities but was so convincing that the bass player immediately canceled other gigs he had booked which would have interfered with the dates of Estefan's tour.* How that bassist eventually discovered the deception is not clear. It must not have occurred to Dempsey that the eventual playout of this scenario was sure to expose him as a fraud, and there was no way Dempsey could profit from this gambit.

The next year, 2004, was our first experience exhibiting our product at NAMM, the international trade show in Anaheim, California. One man stopped, looked at our instruments on display, and said, "Oh, that's a Barker Bass. I played one of those at Michael Dempsey's apartment. He's moved to Georgia now" And walked on.

And that was correct. According to my filefolder of this history, a warrant was issued for Michael Dempsey's arrest in early 2004 and he was eventually located in Georgia where he had written an NSF check. As a person affected by the case, I received many official documents by mail. My next record shows the State Attorney announcing a bond hearing scheduled in spring of 2006, so sometime in that year he had been arrested. Then numerous pretrial conferences scheduled and postponed, a plea change, more pretrial conferences, a subpoena for me to testify at a trial in October, 2007, then a brief note that the defendant had pleaded guilty to the charges.

In January 2008 I called Florida to learn that Mr. Dempsey had been sentenced to ninety days in jail and fined $300. The closure felt good.

I later sold the bass, along with a redacted timeline of its colorful roundtrip journey diagonally across the country, and its adventures in Florida. I bought an Accugroove bass cabinet from Mark, a man of integrity. Above all, Hart was my hero.

TWENTY-ONE

Logistics Intricacies

THE NOT-SO-SIMPLE BOX

Once called "shipping," it's now "logistics." Wags have pondered why a shipment goes on a train car while cargo travels on a ship. I first thought "Bill of Lading" had a misspelled word, but no, it is "Lading" not "Loading."

My needs were simple and clear: I just wanted to put a bass in a box and put it on a truck, UPS or Fedex, and be able to sleep the nights between that moment and my receipt of an enthusiastic "IT'S HERE!" email.

Companies in Portland specialized in packaging products for shipping. I chose one and we designed the box to fit the bass. The rep knew the materials and their purposes and I knew the product and its vulnerabilities. Together we developed a foam insert that the bass nestled in. The instrument was immovable when the lid went on.

As with printing, so with boxes: the more you order, the cheaper per copy. I started with a shipment of fifty. The boxes came flat, but cut and creased so they assembled easily into shape, held with fasteners from a deep-throat industrial stapler. The foam inserts were bulky and bundled as one unit on their own pallet.

My rep from the container manufacturer, Rick Wilcox, was responsible for a brilliant and subtle feature of the box. For a slight upcharge I got corrugated box material that had white paper on one side. That, by Rick's design, went *inside* the box. His thinking was, when the customer opened the box their eyes would be totally focused on the contents *but the white lining in the box would be noticed on a subliminal level and affirm that this was a quality product.* I loved this slightly quirky feature and never regretted the extra expense.

By the time the die fee and the extra material costs were spread out over two orders, I could round-number the box cost at $100 per instrument.

The boxes worked. Eventually over 100 shipments and only one breakage. But first, the dog.

THE STANDARD POODLE

This was the dawn of online shipping for consumers and small businesses, eliminating the tedious visit to a carrier to fill out all the paperwork. I had mastered the computer forms for domestic shipping though it was nerve wracking because so much was at stake: the instrument was my responsibility until it was in the owner's hands.

Then the lady in Germany wanted one. International shipping! Customs forms! Tariffs! Documented country of origin for components! Everything else in the business skidded to a stop while I focused on yet another obscure bit of education: online international shipping! I dreamed of the day I'd have a shipping department. Well, I already did; I just happened to work there, too.

I sat at my computer that spring afternoon, the door open and a nice breeze wafting through. I knew the numbers: Box seventy-two by eighteen by eight inches; thirty-four pounds. Easy, so far. Then I got caught in a Mobius Trip on the Fedex website, round and round like a cartoon carnival ride in a bad dream, clown faces flying at me, cackling. It was lonesome and frustrating. I was despairing of getting this shipping label rendered by my printer, when the dog walked in. A standard poodle, white.

Ribbons on her head, near her ears. She was sweet, self-confident, and curious. She peeked around the counter; I asked her to come over and she did. I explained to her that my last name qualified me as an excellent communicator with a refined command of several canine dialects. She seemed interested but not impressed. She turned and walked back in the shop while I tilted back in my walnut-armed desk chair and laced my fingers behind my head, taking full advantage of the escape from the cloud of stress that gnarled the office air. I consciously did not look at the computer screen; that would have ruined this moment of sweet diversion. Now where did she go?

The dog returned and checked in with me, as if to say that the shop had met or exceeded all her expectations. I was still cupping her head in my hands when a feminine head popped into my doorway. She was wearing a knit ski cap and her straw-colored hair poked out from the bottom in random places. "Have you seen a dog around here?"

"Yes," I answered. As the inquirer came around the counter, I saw a spring-skiing type jacket and jeans. "She's right here."

The young lady's name was Brooke and she and her husband, Paul, owned the company that had recently moved into the unit next door, formerly the foundry. We chatted. She commented that I appeared to be tense about something. I explained.

"I can help you," she said. "I used to work for Fedex, until a couple weeks ago. I'll come back right after lunch and help you through this." And she did. She agreed there was a fault with the web site but she knew a workaround, what highlighted bar to click and when. She breezed through the process.

Triumphantly Brooke hit the orange bar on screen and my printer sluffed out all the documents I needed. We folded them into the openable pouch on the big box with the nice white lining and I delivered it to the closest Fedex dropoff. Another routine miracle!

Paul and Brooke became our friends and good business neighbors. And the box made it to Germany, intact and on time. I owe it all to Treasure, that noble, self-assured poodle with the silly ribbons.

The bass that didn't make it to its owner in one piece was a U.S. Shipment. The box was broken in the middle as if it had been dropped from a significant height onto some large protrusion. The owner of the bass was even more crushed than the box. I sympathized, and was naively confident I could get this handled forthwith.

After I had done all the tedious paperwork for a damage claim, I sent him an empty box for the busted bass and he sent both it and the battle-scarred box back to me. Meantime I went to grappling with the Fedex Machine, me against the typical fine-print exclusions that are designed to make everything bad that happens, the sender's fault. I was hoping for a Deus Fedex Machina intervention. It wasn't happening.

I was in the middle. On the one side is Fedex, playing the delay game that is clearly designed to prompt the plaintiff to give up. On the other, the buyer, who desperately wanted his new bass, intact. It took months of handling his weekly emails beseeching me to just give up and get things moving on our own. I tried to placate him and put my energy toward chasing this issue to the top, if necessary. Fedex had broken my bass and it was their fault and they should pay for it. I have a competitive streak that mostly doesn't show but when it is triggered by an injustice it can persist in my system like uranium's radioactivity. Or the taste of Vegemite. Or farting geese in a teardrop trailer.

My patience was fraying as Fedex and I came to an agreement about the repair costs to the instrument. A win for Barker Musical Instruments, but so far all the people I had spoken to stubbornly refused to replace the box.

After weeks of courteously but unsuccessfully exploring the perverse lower- and mid-levels of jungle vines woven throughout the obtuse Fedex consumer complaint system, I wrote a letter to the company president, explaining in detail the history and integrity of my professionally-designed box, the extent of the damage to the product while it was in Fedex's care, and how much force would be required to accomplish said thrashing. I cited how many times my instruments had been shipped successfully. In painful colors I delineated the frustrating, treacly process I had been through with his company. I noted the cost of the box and demonstrated that in its current condition (photos attached) it was unusable. "It's my box, it cost $100, and *you broke it,*" I wrote. "How can you in good conscience say that you're not responsible to replace it?"

It worked. I got a phone call from a vice president of the company who had my letter on his desk. I went through the points of my case one more time and he agreed to pay the claim, *box and all.* They sent a check. I continued to ship via Fedex because, if something concussive happened to a Barker Bass again, I had the phone number of my favorite vice president of the company. I know I was not his favorite customer because he never invited me to a Fedex chili cookoff.

TWENTY-TWO

The NAMM Shows, 2004-2006

The National Association of Music Merchants presents a trade show twice yearly, in January in Anaheim and in the summer, Nashville. Anaheim is the big one. Eighty thousand people over four days. A daunting thought

We had launched the instrument with print ads in *BassPlayer* magazine and a few other places. *Downbeat* magazine, the monthly bible of the jazz world, did a little piece on the Barker Bass. Every ad and each print mention of the instrument directed the reader to our website.

Every Monday morning I would read the pages of statistics and ascertain things like, how many new eyes had looked at the site, how many pages they looked at, and from what page they exited. The challenge was finding a nuanced way to turn those clickings of curiosity into Barker Bass owners.

(This is why the web has become such a successful advertising medium. All the facts about you and your preferences, purchases, and peccadilloes are a unit package and are for sale.)

A bass player from Portland was intrigued with the instrument but he didn't want to talk about buying one, he wanted me to hire him. "I can tell you exactly who your customer is," he said, confidently. He had my attention. All right! This could streamline my marketing, cancel my out-of-comfort-zone trip to Anaheim, and give me more shop time. Where do I sign?

"That would be $20,000," he said. I scoffed. That much cash was beyond my imagining. If he had said, "Five thousand," I would have offered him a bass in trade. But 20k? No way.

It might have been a bargain. It took years for us to ferret out a flimsy profile of the customer, and that involved a lot of my time and some money poorly spent on advertising that did not appear to contribute to our ultimate goal: Sell basses.

WHAT WE LEARNED ABOUT OUR CUSTOMERS, OVER TIME:

1. Middle-aged men who were gigging regularly and could afford another instrument were our best prospects.

2. Wealthy men whose collecting urge was greater than their musical skills took second.

3. "Tweakers," average players who restlessly sought innovation to set themselves apart from some perceived competition, were next. "Tweakers" is a term used by boutique instrument makers to describe buyers who had suggestions for customization because they thought they knew more than we did. If we wanted to make a sale, we'd do the tweak (often with zero improvement). And, guaranteed, they'd think the result was stupendous.

4. Women bassists who showed up at the shop to try a Barker, bought one, every time.

At this early stage, however, we didn't know this stuff. Even if we did, it would not have been enough. Joel Barker kindly agreed to go to the show and report back.

Conclusion: we had to go to NAMM.

Barker Musical Instruments joined the NAMM organization and opened up another chapter of deep learning, peppered with working on print advertising, improving the instrument and the processes which brought it to life: answering the phone, learning how to accept credit cards, and trying to keep the bills paid.

Booth rental was $5000. The final payment for the January 2004 show was due in October. From Mark at Accugroove I learned that NAMM would allow two small businesses to share a booth, and he suggested I talk to Fred Bolton, a bass luthier in McMinnville, Oregon.

Fred makes four- and five-string instruments as well as extended range basses, meaning many more strings. Like eight, nine, even ten and (gasp!) twelve, at which point they start to resemble aircraft carriers. His market was a narrow subculture of musicians. Bee Basses and Barker Musical Instruments would pair well together as innovative kin targeting separate market segments. It worked, and we became friends with Fred, his wife Petra, and their son Alec.

Linda, in her years managing a flower shop, had been to trade shows. She could visualize what our space might look like. We got giveaway postcards printed.

The setup day before the show is chaos, as is the takedown time. In between, there's a rhythm. You occupy the booth, people walk by, conversation starts. The least you can do is hand them the jazzy postcard.

It was crowded, but we made it work.

A young man with long, curly, black hair and a kind manner saw the bass standing out front of our half of the booth, stopped, and gently asked Linda, "May I play your bass?" Of course. And he did, carefully, respectfully, ear cocked toward the amplifier behind him.

"I'm Hussain Jiffry. I play bass for Yanni," he said, "And he has asked me to find a bass with more sustain. This could be it." More about this later.

THE SECOND YEAR, WE MET MONSTER.

Everything about the NAMM show is in excess. The crowd. The five halls which contain the show. The decibel level, since most booths are demonstrating devices which make sound. The musicians, broadly diverse but bound by their common language, despite its hundreds of dialects. For instance, metal.

At this writing there is a web list of over fifty sub genres of metal. Prefixes include heavy, speed, thrash, power, death, viking, glamour, goth, neoclassical, post, and hair. Convenient one-word entries include sludge, grindcore, drone, crossover, and mathcore.

Monster played metal: Bald, save for an oval of hair at the back of his head, about the size of a goose egg, dyed bright yellow. Dressed entirely in black leather. Columns of metal rings hung from his knee-high boots. His walk generated a clinking sound which could be heard over the droning NAMM noise. Pointy spikes. Clothing features were redundantly laced with more black leather. Rings, some skull-shaped, adorned a working majority of his fingers. A spiky bracelet of leather and metal. One silver earring and tattoos equivalent to the acreage of Yellowstone Park. He wore metal than you could fine on an Evel Knievel X-Ray.

He and Linda, both navigating a crowded aisle at the show, bumped into each other. "Sorry," he said, smiling. "I'm just a bass player..." She handed him a Barker postcard.

"Come see us at booth 1441," she said. And he did. Monster was a sweet, genuine person and he and Linda became friends. His band was "Jugulur" (sic).

Monster's manager, his wife, dressed like an everyday person, a neighbor who would bake biscuits for you. And he was just a guy doing a gig to earn a living. A guy who could not go outdoors and mow the lawn or wash the car without looking kooky. Maybe in their family she did that kind of stuff.

Monster wanted a Barker Bass but only if we would give it to him. He thought it would set him apart. I knew that his stagecraft involved a lot of jumping and exaggerated, physical movement that in no way could be accompanied by an instrument that was not worn by the player. But he kept hanging around. Linda enjoyed him; she still talks fondly of her friend Monster.

I knew this was not our customer. These brutal, depressive, doom, industrial, or deathgrind metal bass players would not be lining up to get their very own Barker Bass, even if I did nail on a few spiky dog collars and steel rings from horse harnesses and paint everything else black. But we loved Monster.

TWENTY-THREE

Will Witt and Gene Simmons

An early discovery in our entry to the world of basses and bassists was the weekend bass event. Part clinic, part promotional event for sponsors, part networking, these Friday night and all day Saturday gatherings would typically draw twenty to fifty musicians, from middle school to middle age, and offer them time to hear presentations by a handful of professional players. Some of those breakout room seminars were chatty didactic sessions and some were "get your bass, get in a circle and we'll do some things together." It was exciting to see Barker Musical Instruments in the lists of sponsors of these events, cozying up to AccuGroove, Alembic, SWR, Zon Guitars, Glockenklang, G&L Guitars, and Gallien-Krueger.

We traveled to and hung our banner at Bass Bash in Bozeman, Montana, and at Bass Quake in Redwood City, and later in Campbell, California, as well as a closer-to-home gathering in Oregon's Columbia Gorge. We would pay a fee and were given a space at the venue to show our wares. It was at these events that we met Dave Pomeroy (Creator of the anthem, "The Day the Bass Players Took Over the World"), Michael Manring, Todd Johnson, Adam Nitti, Gerald Veasley, Trip Wamsley, and others. These are not household names but your friendly local neighborhood bassist can help you appreciate the caliber of these players.

We met Will Witt at Bass Quake in Campbell, not far from his home in Santa Cruz. He was smitten with the Barker Bass. One wouldn't think a young man just getting out of high school would represent a likely sale, but Linda and I were so taken with his genuineness and joyousness that we eventually invited him to work with us in our booth at NAMM.

Will was a church player as well as a student of other styles of music. Gifted but not overweening, he kept a kind of "gee whiz" attitude up front. You couldn't help but like Will, slightly over 6 feet tall and lanky as a full-grown whippet. He ordered a Barker; I took his payments and made him one, a 5-string.

We later invited him to Redmond, expenses paid, so he could star in two YouTube videos about the Barker. Good call. Brian Johnson, local videographer, captured Will brilliantly. Teamwork, wardrobe, success. Lights, camera, action!

Will was a key player on the Barker team at NAMM.

Mid afternoon at the show, a time when traffic often slows a little. Standing at the front edge of our carpet at NAMM, Will looked to his right, down the aisle, and saw a clutch of people approaching the Barker Bass booth. A videographer was backing toward him, camera focused on a tall, broad shouldered man with a slightly puffy face partly obscured by outsize wire-framed sunglasses. Will turned questioningly to Doug Mancini, who immediately recognized Gene Simmons, bassist with the band KISS, whose signature jagged straight-line typeface logo has been appearing on middle school notebooks since the invention of the ball point pen. Will was unaffected by the star's presence, and invited him into the booth to try the Barker Bass.

Doug, directed Simmons to the closest bass, a 5 string. Simmons, his large sunglasses unable to hide his sly humor, pointed to the tuning machine connected to the 5th string. "What's this?" he asked Doug. "I only need four. Why would I need five?" Doug got the joke, laughed out loud.

Simmons played the bass a few minutes, then introduced his son Nick who also played a bit. Having sprinkled its stardust, the gaggle reshaped itself like a band of sheep going around a corner and moved on.

Linda, who had been standing away from the activity: "Who was that?"

Will: "That was Gene Simmons, the KISS bass player!" [pause, hand to forehead] "I didn't give him a Barker Bass handout!" Will grabbed a couple of postcards off the small table at the back of the booth and darted after the gaggle, stopping Simmons, handing him the printed matter, and shaking his hand again. Oh that every entrepreneur at NAMM could have a booth person with Will's energy, enthusiasm and loyalty.

We learned later that the filming was for Simmons' TV show "Family Jewels." Pete Barker managed to record the clip from the show which included the NAMM visit. The Barker Bass segment was about three seconds of it.

Will later worked several years with an innovative amplifier company, Jaguar, in San Diego. He eventually relocated to Portland, Oregon, where he and his wife Elana gave birth to Hazel June. At this writing Will and a partner own a thriving taproom in Hillsboro. He saved his NAMM badges in a scrapbook.

ADVENTURES IN MUSIC | STANZA 8
CinderBlue 2007 – 2009

Rex moved back from his tour of the Tri Cities. We were on the lookout for a new project.

At Jim's summer party with a musical stage we heard a married couple—Jeff and Marlene—and agreed to get together later and try some tunes with them. We did. This group had a future!

Jeff, an engineer by trade, took his guitar playing seriously. He used online teaching resources and practiced diligently, developing a competent solo style that brought interest to our instrumental breaks. He would insert little musical figures at the end of a lyric line, like a musical comma or a semicolon. Artful and sensitive, never overdone. Rex's granite-solid rhythm playing gave Jeff the space to build his skills.

Rex came up with the band name. Brilliant.

The real joy was Marlene's singing. She had not sung much in public but she was gifted with a terrific ear and a voice laced with energy and clarity. She could belt and she could deliver ballads and her delivery was always nuanced and sincere. We'd all get goosebumps when she sang "Dimming of the Day," Richard Thompson's lamentation of love and loss. It was a spectacular choice for the penultimate song of a set, followed by something bright and instrument driven.

We played the usual sorts of indoor and outdoor venues that pepper Central Oregon. A llama ranch,

HOBO'S MEDITATION IS A PLAINTIVE TUNE BY JIMMIE RODGERS

Tonight as I lay on a boxcar just waiting for a train to pass by / what will become of the hobo / whenever that time comes to die / has the master up yonder in heaven / got a place that we might call our home / will we have to work for a living / or can we continue to roam
(chorus:)
will there be any freight trains in heaven / any boxcars in which we might hide / will there be any tough cops and brakemen / will they tell us we cannot ride / will the hobo chum with the rich man / will we always have money to spare / will they have respect for a hobo / in the land that lies hidden up there

The song was short; needed a few more cars on the train. Marlene asked me to write another verse:

When the last train rolls into glory / will the rails be plated with gold / when the passengers step to the platform / and all of their stories are told / Will we sit down at the same table / The rich and the poor, every one / Will we all have our moment in glory / In the place that shines bright as the sun

(chorus out)

a fundraiser for the Humane Society, the county fair, a statewide conference hosted by our local chamber of commerce, a casual wedding. We played several times at a just-opened coffee shop in downtown Redmond and packed the place. Summer evenings, people were standing out on the sidewalk listening.

In Redmond's music world, we were "kind of a big deal." The Dry Canyon Fil was also a big deal years before, but in a different way: Then the town was smaller, and where people gathered for almost any excuse, we were there too, as a given. Years later, town bigger, Marlene could put out the word that we were going to be someplace at 7pm and people would show up.

Twice we played an annual weekend bluegrass event on a farm outside Bend. First time, we were on the "tweener stage," a postage-stamp spot for fledgling groups to play for fifteen minutes or so while the next tested act was setting up on the big stage. A year later we had graduated, given a full set.

We were invited to the annual Wheeler County Bluegrass Festival in Fossil, Oregon, population about 400. Hundreds of people attend. Bands play for a little money and a lot of pride, and all are paid the same. There are bluegrass instrument clinics in the morning two days, pretty good talent on stage all afternoon, and name acts at night, all on the lawn of the county courthouse. We played and were well received although we were not a pure bluegrass band by any stretch. (You can tell a bluegrass band when you see it: four or five people wearing Wranglers, 80% male, who stand in a circle and play as fast as they can while staring at the necks of their instruments.)

Away from the courthouse I observed another band doing their off-site runthrough. A lady there appeared to be coaching them. Later I asked; she was a name bluegrass vocalist, a frequent guest on A Prairie Home Companion. She had quit the touring life to live in Central Oregon. She was their performance consultant!

This observation of a pretty good band getting instruction in the fine art of performing meshed with discussions CinderBlue had had in rehearsal where I had learned that (a) Rex was keenly aware of my skill at performing, and (2) the rest of the band had no interest whatsoever in our performance quality.

I was flummoxed. If you had a band that sounded fantastically good, wouldn't you want it to perform to the same level? I assumed everyone sought to reach their potential with all the resources they could access. Not true. Some get in the boat and row to a goal, some just get in and fiddle with the oars.

There are standard performance practices. These you'll see in regional bands, groups who may not be full-time musicians but are willing to create a polished act in order to be paid well. For instance, the first two songs in a show in a new venue require the band members to be highly focused: You're not only trying to make a good first impression (eye contact, smiling), you're also listening to the blend of the voices and how your instrument is sitting in the mix. Monitor volume too low or too high? Mic feedback? You're checking, checking, checking. And the way to get through this is to start the show with the same two songs every time. And in the same key. When I advocated this common convention, complete with reasonable explanation, They didn't care. Jeff and Marlene: Meh.

A set list is a bit like a one act play. It has a beginning, a middle and an end. The opening song should show the band's nature: it should be right down the center of your playlist, up tempo, played in the fullness of a major key. You are introducing yourself; put your best universal tune first. Follow that with a song with a distinct solo voice to it. This tells the listener where to focus. Third song, introduce a minor key and a bit of melancholy. After that, the comedy bit. Now you have made connection: The listener has been introduced to the members, focusing their attention on one at a time. They have experienced a swing of emotion and have been surprised and entertained. Band and audience are as one.

The climax song of the set is the one before the last. This would be something a bit elaborate, like a medley, or maybe a song with a soaring solo. Or a gripping ballad. Close the set with a tune familiar and rousing and take the break.

We were booked for Music on the Green, Redmond's summer concert series, which had grown from an audience of twenty-five on a postage stamp of a lawn at the Chamber of Commerce office to hundreds at Sam Johnson Park. As the date approached, I blustered my way into complete control of our program, confident that this would cement the importance of my attention to our performance art. We did a fantastic show, a real knockout.

When I got home, a message from the Chamber's concert coordinator on my answering machine: "We have never done this before. This was the best concert we've ever had and we want to book you now for the series next year!" I took this as affirmation. Rex agreed. The other two attributed our success to nothing in particular, just that we were good.

Another difference between unaware amateurs and polished performers: Between tunes, the former talk about themselves (and there's not much there to be said typically) and the latter talk about you, the listener.

You are now written into the story. Tears may come, applause certainly will be robust when the song is over, and you might just be pungling up the fifteen bucks for the CD after the show. Jeff and Marlene could not grasp how this was done or that it was important.

And they thought I wasn't funny. I ended up having to preview my humor bits for them and if they said thumbs down, I didn't do it.

Instead, things like this: We would tackle a new song and by the end of rehearsal someone would say, "Well, that's sounding pretty good. Let's do it Saturday at our gig." I once asked a professional friend how long he likes to rehearse a tune before he takes it out. "When I'm sick of it, that's when it's ready," he said. "Weeks of rehearsal," said another.

I commented about a false start we had done at the previous gig. We started the song and it fell apart. "What can we do to prevent that?" I asked. The answer was, "Nothing! Our fans love it when we have to stop a song and start it again!" Right. I had envisioned a regional band with a polished stage presence that performs at meaningful venues, may travel a few times a year, rehearses and grows, and gets paid well for their efforts. Rex got it; Jeff and Marlene had no such aspirations.

I wanted this band to be about creating a moment for a listener, a connection, an instant when music, or images, or a string of words, brought an inner gasp, a flash of insight, a peal of joy from a dusty bell, a spiritual upwelling that brings with it a longer, deeper view of life. And that's way past ego. That's performer as servant.

I resigned, saw the band through the two gigs ahead of us (which I had booked) and wished them well. They took on a bassist they knew. Rex opted to stay aboard because it was feeding his love of music and he was growing with his constant practice.

Later Marlene told me that, whenever CinderBlue performed "Hobo's Meditation" after I left, she credited me with the last verse. My heart was warmed.

I threw myself into the church music. Eventually Rex joined me there and we were able to continue our joyous musical collaboration and sly glances while we were playing. We share a time-tested bond.

Karen, the music director, introduced me to Alan Yankus, who was playing guitar in a second praise team. I joined, not only because they lacked a bassist but also because it gave me a chance to stand in Alan's shadow and learn from him. His playing was exquisite, appropriate, rhythmic, supportive, and full; never drawing attention to himself.

TWENTY-FOUR

The One That Got Away

At the end of the fourth day of people, cacophony, excitement, promise, and fellowship, the stentorian voiced PA announcer declaims, "the NAMM Show of 2005 is now closed!" The music ends, the rumbling voices fade, and thousands of fatigued people put their hands to dismantling their displays.

On that last day it was just Linda and me and Toby, our Taurus station wagon. Everything that had occupied our display booth had to go in the car just so. That included six basses, plus stands, tables, amplifiers, banners, coiled cables and cords and tools and whatever was left of the Barker Bass postcards and Oregon hazelnuts we brought to give away to all who passed our booth. Last thing in? The handtruck! There was room for everything but our luggage, which made the 1720 mile round trip in the cargo pod atop Toby.

Our flurry of commutes between shrinking booth and increasingly-crammed car was interrupted by a man standing by the back door of Hall E, obviously waiting for us. I knew his name and his legend. According to Wikipedia at this writing he is on 278 albums as the bass player. A few headliner names in that list: Aretha Franklin, The Rascals, Steely Dan, Cal Tjader, Sarah Vaughn, Dizzy Gillespie, Roberta Flack, Peggy Lee, Bob Marley, Bette Midler, Lee Ritenour, Diana Ross, Ringo Starr, Mose Allison, The Supremes, James Brown, Louis Armstrong. I had read his name on dozens of albums during my radio days: Chuck Rainey.

He was appearing at NAMM as an endorser of Phil Jones bass amplifiers, an innovative product which generates impressive bass sounds not from a few big speakers but rather from a bunch of little ones.

He was handsome, gentle, down to earth. He gestured to us. "I want to talk to you about endorsing your bass." We were stuttering, flabbergasted, standing there, unaware of loaded handtrucks going by one way and returning empty. Talking to Chuck Rainey!

Our two-day drive home up I-5 and through Klamath Falls and home was lighthearted. Chuck Rainey! At last we had something to put our product on the map: an endorsement by a legendary bass player. The break we had been hoping for. Our bitter experience with Michael Dempsey posing as Michael Dempsey had nothing in common with this! We had sophomore swagger. Blessed beyond our imagining. The instrument had proven itself in the Yanni orchestra, we had the process in place to produce, finish and ship it, and now we had a person of great, even legendary stature in the bass playing community to bring the final piece of validation. Liftoff!

My topmost job, upon returning home and readjusting to life after having been on Planet Anaheim for a week, was to work out our agreement with Chuck via email. I bullet-pointed my side: (1) I would retain title to the bass and (2) Chuck would furnish me with professional pictures of him and the bass.

That done, I shipped him a Barker B1five with a lined fretless neck. List price $4395; street price $3495.

In our frequent communications Chuck enumerated what was on his future schedule. It included something in New York with Greg Allman, a trip to Japan where he is idolized, European festivals, plus other name-drops. He was generous in his supplying quotes we could use in our marketing: "I like it...looks current...much easier to transport than an upright acoustic bass...with my amps I can make it sound just like an upright acoustic bass...makes me feel more connected to the 'real bass.'"

He had used his Barker B1five on two recordings, we were told months later, though we weren't given any details.

Another person emerged in these conversations: William Zahn, Chuck's "manager," and attorney. Zahn continued to paint the word picture that Chuck loves the instrument and is playing it a lot.

As our product and company became more visible, I was frequently approached by people selling advertising, particularly in magazines specifically for bass players. There was a wider market, too, especially in the jazz world. A magazine sprang up in Portland and, tugged by its geographical proximity and similar startup status, I agreed to place an ad. I would use Chuck Rainey's image with a Barker Bass.

This magazine catered not only to the world of younger bass guitar players but also to upright bassists. The advertising manager told me they might consider a cover story of Chuck and his new and unusual instrument. Joyous business possibilities were piling up around me like water balloons on the last day of middle school.

I knew Chuck had scheduled a photography shoot that included the Barker Bass but I hadn't seen anything from it. The schedule for getting copy and artwork to the Portland magazine was going to be a tight squeeze, so I asked Chuck to get me the images. He sent me to the photographer.

She would not release the pictures unless I paid her $600. This was not the agreement with Chuck, but I was stuck: Days down to hours, I agreed to send her the money. She insisted that I overnight the cash to her and pay the shipping costs. This for a few film prints which then I'd have to digitize. Ever the optimist that this was all going to work out, I did my part. The images arrived, the ad made it in time, I got the magazine proof. The ad wasn't a blockbuster but a good step. I had something in my hand, though having to come up with $600 plus $100 in shipping rankled me.

A cloud moved into the picture of optimism we had brought home from NAMM.

For some other promotional project on which Linda was working (in addition to her day job), she contacted Chuck's photographer about a specific image. The result of that inquiry, done in an acceptable and professional manner, was a scathing phone call to me from Chuck. He insulted us, our handling of the agreement, and dragged in other irrelevancies. It was classic "piling on." Linda was there when I took the call and she said when I got off the phone I was ashen.

In retrospect I can see that Chuck was creating a list to convince himself that we weren't worthy of his time and that the failure was all our fault.

We got things patched up a little with Mr. Rainey, but the trendline was irreversibly tilted down.

Communications with Chuck continued to deteriorate into a lot of back and forth tension that didn't contribute anything positive to my work to get our business endeavor out of the red ink. He complained that the bass was too heavy and that I "need to hollow it out inside." He wanted the strings raised (which would destroy the instrument's common DNA with the bass guitar) and even suggested it have a different stand or, absurdly, a "bent end pin" so he could play it more like a bass guitar! I was dealing with an irrational person.

There is no scientific way for a very small business to assess the value of advertising, especially a one-off like the Portland jazz magazine, so I put my energies elsewhere and tried to forget about that B1five bass and where it might be. It seemed better to try to sell a bass that I had in my hand than to try to get back a used bass for which I would likely have to pay shipping.

A year later I decided to go after that bass which was rightfully mine. Chuck put me off to Zahn, who was always a responsive correspondent. Zahn insisted that Chuck loved the bass and wanted it to be a part of his musical projects. When I said I wanted it back, Zahn said he would pay for it. $2500. He agreed to send me the money, and didn't. Zahn's phone was disconnected and he ceased to communicate. And that's where it is at this writing.

Word gets around in the bass sector of the music industry. Several other manufacturers confirmed that what I experienced with Chuck and the decaying relationship, followed by the disappearance of the product, was a common scenario. The assumption in these narratives was that the endorsed items were sold. I cannot verify that.

Chuck's proclivity for short-term endorsements was noticed by players as well. Bass player internet forums dated 2008 contain posts such as this one: "...when it comes to bass guitar endorsements, no one has put their name and picture in as many ads, (most with some kind of signature model) for varying companies, as Chuck Rainey. Compared to Chuck, [these other guys] are all endorsement amateurs."

This series of events has just blended into "part of the ride" in our business venture. Still, when we talk about it, Linda and I can recall vividly the soaring optimism that gave way to the crushing realization that, from the very beginning, we'd been had.

TWENTY-FIVE

Doug, Eric, Dwayne, and Brian

DOUG MANCINI

He lives in Santa Cruz, California, where he plays bass professionally. It's better to say "full time musician"because most of us aren't. Doug is in three to five bands at once, plus casuals, plus teaching. Slight built, always dressed in black, his wispy long hair responding to the slightest breeze. He exudes gentleness. He has seen more than his share of life's difficulties but has risen above them and given the world a gift: a kind man.

Doug is most at home with the blues, but like any professional sideman, he can get the job done in any genre.

Doug learned of the Barker Bass from brother Dean, who lives in Central Oregon. Came to visit.

From the first note he played, Doug embraced the Barker Bass with his heart and hands.

On his next trip to Oregon, Doug and his brother Dean, a first-call percussionist, recorded some tracks at a Bend studio. We put the tunes on the Barker Musical Instruments website, and bassists commented positively on those recordings over the years.

When I had questions about bass stuff—whether it was something about the instrument and how to improve it, or about my own gigging equipment like amplification and cables, I got the real-world truth from Doug. We were having one of those conversations one day in my office when I mused about some unfledged notion for improving the bass that "might work."I asked him what he thought and he pointed at the door to the shop and said directly to me, "That's what that is for!"I got the message: keep trying! Stay curious!

We used Doug's quotation on one of our postcard handouts:"We've all been looking for the tone...This bass has it!"

Doug went to NAMM with us for two years, where he met his idol, Lee Sklar. That, he said, was a dream he never thought could happen. And it all started when Dean handed Doug a newspaper clipping about this Redmond woodworker who had developed a new instrument.

Our friendship is remarkable. Linda, Doug, and I agree it is difficult to describe. Doug:"It seemed like we all knew each other before." Every time we talk on the phone he says, "I think of you and Linda every day. I love you."

ERIC OWENS

As Barker Musical Instruments was coming in for a landing in 2015, we were selling off our inventory and applying that income to our accumulated debt. Linda, out of the blue, said, "I think, as a gesture of our gratitude for all the experiences we have had, we ought to give a bass away." I agreed. But to whom?We both said, "Eric Owens."

He had been with us from the beginning. At the first Bass Quake event in Redwood City, California, he spent every spare minute with the basses and us.

Over time he bought two basses, a four string B1 and a B45, one of a few Barker bass guitars I built with the signature Barker shape.

At NAMM, he became friends with Will Witt and Doug Mancini.

Eric is now married, with family, has a day job, and still is gigging regularly in Albuquerque. In 2021 he earned his master's degree in education.

He is a big guy, with an impish gap-toothed grin and a deep, resonant laugh. When I was ready to ship him this surprise package,

I called him to get his updated shipping address, told him we were sending him the latest Barker Bass T-shirt.

I wish we could have been there when the delivery driver wrestled that big, long box onto his front porch and rang the bell.

When he called us, later, he was tearful.

He still calls that bass "T-shirt."

DWAYNE DIXON

I was home in the early days of recovering from neck surgery. Linda was at the office when he called. She told me later he was "wildly excited about the Barker Bass, that someone would think to do that!" When we spoke later, a lifetime friendship popped up like a bean sprout in a paper cup in botany class at preschool.

That I would get connected with Dwayne, who lives in a Minneapolis suburb, seems unlikely. Education at Southern Illinois University and Harvard Business School, employed by Microsoft, Xerox, Unisys, Dun & Bradstreet, IBM, among others. And a bass player. When you speak with Dwayne, you experience his fierce focus on you and what you say and how you say it. Not in a critical way, in a welcoming way. The questions aren't on the surface and you know you really matter to this man..

The communications continued and he bought a Barker Bass. But his interest in business and how it bumped up against musicians caught his fancy. He knew we were struggling a bit, and was intrigued by our endeavor.

"How about giving away a Barker Bass?" he queried. "International."

"Sure." He did it all. Acquired the appropriate legal boilerplate, wrote the plan, identified the promotional tracks, set up the digital package so people could fill in a few blanks on the Barker website. The act of entering made them legitimate prospects for Barker Musical Instruments.

Dwayne's idea was a great success. I could monitor the entries and harvest the names and email addresses.

After the contest closed, I printed off a list of the entries, numbered. I hired a notary public to come and sit in my office where we used a random number generator to pick the winner. I called him, a high school student in Chicago, and spoke to his mom. I shipped the bass. And we had the mailing list, just as Dwayne had said.

Contest aside, let us imagine that the Barker Bass was an overnight success, a game changer, a major disruptor of the bass clef universe, the instrument that "made the bass guitar invented by Leo Fender a museum artifact." At that moment, the only person who could have piloted the ship to its deserved destination was Dwayne Dixon. I would have gladly handed him the keys to the wheelhouse and toddled up to my workshop on the second floor of the factory and tinkered away my days, occasionally offering my finely-chiseled features for a sidelit portrait to grace the cover of BassPlayer magazine. I hope those Fortune 500 companies know how close they came to losing him.

At this writing we still have lively, laughter-filled, deeply personal phone conversations.

BRIAN RITCHIE

"Just ask your sons about the Violent Femmes." I was on the phone with Brian, who introduced himself as the bassplayer of that group. He seemed unruffled by my complete ignorance concerning one of the all-time greatest folk-punk bands. The group was formed in 1980 and at this writing, still on. The group had sold more than nine million albums up to 2005. The Violent Femmes are kind of a big deal.

Later, I did ask my sons. Guy said, "Oh yeah, dad, you used to say *'turn that music down!'* when we played the Violent Femmes. A lot!" He explained that it was a power trio, all guys, the name just an attention-getting joke. Much later I heard a musician describe the Femmes as, "Your best possible fraternity beer bust band."

But I am ahead of the story.

Linda was doggedly persistent in her promotion of the Barker Bass in magazines of all sorts. She would do the research about the readership, write the article, submit it per the guidelines, and move on to the next project. One was Horizon Air's in-flight magazine. At the time, Horizon was a regional passenger airline serving the western part of the U.S., including Redmond.

We didn't know it was in print until Kevin Kubota showed up with a handful of of copies. Flying home from conducting one of his photography Boot Camps, he espied the article and, when they landed in Redmond, he picked up copies from seat-back pouches.

The hook for the article: Lee Barker had developed a business relationship with a local guy whose popup lumberyard dealt exclusively in recycled wood, gleaned from sources all over the country. Our deal was, he would bring me a trophy chunk from one of these safaris and I'd identify the wood for him. In exchange for my expertise, he would give me some of the haul. Not enough to clog my lumber rack, but sufficient to occasionally push a special project over the top by festooning it with lumber that comes with its own story.

On one such occasion he brought old-growth Douglas fir, three inches thick, five inches wide and ten feet long. Black and gray, dry and splintery, ugly and boring. It had been carefully milled, a long time ago, with slight bevels on the sides and a wide notch across the grain at one end.

Cut into this forlorn-looking wood, or slice some of the ugliness off an edge, however, and be surprised.

These boards had been staves for giant vats which were used in Oregon's Willamette Valley. The thick round wood bottom, ten feet in diameter, fit into the notch in these vertical side pieces. The vats were used for bleaching cherries before they were re-dyed as maraschinos.

And what happened to the original juice, which was liberated from the cherries? It had wicked up into the fibers of these fir staves, which became pink and beautiful.

Not all the staves were pink. From a large stack at the recycled lumber yard, I selected ten boards from which I got enough wood for four basses, which I built and subsequently photographed.

Linda's story plinked all the right notes for Horizon's publication:The loamy Willamette Valley, fruit, unusual musical instrument, chance encounter with recycled wood, quirky woodworker on our route map.

Back to the Violent Femmes. Brian wanted a Barker Bass. And I ascertained he was a wood guy.

I told him about the pink basses and he was intrigued. Money sent electronically, I shipped the bass. Linda could write another story and I could go build some more instruments.

Brian sent me a copy of his latest CD which was not by the Femmes. He had taken an interest in *shakuhachi*, Japanese wooden flutes. He pursued his curiosity right into the recording studio and made some beautiful music.

Within a year, I got a call from Brian. This is his story, as I remember it:

"I was traveling in Tasmania and I stopped in a little shop which sold bowls and other handmade wood souvenir things. They have some beautiful wood there and I was enjoying the stuff and I started to talk to the shop owner about the unusual looking wood. 'Do you want to see some interesting wood?' he asked.

"'Sure,' I said. He reached under the counter and pulled out a copy of the Horizon magazine, folded open to the article about the four cherry-juice basses."

"Take a look at these!"

"I leaned over the counter, pointed to one of the Barker Basses in the picture, and said, '*That one* is mine!'"

Brian went on to say he loved the bass and its tone.

Later, he called again. The Femmes had reunited and were on the road. Mostly the east coast, he said, and he was playing his Barker, but they had two dates on the west coast, one in Salem. It was not worthwhile to haul his Barker on the plane, but if I would bring one to the Oregon show, he would play it. Easy deal for us to take a bass 120 miles over the Cascade Mountains to the Oregon State Fairgrounds. Joe, his wife Sarah, their baby Lily, and Sarah's sister Carissa caravanned to Salem with us.

Brian is a tall and imposing presence, with long hair and a long face. Gentle, however, and soft-spoken. He seemed relaxed and accommodating as we hauled in the bass we had brought. He made sure we had all-access passes—a big red stickum dot on our shirts—and invited us to come backstage after the show.

Joel came from Portland. Linda cared for Lily outdoors, away from the loudness. My memory is dreamlike, the hard sounds of the music seeming deep in the background, everybody smiling and having fun.

The Femmes are showmen. Not in the costume and fireworks way, rather in a personal openness to the individuals in the audience. Theirs is performance art rather than a presentation of musical art. Brian played a number of basses during the show.

It was the loudest I had ever heard a Barker Bass played. It was a revelation. The tone was just awesome, solid, full, round, big. And it didn't hurt my ears. Subtract my bias or exchange me for someone who listens to bass tones critically and the adjectives will be similar. I became convinced anew that I had built something special.

And the Barker Bass Road Crew had sat in a dressing room and eaten pizza with Brian Ritchie.

TWENTY-SIX

Hello, Brio

J oel and Pete Barker have been stalwart supporters of their dad's
musical adventure. Both are not only market-aware musicians,
they're also competent bassists. When they talk to someone
about the bass, it's a first-person interaction, empathetic, not
a list of boilerplate bullet points from their old man.

In 2005, Joel entered my office and, with ceremonious timing,
laid a yellow pencil pad on my desk.

"We've got to make a bass for under $2000," he said. The price
point on the B1 was often a barrier to a sale.

"We'll lose our image as a top-quality instrument," I retorted,
quickly. I can be resistant, especially when the idea's not mine. But
he was right. A lower-priced model would open us to a wider market,
plus mark our company as dynamic and responsive.

The conceptual first step was easy. The B1 was patterned after
the Fender Jazz Bass, which was introduced in 1960. This new
Barker would be "inspired by the time-tested Precision Bass." And
because the Precision's pickup was different from the Jazz pair,
any bassist could glance at this new model and understand how
its lineage differed from the B1's. Both of Leo Fender's basses had
their singular loyalists, but many players owned both and used
them for different musical settings. Joel's suggestion made sense.

So we studied my B1 parts list, which showed part name, source, multiples per instrument, and cost. We made a blank form: chrome hardware instead of black. A simpler bridge. Imported rather than Warmoth neck.

Fretted instruments of all types, imported from Asia, were making their splash on the marketplace and components followed close behind. Imported arts like the tuning machines and the bridge yielded some savings. The most dramatic item was pickups. The Seymour Duncans I used on the B1s were about $160 per pair. I found a promising line of pickups, made in South Korea.

Samuel Yin made them. His, like mine, was a one-person operation. Communicating was easy; South Korean kids learn English in elementary school. Bottom line on the pickups: fourteen bucks, delivered.

The headstock shape on a brand of fretted instruments is important. Unlike the printing on it, or subtle shapes in the body, you can see a headstock outline from a distance. Leo Fender may have started this all with the Fender Precision Bass. In modern parlance it is the copyrighted "ball and flag" design, which deftly describes its two protrusions. But look at the shape as a whole: *It is the silhouette of the headstock of the upright (orchestral) bass, turned sideways.*

I couldn't compete with that level of brilliance! I adopted the simplest shape I could for the Brio. In another timesaving move the curved cutaway to ease access to the higher notes on the B1 was changed to a straight line on the Brio. Less time cutting and sanding.

The established B1 body had an alder back and cherry front, always bookmatched. (Which is achieved by splitting a board with a bandsaw and "opening it up" to reveal near-mirror images.) Alder for the Brio, front and back, and forego the bookmatching.

To replace the B1's demanding faux-ebony tailpiece detailed elsewhere, I glued a stripe of three or five contrasting colors in the middle of the front, top to bottom. This provided the strong vertical line which I felt gave visual power to the body. I gave up the B1's grooves around the edges, the homage to the violin family, in favor of a simple roundover same as the Fender Precision.

Most Brios got an oil-only first coat, which brought out an amber varnish tone, and a waterborne clear coat over that. Out of simplicity and reliability we'd use the B1 gig bag.

Thus the Brio. Simpler! Lighter! New! At last a Barker Bass with P-bass split pickups! Just what you've been asking for, and here it is!

The only way I could make it under Joel's $2000 ceiling was to fudge on my labor costs. One shouldn't. We were caught in that slack water with not enough income to justify any major expenditures to streamline our purchase quantities or manufacturing processes. Linda had contributed $10,000 from the sale of a house she owned before we were married. Cash contributions came from the Johnsons (our daughter and son-in-law), as well as Rob Anderson and my mom. Bernice van Ammelrooy, mom's companion for the last twenty years of her life, bought me a wide-belt sander for the shop, which revolutionized preparation of parts for the instrument bodies as well as the final body sanding. On we went.

I built Brio #1, optimistically confident enough to stop and develop jigs and fixtures to simplify future constructions of parts that lent themselves to multiples.

I teared up when I plugged it in and played a few scales. Damn it sounded good! Different from the B1, but nothing less. That was a great day; unforgettable. Lots of credit to Samuel's pickups.

So we took the Brio—Italian for Spirit—to NAMM and the world.

It didn't set anything afire. I was not immediately out hiring ten employees and moving our facility to one twice the size with a mezzanine office from which I could look down and watch my finely-tuned workforce happily sawing, sanding, finishing, bagging, and boxing the new, astoundingly popular instrument.

But the Brio had a lot of intrinsic fun in its DNA. I felt freer when I was building them. One I painted machinery gray and embellished it with a life-sized tire track curving across the front. We called it "Roadkill." We took it to NAMM and then sold it to Jim Bull, a local bassist and professional sound guy.

I made a Brio for myself and used it at church. I fancied up the electronics with a neck pickup like the B1 and a P Bass pickup at the bridge. It was a dandy and I loved feeling its sound through my feet.

ADVENTURES IN MUSIC | STANZA 9
JazCru 2010-2015

I told Alan I had parted ways with CinderBlue. He leaped: "Want to get together to try some stuff?" Well YES!

In my year plus with Ed Casias I loved the easy swinging tunes like "Dancing on the Ceiling" and "Satin Doll," and that genre was dead center for Alan. We bought copies of the legal Jazz Fake Book and dove in. It was a joyous mutual exploration of music we had both grown up hearing on the radio. As our book increased, I was getting stretched, a lot.

Alan's wife Maria was a classroom aide for students with disabilities and Alan was a coordinator of services for the Deaf and Hard of Hearing. He often worked as a classroom interpreter for those students he served. But music was his passion and he pursued it vigorously. He could walk into nearly any setting and play guitar, bass, saxophone, flute, or keys. He frequently played guitar in pit orchestras for Central Oregon musical theater productions, usually had some kind of '70s-'80s classic rock band going, at least one church thing, and us, *JazCru*.

The name popped out of an email exchange we had wherein each successive response built on the one before. Linda came up with the logo. Alan got postcards printed, snap-brim caps embroidered, and even coffee mugs. We were on!

We wondered about a percussionist. I liked the tradition of it, the archetypal jazz trio, but the duo seemed so sweetly streamlined, free of drama, and an easier sell than three. We auditioned a drummer and hired him on. He was a good harmony singer—Alan had worked with him before—and his playing brought interest to our book but, alas, drama walked in one day to a steadily increasing beat and presto! We were back to two and cool with that. We played mostly casuals like wine bars, wineries, and small restaurants. One wedding, which is one more than I wished for, but it was ok. Ask any musician: they can be grim.

Later, a New Year's Eve at a Bend country club: We suspected there would be dancing, so we hired Sophie, a young post-high school percussionist. Very sharp. We'd rehearse a tune, sometimes just the beginning and ending and enough of the head to establish tempo, and Sophie would make a few written notes. Gigtime, she was spot on. Everybody loved us that night, a perfect pairing of musicians and appreciative listeners.

Alan was brilliant in bringing out the best we had through our Bose L1, a minimalist but competent PA system. I brought my little Genz-Benz rig with a ten-inch speaker. Load in and out was breezy with the three Bose bags plus instruments, two mic stands, and two stools. Our compact stage plot had an intimate, living-room concert feeling. Alan's soothing voice announced the tunes but mostly we just played and enjoyed ourselves and let the music draw us through time. You were welcome to come along.

Alan and I agreed that dressing better than the audience was important. We wanted to *show* this performance was a special occasion. It was always black

PARTIAL LISTING FROM OUR BOOK:

- The Girl From Ipanema
- On Green Dolphin Street
- Misty
- Fly Me to the Moon
- Watermelon Man (again!)
- S'Wonderful
- Fever (Alan's arrangement featured 6 key changes)
- Tangerine
- Satin Doll
- Georgia
- All Blues (I learned the complex, iconic bassline for this Mile Davis gem)
- Light My Fire/Moondance (We introduced this as our "Morrison Brothers Medley")
- God Bless the Child
- Take Five
- Route 66
- Scotch and Soda

slacks and black shoes and we varied the top story with similar Hawaiian shirts or solid colors. I wore double panel shirts untucked, favoring one that was black with small gold martini glasses embroidered on white panels. I was a jazz dandy and damn proud of it.

We played the high-toned Tower Theater in downtown Bend for a Deschutes County Library presentation by Amor Towles, author of Rules of Civility, set in 1938. Our music was spot-on and we wore just the right sport coats. Dapper cats we were, togged to the bricks!

As a radio personality I detested the term "background music." Imagine the cocktail party chitchat: "Oh, you're in radio! I love to listen. I have it on as background whenever I'm home." Hearing that would cause my adenoids to suck up under my inner ear so tight I could barely hear the clink of glasses. Music is for *listening*, dammit! But that was when my ego was wound up tight with my profession, coated with the lacquer of insecurity. In order to step up to a microphone every day and commune with a faceless person as a disembodied voice, one has to jack up his self confidence to *believing absolutely* that there are ears next to the speaker and minds hanging on every syllable one utters.

But now JazCru was background music. And I loved everything about it, deeply and enthusiastically.

At casuals like coffee shops and wine bars, I was playing background music. I played for the composers, I endeavored to pave the way for Alan's artistry, and always for the sheer joy of making music in a drama-free zone. If a few people applauded after a tune it was a nice interruption and we'd acknowledge it.

A Foggy Day in London Town, another notable arrangement by Alan. He'd do the first quatrain ad lib (freely, strum a chord, sing a few words) then I'd bring in the bottom end, following his lead. When we neared the end of the verse we'd hit the beat crisply eight times, make the turnaround and launch into hyperdrive. Technical musical term: fermente. "Furiously." It romped. Then we came down to earth at the final "...and in foggy London town the sun was shining ev-ry....w h e r e." (five beats, five different chords).

About a third of the book was instrumentals. We had pocket for a bossa nova tempo that felt like a breezy walk down a sunlit slight slope.

Everything about JazCru the duo was easy. Rehearsal was in my living room. Alan would stop by on his way home from work and bring in a guitar and his little Fender amp. The instrument might be his Fender d'Aquisto, a slightly unusual acoustic electric with a buttery character in its sound, or it could be his Epiphone ES 335, a classic model that brought a little more bite and clarity to the mix. Both were wondrous tools in his hands.

I'd set up my little bass and amp and two stools and we were ready to cook. I recorded tunes at rehearsal so I could practice all week playing along. We got stronger. "Like a well-oiled machine," a listener once said.

Nate Hygelund, a local retired bassist who had toured Europe in the '60s with Thelonius Monk, commented after a gig, "You and Alan are both real solid." (Nate owned a Barker Bass. Just thought I'd mention that.)

The day of my Big Musical Epiphany of Jazz: I asked Alan a simple question, similar to one I had asked in other groups: "What do you want me to play during the verse and bridge to give you what you need to build on for your solo?"

He looked at me, paused, and said, the lift on one side of his mouth betraying his savoring the moment, "Play whatever you feel at the time." Whoa. I thought I was in a musical setting that couldn't possibly get better and it just did. He encouraged me to express myself, musically! I was humbled and overjoyed.

After the first year of our collaboration, I could relax into a bassline and experience moments of "flow" when I felt buoyed along on the pleasant current. As my grasp of structure improved and my sensitivity to aural clues that point the way forward grew, I could enjoy better our artistry. It is those moments which remain in my heart, ineffable. We might glance at each other simultaneously or one might be aware the other was glancing and meet it. Our purest musical selves were honoring the composer.

Bluegrassers make a big show of the lead guy lifting a brogue a foot off the ground to signal it's the last time through the song (so everybody play faster and louder. No, just kidding.). Alan could cue me with a glance and the tiniest nod.

Most memorable of the gigs was a many-decaded wedding anniversary celebration for a couple long a stalwart of the Redmond community. It was outdoors at a winery, a beautiful summer afternoon, and we were in a small copse of lilacs. The shade moved slightly and we moved with it, which was the only break we took. Four and a half hours straight. Many spoke their appreciation.

Jazz settled down inside me as a happy discipline of exploring what wonders lie below a beautiful melody hung on a series of inviting chords. Every tiny bit I learned, what might I play, what not to play, what attack, how long to let the note be a note, where to point myself now, the blizzard of choices that not only make the music live, they also mirror the decisions of a life.

Neither of us was going to give this up. The decision came from elsewhere: the market for our art faded away. Places where we had played no longer had music. No easy explanation. Styles change, consumers change, management changes policies. We loved making the music and rehearsing but for the artist, that's an incomplete circle.

Concomitantly I was experiencing decreasing facility with my aging tradesman's hands. To imagine a bassline and not be able to play it with pellucidity was becoming real. I did not want to apologize for my playing, even if it were a mere chili cookoff.

Alan and I reluctantly unplugged it, formalizing the moment with an email exchange, excerpted here.

From Lee to Alan:

"You are...the most gracious and most talented musician I have ever had the joy to play with. What I appreciated most was that you always practice. And you were always on time, ready and eager...

Thanks for a delightful run, a chance to learn and grow with your nurturing, the friendship and the richness that seems to be unique to a musical ensemble experience. If this is the end of my musical giving, and I suspect it is, it couldn't be better."

Reply from Alan:

"You allowed me to do something that I had often dreamed of, but never really thought would happen...I found a vocal niche that had previously evaded me and I love it. The "art of the duo" is a special experience....JazCru will hold a high place among my musical escapades. Thanks for a great ride into older, real jazz. You have been a gracious and understanding partner allowing me the liberty to express myself with music and arrangements. You are a true friend and brother."

TWENTY-SEVEN
Venus and Mars
Andy and Tony

AT THE ROSE GARDEN, PORTLAND

oel Barker had treated Linda and me to a night at a refurbished boutique hotel in downtown Portland, Oregon. We were there for an evening concert but the afternoon before was spent driving under sunny blue skies through some of the gentrified sections of Portland looking for a nice coffee shop where we could have a bite to eat and a beverage. The driver was a Portlander, Thomas; in the passenger side, his friend of many years, Hussain Jiffry.

Since our first meeting I had learned a lot about Hussain. He had toured with Sergio Mendes, who hit the charts with a group called Brasil '66 in, well, about 1966. I had played bucketloads of their music on KALL, all of it recorded on Herb Alpert's label. Later Hussain toured with Herb, supporting his album "Steppin' Out," which was released in 2013. They played the Tower Theater in Bend in 2019, and we got selfies with Hussain after the show. But back to Portland, 2004:

Linda and I were in the back seat, mentally pinching each other, blinking in disbelief as we chugged through intersections and past sidewalk cafes littered with the Young and Beautiful of the Rose City. We found some pastry and cappuccinos. It was a charmed, wispy afternoon.

They dropped us off at our hotel just before five. We had to dress for the concert.

And here I was, my stunningly beautiful wife at my elbow, stepping through the thick, tall double doors of the Heathman into the slanting sunlight of a gentle May evening.

Just outside the hotel we boarded Max, Portland's light rail system. Paralleling the Willamette River and then crossing the Steel Bridge. Linda was ecstatic, drinking in every moment, every view, every sound, enriching her experience. Even though this girl had experienced a lot of life since her childhood in rural North Idaho, no plumbing, water carried in a bucket to the house from a nearby spring, she could still bring that childhood wonder to moments like this.

I was unsure, uncomfortable, nervous, withdrawn. We were a poster for "Men are From Mars, Women are From Venus," John Gray's book about hard-wired gender differences.

There were thousands at the Rose Garden. People everywhere. Programs, hawked in the lobby, were twenty bucks apiece and I bought two. In the center of the collage of the musicians in the centerfold, a joyous Hussain Jiffry playing the Barker Bass. We found our seats.

Yanni is a creative artist who composes music on a grand scale and has the chops to deliver it to a massive, loyal, CD-buying, adoring, often teary-eyed, mostly feminine fan base.

His orchestra that night included accomplished musicians from all over the world, many playing unusual instruments. Lots of drama with lights. Yanni conducts from a cluster of keyboards resembling the bridge of the Millennium Falcon. On occasional tunes he moves to a Steinway Grand, about the size of Massachusetts, even from our way-back seats. He occasionally waves a conducting hand. He knows the music—he wrote it all.

The ballads can be mournful if not soulful, at the very least gripping, with an occasional economy of restraint. On the other end of the tempo spectrum, the high-octane raceway music often involves two soloists playing at, against, or with each other. The exchange of energy in these confrontations is beyond verbal description.

And then it was over. The applause subsided and we exited the building. Headed for the Max station, just across the parking lot.

"How do you feel?" asked Linda. She let go of my arm and flitted like a junco just noticing a freshly-filled bird feeder. I had no answer. Likely I shrugged. She circled around in front of me, fingers curled into my jacket, and we stopped. She was crouched a little; I looked down at her. Silence.

In concert: Yanni, Hussain, and the Barker Bass

"Don't you see!" she said. "Don't you get it? You just saw Hussain, a world-class bass player, play an instrument that you built, in an internationally-known band, in front of thousands of people! Thousands! Don't you get it? With your hands! YOU BUILT IT!"

She was King Hell Solid Correct. I straightened up, as did she. As we fussed with the self-serve ticket kiosk, we stole glances at each other. It was a fantastic experience, unforgettable, a very high point from those first tiny shuffling steps when we decided to unplug Great Ned! Woodworks and screw a light bulb into the "Barker Musical Instruments" sign.

We boarded the well-lit train back to downtown Portland. I had heard my instrument and, better, I had been encouraged to celebrate this moment. I built it! I built it! Making an unusual instrument, many can do that. But this, this was a big deal.

Before Andy Pfaff bought his Barker Bass, he took a picture of one into the office of the outfit that books him for gigs in New York City. Appearance matters. "Would this instrument be ok if you ask me to play upright?" he asked.

"Certainly," was the reply. Permission granted. So Andy, New Jersey high school teacher by day, now takes his fretless B1four into the City for upright gigs. Like the day he was booked to play for a wedding reception at the Pierre Hotel. For Regis Philbin's daughter.

Linda the Librarian formerly worked at, and eventually managed, an established downtown flower shop in Bend, Oregon. She is an accomplished floral designer, calls flowers by their scientific names, and often raids the neighbors' flower beds when she's doing up a centerpiece for some weekend special occasion.

It was that background that triggered her interest at the library the day that a new book came out of the back room, ready to be shelved: Inspirations by Preston Bailey. Mr. Bailey is, quoting from the flap of the sixty-dollar coffee table book, "*the* event planner for clients who wish for a spectacular celebration." Those clients are "celebrities and the affluent."

AT THE PIERRE HOTEL, NEW YORK
Cast of Characters:

PRESTON BAILEY	TONY BENNETT
ANDY PFAFF	THE BEAUTIFUL AND CURIOUS LIBRARIAN
REGIS PHILBIN	
NEIL SEDAKA	

Leafing through the book she noticed "Regis Philbin's daughter." The text described the ballroom where Neil Sedaka did a set for the guests, and "...the one and only Tony Bennett was truly the icing on the cake, singing a surprise serenade to the blushing bride."

It's a two-page picture, 156 and 157. Pale pinkish-orange flower-festooned chandeliers, crystal tableware, star shapes projected on the ceiling like a planetarium show, elegance beyond imagining. No guests are present, but in the background, right at the fold, you can see the band is on stage, getting ready. And there, if you look close, is Andy. And his Barker Bass.

She called, I stopped what I was doing at the shop and drove straight to the library.

TWENTY-EIGHT

Oregon Art Beat

Pride in our state got a weekly booster shot Thursday nights on Oregon Public Broadcasting television. Eight o'clock was Oregon Art Beat, followed a half hour later by Oregon Field Guide, a portrayal of almost anything human beings do throughout the beaches, mountains, valleys, rivers, lakes, and high desert of this 98,446 square miles of Earth. Oregonians who watch these tandem productions get a double dose of regional Emmy award winning video explorations of our state and its artists.

The apotheosis of Oregon Field Guide's three decades of history was the reporting, in 2016, of a heretofore unknown, to non First-Nation Americans at least, slot canyon in the Mt. Jefferson Wilderness, only sixty miles south of Portland. It was first spotted from the air when Mike Malone, a helicopter pilot working a nearby wildfire, had to detour because of smoke. He got permission to fly over the Wilderness and noted what looked like a 100 foot waterfall.

In 2015 OFG mounted a twenty-four person expedition to explore and map this anomaly. They discovered *three* waterfalls over 100 feet each in a steep-walled, misty, mossy canyon fringed with ferns and trees. This was a modern map-changer of the first water.

Less remarkable and years earlier, Oregon Art Beat discovered the Barker Bass. In the lead segment of the January 8, 2009 program, host KC Cowan, owner of a mellifluous voice that gets easily animated, introduces the story. She says, at the getgo, "We had a *blast* filming this segment," and that, as well as the story that gets told, is accurate. It was a terrific day and I wouldn't change a thing in it or in the program broadcast later throughout our state as well as southwest Washington.

It was a fortunate coincidence and a bonus for everyone involved that we were in rehearsals for the Patsy Cline show at the time of the filming. The Oregon Public Broadcasting crew came to Redmond the day before our scheduled shop shoot and that evening music director John Haverly, my bandmates, and the amazing Sherie Neff graciously welcomed them into the basement of the American Legion Hall. We were rehearsing the music for the later production of "Always, Patsy Cline," a Broadway show about the pioneer singer who bridged the gap between country and pop music. The underbuilding was acoustically not ideal but period-perfect to the history of Miss Cline, who released her first record in 1955 and died in a plane crash in 1963.

The OPB film experts got superb audio of the instrument's low frequencies in the context of an ensemble and they used two clips from the evening's takes in the final program segment. (Getting this kind of footage indoors is much easier than, say, at an al fresco chili cookoff on a sloping field of mature cabbages grazed by both fainting goats and peahens.)

My prior experience as the acquired target of a video camera was limited to acting in a few television commercials during my radio years in Salt Lake City. In those instances I never had a speaking part. (Hm. Odd they would hire a radio guy and not let him talk. Must be my finely-chiseled features that got me the gig.)

That spring day in Redmond I was both calm and curious about these technical people from the Big City. (That calmness is a defense mechanism borne of my dislike for feeling disappointed during playback coupled with my experience with how many things can go wrong in the world of broadcasting. Going with the flow takes less energy than fretting about how one looks or sounds.)

I prepared for filming day by (1) cleaning the shop, (2) cleaning the shop some more, and (3) getting several basses to different levels of completion so the OPB crew could film steps in the process. They had requested this in advance.

Tom Shrider shouldered the camera and tended to the lighting while William Ward collected the audio. The audio in particular interested me. KC and I were wired with mics. William wore headphones and carried a control box, festooned with dials and volume controls, which was slung about his waist like a fanny pack 180° out of phase. He was connected to a master control unit via a hefty umbilical which, as he moved, snaked along my sparklingly clean floor. As William maneuvered close enough to be in tandem with the camera lens but far enough away to be out of the picture, he was tightly focused on finessing the speakers' volumes.

There was no preconceived sequence for the shoot. We'd set up in one area of the shop and KC would offer some potential questions she could ask on camera and I'd respond to them not with answers, but with exposition for the crew of what I might say and what props we might have for a particular question-answer diad. Then we'd just do it. My lack of self-consciousness in front of the camera seemed to surprise them. We went with alacrity from location to location in the shop. They loved the sequences when I was using power tools, especially those that made the chips fly.

After the morning's film was "in the can" (I don't think anyone says that except in the movies), we had lunch at a downtown cafe, walked to the library so the crew could meet Linda, and then went to our house for the "artist at home" part. That was the great moment for our scruffy pound-hound Wanda to get her cameo, shuffling past me to request some quiet time in the back yard instead of feeling displaced by all this technology that was invading her living room.

KC asked, I answered. Rinse and Repeat. Cables were coiled and cameras coddled into black cases and loaded into the van.

KC said that she was pleased with what they had captured. "You sure had a lot of people wanting us to come do this shoot," she said. I was flattered, and surprised. Where had those requests had come from? "Letters," she replied. Aha. Linda had done that; sent a packet of stuff. Later our longtime friend Leanne Latterell told me she had written to KC suggesting the story.

It was January, the next year, when Linda and I made ourselves comfortable on our sofa and clicked on the TV. We watched a lot of PBS stuff on OPB those days, eschewing crass commercialism for the peccadilloes of Doc Martin, the animated and emotional news reporting by Gwen Ifil and the thrill of victory and agony of defeat on Antiques Roadshow.

Linda pinched my arm as the show started. "Can you believe it?" YOU are on OREGON ART BEAT!" I muttered something. I was shaky.

KC says, "We had a *blast* filming this segment..."

And it was wonderful. At this writing the Barker Bass episode can still can be found on the Oregon Public Broadcasting site on the web.

TWENTY-NINE

Ed Friedland

"Enterprising" describes this accomplished musician, writer, critic, and educator. He has taught at Berklee, one of the top schools in the country. He performs, records, and teaches both electric and upright bass.

Along the way Ed had written some dismissive remarks about the Barker Bass. I took on his attitude toward the Barker as a project. At NAMM he was upstairs at a big-name bass manufacturer's booth as an endorser. I chatted him up and invited him to come down and actually try a Barker. He consented and showed up as we had agreed. The show had not yet opened. I was out of his line of sight, across the walkway. He thoughtfully played two basses, a fretted and a fretless, back and forth, and stopped. He pointed to the fretless that he had just played, let both his hands drop, turned to me and said, "Lee, I get what you're doing." I was wearing a pullover; otherwise, my buttons would have popped. It was a personal victory for sure, and it also served as a micro example of our macro marketing challenge.

I had my own peripheral product during the bass years: The Barker Mutes, a set of two. JD Grinnell helped me develop the product and the presentation.

While we spent a lot of time bragging about the bass's sustain, there were folks who wanted to recreate the early James Jamerson R

& B sound and that required muting the strings. Early Fender basses had a piece of dense foam glued on the metal plate which covered the pickups, and you can see that pickup cover on almost every picture of Jamerson with his bass. In the 80s, Fender abandoned the metal plate. The muted sound was out of style.

My mutes, which were not my invention, slid under the strings right at the bridge. The mutes were made of three different kinds of foam: A dense but flexible base, a three-color laminate (black and two others, red or yellow or orange or green, each color .0625 inches thick) in the middle, and an open-cell top. Each was about five inches long and .675 inch high. They were different widths, .675 and .750, so one would have different qualities from the other. Shipped in a fake velour drawstring bag, the "matched pair" arrived at your mailbox, postage paid, for $15.95. People loved them and advocated for them. They were just as effective on a bass guitar as they were on a Barker.

The fanciful construction had little to do with the function. The more impressive they looked to the player, the better they sounded to the ears attached to the eyes which saw them. I glued them up in twelve-inch square sheets and cut them to size on the bandsaw. Thirty-two mutes in an hour and a half.

Friedland loved them and even plugged them on one of his YouTube videos. At this writing the marketplace offers more sophisticated versions of the basic foam mute, so the Barker Mute Set has faded into the dark place where foam fads fall.

One could argue that the mute sidetrip was a demonstrated loss of focus. But in the world of innovation, quirky things can happen, and are more likely if you explore side-products. You already have a prospect list and your product will at least make sense to them, maybe solve a problem. Ed Friedland was an unexpected bonus.

Ed's life changed, but not because of any of my insignificant, sandwich-foam interventions. His column in Bass Player Magazine, entitled "The Art of Being No One" lays bare his transition from versatile, in-demand freelancer to touring internationally with "The Mavericks." Now he has only one identity and plays the same music every night, and instead of finding that a stultifying, ego-starving career in faded headlines, he discovers the juice in being the bass player in a nine-piece, song-driven band:

"When your goal is to be as unobtrusive as possible, what do you strive for musically? My first impulse was to dig deeper into the rhythm to find the sweet spot for the groove. It is a continuously moving object, and you ride it much like you would ride a horse—guiding it, knowing full well that it has a life of its own. Taking the next step, my intention became to fill each note with what I call "life force." This "stuff" of the universe surrounds us, and playing music is an excellent way to work with it."

But he doesn't leave us up there in the hayloft. He brings it right down into the barn:

"How exactly does one do that you might ask? For me, it's part physical understanding of the music, mental awareness, and listening deeply. By anchoring all the pieces, I'm able to centralize my position in the feel and more effectively control and react to what's going on. From this location, I encapsulate everything that is played—every note I play is the entire band. Once merged with the music, I cease thinking about bass. No, I don't need to invert that triad. No, I don't need to go up to the higher octave now. No, I don't need to do anything to make the bass line "interesting." All I have to do is play what sounds right, and play it perfectly. When you give up the agenda of putting your personal stamp on everything you do, you begin to understand the Art of Being No One."

This slip-fits beautifully with my 'performer as servant' notion expressed elsewhere in this work.

We are both talking about "settling," which is a good place to find, to play music from, and write from. He gained it, in part, by staying in his career and bouncing gently off its borders. Some of us bounce too hard and pop through the other side and go do something else. Our settling may come later.

THIRTY

The Sweet Ending of Barker Musical Instruments

SLOWLY SLOWING DOWN

As a woodworker, I had survived downturns. I blithely opened my business during the early eighties economic slide, slowly gained ground, and rolled through recessions in the early nineties and early aughts. However, those accomplishments did not insulate me from what was happening in 2008.

There was plenty of talk, on National Public Radio and elsewhere, about the national economy. Just as Central Oregon, through its growth and diversification, had become more vulnerable to national and even international economic vicissitudes, so had I.

I looked at the colorful pins in my world map behind my desk: Germany, Mexico, Japan, Canada,Venezuela, Australia. There were pins in nearly every state in the U.S. We had done well, and I wanted to keep trying. But I wondered if it would all wind down, or maybe even THWACK to a halt like when a go kart chain comes off its sprocket and wads itself around the axle.

My bass-buying prospect looked like this:

Middle aged guy, serious about his hobby of music, played out some (performed for an audience, perhaps was paid), actively involved in online groups around music, but kept his day job. If he liked innovation and had some disposable income, he might be serious about adding a Barker Bass to his assortment of instruments.

And now, all across the land and beyond the oceans, sales of all kinds lagged, money flowed like midwinter treacle, and jobs teetered as if balanced on the point of a uselessly bent circle-drawing compass found in the darkest corner of a fourth grader's desk.

Mortgages turned upside down. Desperation descended on the innocent as well as those who had overextended themselves, the latter described by a friend as people who are, "...one flat tire away from bankruptcy." That B-word scared me in its ubiquity.

Linda and I had reluctantly decided that our best economic move was to file for my Social Security. Through my years of self employment, with the encouragement of our devoted CPA, I had been diligent in reporting my income and paying into the system. The monthly SSI check would be less than if I were to wait a few years but I could still earn some money without penalty. We hewed to that goal.

So as inquiries from musicians slowed and sales sputtered, I returned to weekly ads in the still-viable Redmond Spokesman, rebranding myself as a furniture repair guy. Got a new set of business cards. And it worked. Sometimes just a busted table leg, sometimes five out of six dining room chairs had the wobbles. Lots of hard-to-carry broken drawers. I wove these jobs into a business week that included marketing and selling inventory basses as well as making furniture and cabinetry on commission. I wasn't alone in making these kind of adjustments Many people in our community were struggling financially and seeking creative ways to just get by. Having been born to parents who survived the Great Depression came into crisp focus in 2008 and following.

One call was about repairing some basic dining chairs, no upholstery. I went to the client's home to survey the work and was relieved to see that the chairs were factory made, probably in the fifties, and were screwed together at every joint. This would be pretty straightforward: Remove the screws, loosen all the glue joints that weren't already wobbly, clean the parts and reglue and clamp. I gave the lady my price, she agreed, and I toted the chairs back to the shop.

Patient Number One was on the table, legs pointed at the wall, and I had scrubbed in and was ready with my screwdriver to begin the surgery of dismantlement. That screwdriver kept slipping out of the slot. I have quality tools; this shouldn't be happening. Peered at the screw. Not much of a slot. Probed with an awl. These fasteners were not screws at all; they were nails with a cheesy faux slot in the head, designed to show the customer in the showroom that these chairs were "quality built." A nail in a chair joint is about as useless as a flush toilet in the International Space Station. And it is very difficult to remove a nail from a piece of furniture. They have to be dug out, which can leave an obvious scar.

I gouged out all the nails, cleaned and reglued the joints, and then enlarged the nailholes to accept small dowels, which I glued in, cut flush and stained to match.

She was happy and I got paid. The fundamental joy of the repaired mailboxes on Phylden Drive in Salt Lake City had no sell-by date.

Before every repaired piece got returned to the owner, I'd study it as a whole and try to make it look right. If the repaired part looked too new, add a few understated nicks and dents. If I had refinished part of the piece, I'd blend it with the old. Final wax, either carnauba paste wax or—true confession alert—Pledge.

TAKING RESPONSIBILITY

The best part of this period of financial anxiety in my professional world was the chance discovery—I saw a poster—of the Dave Ramsey program, a systematic approach to controlling your household spending while getting out of debt. Linda and I knew we were behind the curve, and that it might take time, but we could improve. We weren't looking for a miracle. We signed up for the class, which cost just under $100. It was life-changing.

We had borrowed from my mom, we had sucked the inside out of my life insurance policy, refinanced our home, and invested our cash resources. Our kids had contributed help too. The total of our obligations made me go pale: Over $50,000. I didn't regret any of the spending—we hadn't bought a half million dollar motorhome and done a graphic vinyl wrap showing the Barker Bass several orders of magnitude larger than life—but I was guilty of not paying attention to the monthly reports I was getting from our bookkeeper. Missing the big picture.

We explored bankruptcy. Linda's conversation with our banker confirmed our bias: we could avoid it. And he would help us.

Meantime, we had basses to sell, and I turned up the heat on that part of my day, still weaving in the repair work and new stuff. The shop was well organized for bass making but there was enough space, and basic power tools, to easily accommodate the new work flow.

Linda's job at the library was rock solid and the library district takes good care of its employees. Without that stable platform, we would have wobbled until we lost it all.

We made it through. The debts were paid. It took well over a year, and the best part was how this process strengthened our marriage. That we both came from households with humble incomes was a gift. We enjoy the challenge of living within our means, living well, and continue to employ Ramsey's "envelope system" with monthly success. Mark Greaney, our stalwart Ameriprise financial advisor, saw us through with solid granite counsel and reminders to protect our retirement savings.

Looking back at this whole musical instrument adventure, whose antecedent is Linda Barker's forbearance of a husband whose side job was playing the bass, it is clear that the top third of our success was the direct result of Linda's involvement. I got us in; she got us out.

I could have built the instrument and tweaked it and figured out ways to build it with reasonable efficiency but that would have left us with a garage full of unsold basses in 2008. Failed manufacturing endeavors can end that way. And then there's the issue of the acquired equipment. Auction or craigslist, you just have to get shed of it. And even with all that in the rearview mirror, I would still be dragging the rusty chain of failure to this day.

Linda made the difference.

She is an artist, and was born that way. She can't help seeing art, hearing art, experiencing art. Some of us have to switch on a few inactive circuits in order to see and appreciate something as banal as a Norman Rockwell cover on the Saturday Evening Post. Not her. She gets art, and quickly. It's her life.

So when photos had to be sifted through for a postcard handout design, or we needed a logo for the bass, or a ginormous banner for shows, she did the artwork and it was always spectacularly right.

I am an introvert. I'd rather be alone, at home or in my shop. She's the opposite, drawing energy from her encounters with other people. When my inherent reluctance was holding me back from some kind of outreach that might help the company (sell a bass!), she would cajole and nudge me into action.

Though I often quote myself with, "I don't want to die saying I had a good idea and didn't do anything about it," without her, that would have been the case. She used her vacation time from the library for our trips to bass workshops and NAMM, never complaining. She was invaluable 100% of that time, whether setting up and tearing down the display booth or suggesting what I wear. She could talk to anyone about the Barker Bass—like Monster, or Ned Steinberger, or Hussain Jiffry.

We have no regrets. She said, "We came out the other side with rich life experiences. We are better people because of Barker Bass. I'd do it all again."

IN WALKS JOE

Every year since its inception, my business, a sole proprietorship, received a Personal Property Tax bill. All the business's assets are taxable and I as the owner was responsible to pay. This was neither burdensome nor depressing. As I continued to purchase tools and equipment I would annually be reminded of the size of my accretion of cool things that plug in and make whirring sounds and change the shape of wood. Yes, I had to pay Deschutes County tax, but in the back of my head, the final chapter of my unfolding exit plan would be the sale of these high quality, well-maintained tools. It would hardly amount to a corporate golden parachute; perhaps more like the umbrella in a piña colada. But this is often the trade for being able to make—and be solely responsible for—one's every business decision, every day.

There was no Barker Musical Instruments business to sell. The company's indebtedness far outbalanced the sales. In economic climate of the time, there was little future for someone wanting to take over what we had struggled to get up and rolling.

Imagine our surprise, then, when stepson Joe walked into my office and said, referring to his sister and two stepbrothers, "We hear you saying the word "retirement" but we know you never will. So how about I move into the back of your shop here and push you out the front?"

Joe had been employed by the Opportunity Foundation (OFCO), a nonprofit organization which served people with developmental disabilities. He had worked his way up to managing the mill, which employed the Foundation's clients and manufactured things like survey stakes, frieze blocks (a component for truss roofs on residential housing), and, of late, wine boxes. They were made of thin pine with sliding tops, often adorned with a burned-in image of the winery's logo.

Upper management wanted to dispose of the wine box segment of their production picture and Joe got a vision that he would never regret pursuing: Purchase that business's assets and blue sky (goodwill), quit his job and become self employed making wine boxes. And all this would be in Lee's shop, which he wisely intuited could be purchased.

It worked; a genuine miracle. OFCO made the first part easy for Joe to acquire the customer list and much of the specific tooling, including the branders and existing brand plates.

He sweetened his offer to me by saying, "...and you will always have a workbench here and can come in anytime and use any of the tools for anything you want." This was a compelling sales pitch for me. Since my entry into construction in the mid-seventies, I had gathered most of my self esteem and sense of self from making things with my hands; Joe was saying I could slow down, still get my esteem tank topped off, and what, get money for my tools? Whoa! I couldn't say yes any faster unless I was the guy reading the side effects list at the end of a prescription drug commercial.

This was 2012. We worked out a price for the tools and materials, memorialized it in a signed contract. Joe paid it off ahead of schedule.

I also had the unexpected privilege of watching Joe get his feet on the ground in establishing his business and shaping his own entrepreneurial dream. He manufactures. He likes multiples. With the boxes, he didn't have to fuss with coatings like lacquer or varnish. One client's order could mean a month's work. His first order, realized, was eight pallets, four feet square, seven feet high, shrink-wrapped and loaded on a semi truck with a fork lift. At this writing, eight years of success.

Some people's retirement stories include loss. I had none of that pain. The shop area was Joe's, but I had the office, and I went there every day for almost a year. I sifted through files, threw papers, plans and old contracts away, and felt useful when had a question. I would come home in the afternoon, earlier and earlier, as the months rolled on. Then one day I didn't go.

THIRTY-ONE

Ginner Goes to Delafield

DECEMBER 30, 2019, NEDSON WOODWORKS,
REDMOND OREGON

The microfiber cloth picked up the persistent dust that accumulates readily on a stringed instrument. It was easy to see it on this six foot long bass that laid on a scrupulously clean pad on the workbench. I slipped the cloth under the strings and gave a little "Chattanooga Shoe Shine Boy" brightening to the brass frets and the rosewood fingerboard, then eased farther down and angled it around the pickups and the bridge. I buffed the faux ebony tailpiece. It felt like sweet satin as the microfibers warmed the wax finish.

I stepped back and cocked my head to get the light just right to check my work. I had played this bass regularly for several years, mostly at church, but also in JazCru, the jazz duo. There were worn spots on the finish where my right thumb rested. "Ginner" had a few dings and marks on the body and had been host to several different electronic configurations, a testbed for pickups and tone-shaping gizmos. The cherry body had darkened to a warm, horse-chestnut brown.

She was named after my mother, Virginia, who died in 2008, an emblem of spunk, but weary and worn. She had carried aplastic anemia, with which one's immune system attacks the bone marrow, crippling the production of blood cells. It is typically fatal, but she, with difficult experimental treatment, kept it at bay for over twenty-five years and lived to be ninety. She was a tireless supporter of my wild-assed venture into the world of musical instruments.

The control knobs on the front had glass jewel-like inserts, blue, her favorite color. A little lump in my throat as I shined them. I would miss this bass and the way its presence with me had honored my mom.

I eased the instrument gingerly into the maroon gig bag, zipped up and laid it in the extra-thick cardboard shipping box waiting on the other side of the workbench. I set myself to bracing everything with Styrofoam blocks and eggcrate foam. I jiggled the well-fitting lid on and circled the closed box with four lengths of half-inch wide strapping tape, fastened with nylon buckles. I used pliers to pull the tag ends tight.

I peeled and stuck the eight "Fragile" stickers on, all sides, wishing the computerized conveyor belts at the UPS hub could read. Finally the delivery label: "Todd Wenzel, Delafield, Wisconsin."

As I stood at my old worktable, now Joe's, boxing task complete, the memories came back, roiling up like Mentos in the Coca-Cola.

In the past sixteen years on over a hundred twenty occasions I had performed this same boxing-up task, each time focused on every detail of the packaging process. Those basses, new, went to someone I had met or conversed with online or on the phone. They may have never seen or touched a Barker Bass before, but all had sent me a check or given me a credit card number. And one day that tall box showed up on their front porch.

On this December day I thought of the mysterious female bassist from Germany who bought the only BiFour with a sunburst paint finish by Lou Brochetti.

About Steve Legersky in Colorado, who developed a herniated disc from playing bass guitar, got it repaired, and now owns two Barkers. He thanked me for saving his career. "Switch to Lee's bass," he advises, "before you injure your body!" Similarly, the lady in northeast Oregon who could no longer play a bass guitar because of a shoulder injury. Her playing was over, she said, until she found the Barker Bass.

Eric Owens in Albuquerque, with his "full set" of Barker Basses.

The owner of an architectural millwork company on the East Coast who read about the instrument in an industrial woodworking trade magazine and ordered one. He insisted that it be "absolutely perfect." He wasn't a bassist; he would display it in his office, and it would never be played. He sounded like the kind of guy who would send it back collect if he found a teensy flaw somewhere. Or the widow of the man who had found church bass playing after he retired. When he bought the bass, he was immobilized while he healed from a broken ankle repair. She called a few months later to tell me that he died from a pulmonary embolism following that surgery, but she was keeping the bass and would display it by her grand piano in their New York apartment.

Eduardo Kelerstein, Mexico City, who died in 2017.

Then the email from Rob Mccloskey in San Francisco, which reads in part, "it has been my unique and lasting pleasure to not only play and own one of your wonderful instruments, but to actually get to know the inventor of the greatest contribution to electric bass since the Fender Precision.

Ed Goode, Georgia: "Thank you Lee for your fantastic workmanship in building this beautiful bass"

Leo Goff, iconic bassist on Beale Street in Memphis, plays the blues fulltime and keeps a full recording schedule as well. He bought one, unpacked it, noodled for twenty minutes, and took it to that night's gig. He loved it. Later we developed the Leo Goff signature model with some unique electronic features and his name inlaid on the fingerboard in abalone. At this writing I still chat with Leo from time to time about basses, music, and motorcycles.

The last new Barker Bass to ship left Redmond in 2013.

But the one to Todd Wenzel was not only the punctuation on that sentence, it was also a concurrent beginning. I was seventy-five years old and my bumpy and scarred blue-collar hands would no longer respond to playing the instrument as I willed them to.

Todd had purchased the right to produce (and improve!) the Barker Bass. I had sent him all the parts, jigs, fixtures, construction documents and ephemera which I had saved high on a shelf at Nedson Woodworks.

Ginner, borne of two wrists who wanted better days and pain-free nights, had served me for years through thousands of musical hours in Central Oregon. Now she lives in Delafield, connecting one 9-year stretch of history to another stretch, as yet unwritten.

Todd, may all the joys this adventure has brought Linda and me, be yours in double.

Life Goes On

I built my shop in the garage at home. Linda was supportive in every way, knowing that I would not be good 24/7 company if I didn't have a place where I could make, repair, or make and break, things. We built a year-round, welding-friendly shop, heated, insulated, ventilated. The heavy lifting carpentry part was done by Ace Carpenter Rex Gatton, my frequent musical partner.

Between tinkering projects, time to reflect. Not much wasted on what-ifs. More about celebrating the high points and accepting the low points. Learning from the mistakes now is a waste of time but appreciating those people who helped me past them, gave me encouragement to keep an even strain on all moving parts, spoke to me when the more timid wouldn't, that matters. They helped me thrive.

Author M. Scott Peck, in his popular book The Road Less Traveled, published in 1978, speaks well of one being comfortable with delayed gratification. I agreed then, and I still do. Work now, play later. It breeds hope in a positive state of mind.

Through these stories wends a thread of Peck's notion. For example: At two hundred dollars a month for forty-eight hours a week in 1966, I was earning $1.14 per hour. Average wage in the United States: $4.50. The difference equaled the dues I paid to begin a career in which, at times, my mouth was an open wound.

After 2 years, I was making $400. That could have increased had I stayed in Dillon, but I wanted more than that setting could offer.

Salem filled the bill. The bonus was appreciating McCarl's intentionality in creating his best of all possible jobs for himself. But for me, Salem lacked the vitality I had felt in Salt Lake City. Returning there was not homecoming; it was a career move that taught me how exciting and challenging this line of work could be. And how fragile.

IN REDMOND, I THRIVED

If I had found Redmond, or equivalent, sooner, would it have been a more settled life? No. It was all that went before that let Redmond fall into place like the last little piece, three tabs and one hole, that fits into the Dogs Playing Poker jigsaw puzzle on the card table in Bernie's living room.

I thrived because, all along the way, I have heroes. Fred Olness, sousaphone player in high school in Big Timber when I started on tuba.

College Buddies: Route. Holbrook.

Heroic Heroes: Charles Lindbergh.

Humorists: Steve Allen. Stan Freberg. Peter Schickele. Spike Jones. Stephen Potter. Lou Gottlieb of the Limeliters.

Musicians: Jim Erickson and Mike Sutherland. Alan Yankus. Ed Casias. Hussain Jiffry. Doug Mancini.

Radiodians: Martin Doerfler. Bruce Bell.

Activists: Jane Schroeder. Martin Luther King Jr. Barack Obama.

People Who Live Well: Frank Musgrave, friend since Salem. Steve Cross, family doc in Redmond. Doug Potts, brother-in-law by serendipity. Bernice van Ammelrooy, my mom's companion for many years.

And you, dear reader, thank you for offering up your time for my stories.

Liam, Emily, Bjorn, Juni, Lily and Maya: For you, I wrote the story of my work. I trust you to extract any truths, bad habits, dietetic propensities, peccadilloes, spiritual sideroads, or political kneejerks that will suit you and your life. Know that your grampa loves you, bigger than the elm tree you climb in his back yard, louder than a golf ball exploding in a microwave, and sweeter than fresh honey

ACKNOWLEDGMENTS

This book would not be in your hands if it weren't for David Brock, Margaret Green, Will Peet, Willa Goodfellow, Joe Federico, Kate Van Voorhees, Andy Pearson, and their collective and singular help. They are the best writers' group one could hope for and I am forever in their debt. Simultaneous appreciation goes for the faceless people behind Zoom. All of us in the group would have been stymied for two years if we couldn't have interacted for two hours a week during the pandemic.

Diana Barker, who, in addition to being the mother of our sons Peter Guy and Joel, brought emotional and financial support to our family when my career sputtered in Salem and we risked the move to Salt Lake City.

Mary Clark, whose eye for precision and gift for proofreading brought this manuscript to a level of professionalism which it may not have deserved, but which it is not giving back. Mary is a good friend and a dependable neighbor.

Lisa Dorn, extraordinary designer, who took this typewritten, three-hole-punched pile of bricks to candidacy for a gold medal at the Olympics of Bookossity.

The people of Redmond, Oregon, who welcomed me and my flimsy business in the tattered old Ice House. You are an open, supportive community which cares about its own, and I felt that keenly those first twenty-two years.

Every bassplayer who pungled up their hard-earned spondulacks to take delivery on a Barker Bass. So fine of you.

The Geezers: Jim, John, George, Bruce, Anthony, JD, and Chris. You kept my mind from enfeeblement while I was at a crossroads looking for my remainder biscuit which you found on its own petard.

The Star Spangled Banner is next, but we're waiting for the sousaphone player to get his horn out of the case and assembled. So please remain seated.

Improbabilities

I

Cheery Mrs. Berry was our Carleson Hall dorm mother at Westminster College 1962-1966. She was in her early seventies then. She had published two novels.

I am in a thrift store in Madras, Oregon in the 1990s, and my hand falls on a paperback copy of <u>High is the Wall</u> by the very same Ruth Muirhead Berry, published in 1955 when it sold for $1.25; I gave a buck for it. Her work keeps its value. And I kept the book!

II

In the late eighties sons Joel and Guy and I flew to Cadillac, Michigan to visit my sister Cathy. I purchased the Sunday paper. From the boy with the Rotogravure funnies: "Hey Dad, look at this!" He pointed to Ripley's "Believe it or Not."

"Abe Johnson of Redmond, Oregon, also known as The Birdman, can call in certain birds with calls unique to each species!" There was a drawing of The Birdman holding out his hand with birds hovering above. We didn't get that feature in our regional paper at the time and that was my only purchase of a newspaper that trip. Everybody loved the Birdman. At his passing, I built his casket.

III

In 1979 en route to the Oregon Coast, my wife Diana and I stopped at a sprawling bookstore in Grand Ronde. Both being capable of becoming lost in such a place, we agreed on five books apiece and be out of there in twenty minutes. All paperbacks so we wouldn't dent our Mo's Clam Chowder budget for our beach visit.

Once established in our motel, I scooted a chair to the seaview window and plunked down my stack of reads. Mindlessly I selected the top book, The Swiss Account by Leslie Waller. Page 1: Flyleaf with a blurb about "...billion dollar barons gambling for the world." Verso: blank. Recto: The title page with all the publishing information (1976, ISBN, etc.). Page five: The Dedication.

"FOR LEE BARKER, IN MEMORIAM"

Later I wrote Mr. Waller recounting this occurrence. The Lee Barker in question was "LeBaron Barker, editor in chief at Doubleday for many years...he died in the middle of my writing The Swiss Account."

But wait! There's more! Same bookstore, different wife. This would have been in the nineties. Linda had heard the story and knew the bookstore and yes, we were on our way to the Oregon Coast. Her interests were photography, art, and decorating.

I had my choices, and went to find Linda, who had selected several books. I asked her about and she said, "I'm not sure I am going to buy it."

"I think you should buy it."

"I am not sure I want it."

"I think you should buy it." And, I thought, take it home and put it on the shelf next to The Swiss Account by Leslie Waller. Her selection was about furniture and interior decorating. Written by Linda Barker, a British designer, TV personality, and author. Think Martha Stewart without the prison time.

On we went to the charming and relaxing Oregon Coast. We still have all three books. Grand Ronde, Oregon, it is 251.1 miles from the Oregon Vortex, "a strange world where the improbable is commonplace and everyday physical facts are reversed."

This recipe was simmered to perfection by the Donaldson Family of Sausalito, and celebrated weekly by son Loren and his wife Barbara. And their offspring too. Too good to hide under a colander.

You'll never go back to buying the jarred blandness mislabled 'pasta sauce.'

- 4 T olive oil
- 1 big onion
- 1/2 bell pepper
- 2 cloves garliC

Chop and cook low, 15-20 min

Then add

- 2 ea 15oz. cans tomato sauce (or 1 thirty)
- 1 ea 6 oz. can tomato paste
- 1 bay leaf
- 1 t chili powder
- 1/4 t leaf rosemary
- 1/4 t oregano
- 1/4 t black pepper
- 1/4 t.hot sauce
- some salt
- Add browned ground beef, if desired.

This will work for 2.135 adults. Following is my version, whose flavor is descendant from the original. Perfected when teenage boys comprised the Flavor Panel. Will fit nicely in your basic crock pot; put it in there midmorning for an evening meal.

- 2.87 onions; yellow, white, purple, any
- 6-8 cloves garlic
- 2.3 peppers

Chop and saute until just right

- 2 each 30 oz. cans tomato sauce (or four fifteens)
- 2 or 3 each 6 oz. cans tomato paste (this determines the thickness of the sauce)
- Optional: black olives and/or mushrooms, sliced
- 2 bay leaves
- 2 t. chili sauce (if you want more heat)
- A scant palmful each of rosemary, oregano, & basil. Thyme, if you wish to take it.
- Rub and add add hot sauce and black pepper. There's enough salt in the canned tomatoes

Add any combination of cooked burger, sausage, or TVP anywhere along the way.

THE SIX CONSIDERATIONS FOR CUTTING WOOD
(suitable for framing)

1. Characteristics of the material
2. Condition of the cutter
3. Angle of the cutter

4. Speed of the cutter
5. Rate of feed
6. Chip dispersal

WHY I TEND TO BE FUNNY

The early part of my mother's life was laced with tragedy. Her father Leo, my namesake, was a coal miner in southern Illinois. Work was not always regular. There were strikes. They had no car—he walked to the mine. Mom told me how she and her dad would wander the alleys of Pinckneyville picking lamb's quarter, an edible plant, their vegetable at the next meal.

When she was six, my mother's mother died. Little Virginia was shuttled from family to family, always taking with her a wooden box about the size of a footstool. It contained all her possessions, including clothes. We still have that box.

Eventually her father remarried and that didn't do much to stabilize things although Ginner, as she was known as a child, did very well in school. Her straight A report cards are a legend in the family, as yet unmatched.

My father met her when she had graduated high school and the smitten couple were soon married. They were a portrait of opposites—he the gregarious, jocular, extroverted printer's apprentice, lover of language, and lifetime autodidact who could converse with nearly anyone about almost everything and usually had a humorous story to add. He could dress dapper.

She the dark-haired beauty, quiet and shy, self conscious about her slightly large front teeth. She was out of her comfort zone if she was away from the house and the tasks that defined womanhood of that era. (This hid from everyone her mathematical mind and engineer-like ability to solve mechanical and spatial problems.)

Years passed and Bernos Jane was born to them, bright and chatty, the apple of her father's eye. He was an involved dad who enjoyed nurturing their mutual love of music. Bernos was two when I was born.

Sitting in my apartment my last year of college: my dad shared: "You were two years old, and your sister was somewhere else in the house. Your mother and I were outside the bedroom door, which was just ajar. We saw a small hand from inside the room reach through and grasp the door and slowly pull it open just wide enough for you to walk out of the bedroom wearing nothing but a pair of yellow mittens, which were on your feet."

"And that," he said with gentle finality, "was the first time I heard your mother truly laugh." Further, I would add, it defined my Family Job and shaped my life.

According to The Book of Lists, published in 1977, most people would rather have cancer than appear in front of a group. The attention I got, at age two, actualized my romance with entertaining people, making them laugh, lifting them up.

GEARHEADS AT LARGE
A Drama in Eight Scenes

FROM THE URBAN DICTIONARY:

A Gearhead is someone who has a tendency to want or to be interested in mechanical things; to understand, or to be able to work on, things of a mechanical nature, or things with gears.

Redmond, Oregon SUMMER, 1997

The Cast in Order of Appearance

LEE, an audience favorite, who has a motorcycle for sale.

GABBY, motorcyclist, who rides by with Junie on the back.

DENNIS CARPENTER, mailorder seller of reproduced parts for Ford trucks and Cushman scooters.

LOU, who thinks that the movie "American Graffiti" is about him, but his name was changed to John Milner.

DAN, who owns a wrecked ultralight aircraft and lives on the Cline Falls Private Airstrip.

SUNDAY, JUNE 29

I had been advertising the Honda CB700SC Nighthawk for a couple months; no takers. I pushed it out to the curb, made sure the FOR SALE sign was well-adhered to the windshield, feeling hopeful because the best months of Central Oregon motorcycling lay ahead.

Later that day, Gabby rode by on his Honda 900. Junie, his new squeeze, hung on as he slowed to a stop and parked. Junie and I visited while he took the snappy Nighthawk for a brief test ride.

"I like the 900 for me and Junie but I want to do a little sport ridin' from time to time and this here 700 would be just the ticket," he said, stepping back to get a good look at the crisp lines and nearly flawless condition of the 'Hawk. We dickered, came to an agreement, and they rode away. Despite Gabby's being a little vague about when he'd be back, I sensed my life was about to get simpler. One less motorcycle and some cash.

The money was earmarked: buy and restore a Cushman motor scooter. I liked the low initial investment and the simple mechanics. And the best part, a visionary named Dennis Carpenter had purchased all the tooling and rights to reproduce parts for the obsolete scooters which had ceased production in 1966. Yes, I had owned a Cushman in high school. But I had never owned a Cushman Eagle, the coolest model of all. A textbook case of delayed adolescent dream fulfillment, common in men of my vintage.

And I waited for Gabby to be back.

FRIDAY, JULY 4

I had not heard from Gabby.

Lou Brochetti came to our house for some all-American holiday barbecue on the deck. I told him about my Cushman idea, and he resonated with it. "Wouldn't mind having one of my own, too," he said. Would he help me with the painting part of the project? "Sure."

SATURDAY, JULY 5

Gabby called. "Wanna trade that there Honda sport bike for a '69 Ranchero?" he asked. "It's a beauty. New paint, 351 cubic inches, new tires and brakes. Nice enough to take to Show And Shines around here; lots of fun. Wanna take a look?"

The Ford Ranchero appeared in 1957, uncertain whether it was a pickup. It was built on a car chassis, but had only a bench seat. The trucklike bed was carlike. The model had a long run, despite its identity crisis, disappearing in 1979. Chevrolet,  in a copycat move typical of the era and the industry, responded with the El Camino in 1959, which lasted until 1986. They were automotive hybrids in an era when that term was used for mules, ligers and corn, and referenced something produced from two parents of different kinds.

"Sure," I said, my enthusiasm several orders of magnitude south of his. Looked like the Cushman dream might be fading. "When?"

"I'll be over in 20 minutes."

The Ranchero was several orders of magnitude greater than what I expected. It was beautifully restored, bright white, so clean under the hood you could do cardiac surgery there, and ooooh those dual exhausts with glasspack mufflers. They burbled happily at idle.

I drove it. Having a show car had never been much of an urge for me, but I could visualize having this for maybe a year, then selling it. The Cushman would become delayed gratification. I just didn't want to throw any cash into the deal and it was obvious that was where we were headed. Gingerly I broached the question: "How much to boot?"

You could have knocked me over with a pair of fuzzy dice when Gabby said, "Straight across." We agreed to meet at 4 pm Monday at my house to sign some papers and swap some keys.

SUNDAY, JULY 6

I told Lou about the Ranchero. He asked me a lot of questions about it. He was looking for something larger than his Mitsubishi pickup, a vehicle he could camperize so he and his yellow Labrador Sam could leave town at a moment's notice and head for a trout stream and stay put for a while.

MONDAY, JULY 7

2:30 PM. I'm at work and Lou flies in, feet not touching the ground, waving a business card, more adrenalin than a unicyclist carrying a Volvo trunk lid in a stiff sidewind in scattered traffic on the freeway. I FOUND A CUSHMAN EAGLE FOR SALE COMPLETE ON A TRAILER YOU CAN HARDLY SEE THE FOR SALE SIGN AT DESCHUTES JUNCTION I TOLD THE GUY YOU'D COME BY OR GIVE HIM A CALL HERE'S HIS BUSINESS CARD!"

Lou left, clouds of dust everywhere looking for places to land. I couldn't leave! I was waiting for a lumber delivery! Stuck!

With diesel exhaust wafting about and the squartch of airbrakes, my material arrived, the driver and I unloaded it, and I locked the doors and raced south on Highway 97, found the scooter, made a handshake deal. Said I'd be back before six.

4 PM. MY HOUSE.

Present are Gabby, Junie, the Ranchero, and Lou, who is all over that vehicle, looking, touching, crawling under it, asking questions, being twitchy. I ignored him, focused on the motorcycle title, putting the mileage in the little box, filling out a bill of sale. An earlier thought: There is something fluid about the dynamics here. Do not sign the Ranchero title.

Junie left and Gabby rode off on the blue and black Nighthawk while I allowed myself a minute to say goodbye to the most fun-to-ride motorcycle I have ever owned.

"Lou, I've got to get downtown to the bank to get cash for the Cushman."

"I'll lend you the money if you'll let me drive the Ranchero out to my house to get it," he countered.

"Ok." I flipped him the keys and slid onto the passenger side of the black, roll-upholstered bench seat. I am twitchy. I don't have the cash yet, and it's a half dozen miles out to his house at Cline Falls Air Park. I'm due at Deschutes Junction before six or else, in my unreasonable reasoning, I'll never own a Cushman. Ever. Messing with destiny here.

And we creep along. I ask Lou what he thinks of the car. He shushes me. He's listening to the engine, the glasspacks. Tugs the wheel a bit, this way, then that, feeling the front suspension.

Forty miles an hour? I just didn't get it. Hand me the key to my new motorcycle and I'm on it and through the gears and looking for some open road so I can turn up the wick and get the full, high-caliber, high-velocity experience that this two-wheeler and its churning powerplant between my legs can offer. We are speed dating, this steed and I. Quite unlike this ponderous, achingly slow, retrograde parade-speed creep. So unlike Lou.

I mentally returned to the front seat of the white Ranchero on Highway 126. Everyone is passing us. Lou is staring straight ahead, somber-faced.

Six agonizing miles later we pulled into his driveway; he went in and got the money. Headed back to town, he turned to me and said, "I'm John Milner."

OK, I got it. He is back in Southern California, teenager, cruising downtown streets at dusk. Which is all about being seen. I shut my yap and let him bask in the Ranchero Experience. I think he might buy it.

We pulled up at my house, traded the glasspacked Ranchero for my practical Toyota flatbed, and headed for Deschutes Junction. On the way, he wanted to know how much for the Ranchero. "You can have it for the asking price for the bike." Deal.

In the parking lot of the industrial building at Deschutes Junction, I got a closer look at the Cushman. It was an Eagle, 1959. The Art Deco back fender/taillight/luggage rack design made my heart flutter.

We'd unloaded the Cushman as Linda arrived home from work that July evening. "You two and your horsetrading," she said, after we showed her the rusty trophy. She turned toward the house, stopped, turned back and said, "And I want to drive the Ranchero to work in the morning," Of course!

Lou said, "So when do I take possession?"

"Wednesday," I replied. I still had the unsigned title.

WEDNESDAY, JULY 9

Lou showed up after dinner, took the title and the keys. Putting a camper on it would not be the right thing for the car, he said, but he'd keep it for a while. Linda and I stood on the sidewalk as he cruised gently away.

THURSDAY, JULY 10

Lou drove the Ranchero to the other end of the Cline Falls Air Park to borrow a cement mixer from Dan, a middle-aged tradesman in the aeronautical world, whose hanger contained a variety of vehicles on wheels. Dan heard those glasspacks and burst out his front door.

"Brochetti! What? Is that yours? I have to have it! What do you want, name your price!"

Lou stayed cool, thankful he hadn't signed the title. "What do you have, Dan?"

They inventoried his garage. Dan pulled the canvas off his exotic kit car. Very flashy, like a vintage European something, powered by a Volkswagen engine in the back.

Lou: "No."

They stepped over to the big Dodge truck, 4x4, gas guzzler for sure.

Lou: "No."

"Ok," Dan said, exhaling. "That leaves the blue Chevy S10, big V-6, long bed, wired for a camper."

"Well, yes, but it would need some work. How about throwing in your crashed ultralight aircraft?"

"Ok," said Dan, relieved.

Lou sold parts off the ultralight for cash and got the S10 squared away and planted a camper on it, which left him time to tie flies in the evening and ponder his next weekend fishing campout.

Dan signed the title, did a cosmetic onceover on the Ranchero, and shined and showed it in the Shari's Restaurant parking lot where balding guys in paunchy satin jackets gather on Saturday mornings in the fall.

I restored the Cushman, painted it light blue, rode it in a parade, racked the whole experience up to fulfilling in midlife a childhood dream. Glad I did it.

QUOTATIONS GUARDING THE AERIE
ON THE FLYING BUTTRESSES UNDERNEATH
THE CROSSROADS OF TRUTH

"You spend the first half of your life learning to love and the second half learning to let go." —Anon

"They study to pass, not to know, and outraged science takes her revenge: They do pass, and they don't know."
—E. Brentwood Barker

"I have reached a plateau of great serenity." —P. L. Senger
(trans: I don't give a shit.)

"A prophet is without honor in his own country." —Mark 4:6

"That I do not know, and for fear of deviating from the precise truth, I feel a delicacy of articulation, and therefore withhold my response." —Samuel E. Davis and E. Brentwood Barker, conflated
(In answer to a difficult question)

"Always buy your hardware first."
—Robert Miller, furniture maker, referring to woodworking

"Looking back on things, the view always improves."
—Walt Kelly, creator of Pogo, a print cartoon

"Things are more like they are now than they ever were before."
—Dwight D. Eisenhower

"I scarcely can think of a food which cannot be improved by the addition of garlic or whipped cream." —E. Brentwood Barker

"Most writing is just bullshit set to music." —Ern Pedler

"We don't build the pianos, just the boxes to put them in."
—Rick Barnes, referring to standards of precision in framing a house

"Ya make money, ya spend money."
—Parke "Burley Route" Miller

"Nothing is so astonishing in education as the amount of ignorance it accumulates in the form of inert facts."
—Henry Adams, circa 1900

"Play what you feel like playing." —Alan Yankus, musician

"Keep an even strain on all moving parts!" —Rick Barnes

"Confusion always precedes enlightenment."
—P. L: Senger, referring to learning

"Space." —Miles Davis

HOW TO INSULT A TRADESPERSON
SAY, "BE CAREFUL."

As the plumber is about to insert his thorax under your kitchen sink to repair something that has baffled and infuriated you, say those two words and risk getting a Stillson wrench dropped on your left Gucci. Or your right Jimmy Choo.

As your neighbor, who cleans chimneys for a living, is ascending your ladder to your roof to reclaim your daughter's Frisbee, say those two words and plan to never ask him again.

While the landscape maintenance guy is gassing up the aerator in preparation for pulling those little sod plugs out of your lawn, say, "be careful of the sprinkler heads."

When the vet tech scoots your Airedale around on the stainless steel table and prepares to trim the nails of her forefeet, say, "be careful you don't make them bleed."

My point: What we workers do every day is be careful. We don't want to hurt ourselves or damage something that doesn't belong to us or something that we hope will soon belong to you. We assess risk and then do our job. Risk does not prevent us from accomplishing work; it is a consideration, something we take into account. Always there, never ignored.

Take comfort in this fact: we are well aware of the condition of the ladder and exactly how it is leaning on the edge of the roof and we know that if the ladder starts slipping sideways there is no way that you, standing below, can do anything about that; we know how easy it is to bump one's head on the kitchen sink cabinet and how long it takes to repair a busted sprinkler head. Be thankful you are being helped. Bake some biscuits for those who help. Or pay it forward.

That's all. Oh, and be careful turning the page. You might get a paper cut. And bleed.

Oh never mind. No more pages.

Made in the USA
Middletown, DE
29 November 2023